Origin Narratives

The first of its kind, this volume unpacks the cultural construction of transnational adoption and migration by examining a sample of recent children's books that address the subject. Of all European countries, Spain is the nation where immigration and transnational adoption have increased most steeply from the early 1990s onward. *Origin Narratives: The Stories We Tell Children About Immigration and International Adoption* sheds light on the way contemporary Spanish society and its institutions re-define national identity and the framework of cultural, political, and ethnic values, by looking at how these ideas are being transmitted to younger generations negotiating a more heterogeneous environment. This study collates representations of diversity, migration, and (colonial) otherness in the texts, as well as their reception by the adult mediators, through reviews, paratexts, and opinions collected from interviews and participant observation. In this new work, author Macarena García-González argues that many of the texts at the wider societal discourse of multiculturalism, which have been warped into a pedagogical synthesis, underwrite the very racism they seek to combat. Comparing transnational adoption with discourses about immigration works as a new approach to the question of multiculturalism and makes a valuable contribution to an array of disciplines.

Macarena García-González has a Ph.D from the University of Zurich, Switzerland, and is currently a lecturer at the Catholic University and Diego Portales University in Santiago de Chile. She has published in journals such as *The Lion and The Unicorn* and *Children's Literature Association Quarterly,* and she is co-author of *La Era Ochentera TV, pop y under en dictadura* (2015).

Children's Literature and Culture
Jack Zipes, Founding Series Editor
Philip Nel, Current Series Editor

For a full list of titles in this series, please visit www.routledge.com.

Origin Narratives

The Stories We Tell Children about Immigration and International Adoption

Macarena García-González

Routledge
Taylor & Francis Group

LONDON AND NEW YORK

First published 2017 by Routledge

2 Park Square, Milton Park, Abingdon, Oxfordshire OX14 4RN
52 Vanderbilt Avenue, New York, NY 10017

Routledge is an imprint of the Taylor & Francis Group, an informa business

First issued in paperback 2019

Library of Congress Cataloging in Publication Data
CIP data has been applied for.

ISBN: 978-0-415-78548-8 (hbk)
ISBN: 978-0-367-34634-8 (pbk)

Typeset in Sabon
by codeMantra

Contents

List of Figures

Acknowledgments

It is untrue that writing is a solitary job. Writing, at least writing this book, has been the product of a permanent exchange with many people from all over the world. Some of them are acknowledged in the citations in the next pages, but the most important are not, so here a note to acknowledge my gratitude to them.

I should start with Ingrid Tomkowiak and Jens Andermann, the two generous advisors of my doctoral dissertation at University of Zurich, who were always there for me, giving invaluable comments and advice. I am thankful for each of our meetings, their comments and annotated copies of my draft. Their intellectual gifts are scattered all through this book, which was firstly written as a doctoral thesis.

Lies Wesseling, the supervisor of my Master's at the University of Maastricht was who brought my attention to the narratives of transnational adoption and introduced me to a number of the theoretical insights I use in this work. I'm thankful for working with her and Maaike Meijer, who was then the director of the Center for Gender and Diversity of the University of Maastricht, where I also met inspirational colleagues when I was considering an academic career after many years in cultural journalism.

During 2013, I made a six months research stay in Barcelona. I'm really grateful for all the outputs I got for my work and for the wonderful people I met there: Diana Marre, Beatriz San Román, and the researchers of the Grupo AFIN a very stimulating group to share this work with and to learn from; Teun van Dijk, who read and commented my chapter on immigration and introduced me to the young researchers of the Discourse Analysis seminar. I am also thankful for the welcoming of Teresa Colomer and the Grupo Gretel at Universidad Autónoma de Barcelona, a leading group on children's literature research in Spain. And I'm especially grateful to the very kind and open team of the now-defunct Centro Internacional del Libro Infantil y Juvenil of the Fundación Germán Sánchez y Ruiperez in Salamanca, especially Luis Vásquez and Luis Miguel Cencerrado, for opening the doors of the institution for my field work.

I am thankful for being a part of ISEK, the Institut für Sozialanthropologie und Empirische Kulturwisssenschaft at the University of Zurich, formed by nice people who made the everyday rituals of reading and writing so pleasant; I may specially mention Gianenrico Bernasconi, Christian Ritter, Manuela Kalbermatten, Brigitte Frizzoni, Christine Lötscher and Aurelia Ehrensberger.

Earlier versions of this manuscript have been presented in numerous settings, and I wish to thank all the readers and audiences around the world for their invaluable inputs and comments. I may mention here Júlia Vich-Bertran, Nina Alonso, and Xavier Mínguez—Spanish academics with whom a fruitful intellectual exchange continues to this day.

To my great friends and intellectual partners in Zurich: Ieva Bisigirskaité, Megan McDowell, and Noelle Paulsson, for all the complicities shared, the conversations to be continued, and that faith that changing the world is a day-to-day business. Special thanks go to Noelle, who copyedited this book in what was the most torrid summer in Zurich ever since.

Very importantly, to the Routledge team and the peer reviewers, whose comments helped to sharpen the arguments here. And especially to Phil Nel for welcoming this book in this wonderful series.

Last but not least: my son Álex was born few months before I started this project and had himself carried around to numerous libraries and meetings throughout his very early childhood. I'm grateful for his patience (which he had, sometimes...) and for his passion for that Ikea Leka baby gym that gave me so many hours of almost uninterrupted reading.

And, of course, to Ricardo, the best partner in life I could possibly have.

Introduction

"I remember a time when I too felt unbeautiful. I put on the TV and only saw pale skin; I got teased and taunted about my night-shaded skin. And my one prayer to God, the miracle worker, was that I would wake up lighter-skinned." These two sentences were part of a speech given by Hollywood actress Lupita Nyong'o that went viral after she won the Oscar for best supporting actress in 2014. "A Hollywood star is born" proclaimed *The Guardian* on the other side of the Atlantic, and a Nigerian-born journalist explained how much Nyong'o's skin color mattered to Black women around the world. The shared feeling of having passed a milestone was seen as a continuation of the trend of breaking down color barriers that was also and particularly evident with the election of the first Black American president. On an online forum where questions of gender and 'race' are discussed, one user, recalling those post-Obama-election days, commented that 'race' will be overcome the day that a Black president could be as mediocre as his predecessors.[1]

Nyong'o's speech was quoted and reproduced in different countries with diverse backgrounds in terms of cultural and racial diversities. Many shared Nyong'o's hope that she could become a figure of identification for black girls and reproduced that belief through identification—the feeling of being identified, represented by someone—as the most important means for self-confidence. Indeed, in the speech quoted above Nyong'o recalled how her life changed after a Black model, Alek Wek, burst onto the international scene: "A celebrated model, she was dark as night, she was on all of the runways and in every magazine and everyone was talking about how beautiful she was. Even Oprah called her beautiful and that made it a fact. I couldn't believe that people were embracing a woman who looked so much like me as beautiful."[2] Our subjectivities are shaped by discourses that compete and shape what we do, mold what we desire, and sketch our own constructions of who we are. Children, therefore, are also exposed from very early ages to competing discourses of gender, 'race,' and class, and they negotiate possibilities for themselves as gendered, "racialized," and classed beings (Naughton et al. 36).

In this book, I inquire into the forms in which ethnicity and 'race' are (re)presented and narrated in recent children's books. Children's literature today is regarded as fundamental not only in the classroom, but also in parenting practices and public programs, and a great deal of attention is devoted to whether and how children's media portrays the increasing diversity in today's migration societies. Some fifty years ago, American scholar Nancy Larrick published "The All-White World of Children's Books," an essay that sounded a call to authors, publishers, and illustrators to pay attention to the 'racial' imaginaries in their books. Despite the numerous references to this essay over the decades, the actual advances have been rather modest: characters of color are still uncommon in recently published books and when represented are most often subject of stereotypes and lack agency (Lee & Low Books; Cooperative Children's Book Center; Koss; Myers). In 2014, the American author and illustrator Christopher Myers wrote a piece on the matter for the *New York Times'* "Sunday Review" under the provocative title of the "The Apartheid of Children's Literature" (Myers).

Even if young children are often described as color-blind, research on processes of racialization reveals that they acquire notions of 'race' related to structures of exclusion from very early ages (Naughton and Davis "Introduction: Thinking Differently: The Call and the Desire" 2). The first studies on the psychological development of children's 'racial' awareness and self-identification were those conducted by Mamie and Kenneth Clark in the United States in the 1930s. The Clarks' original experiment confronted preschool children with black and white dolls and asked the children about racial preferences and identification, utilizing questions such as: "Give me the doll that is a nice doll" and "Give me the doll that looks like you." In studies across the decades, several researchers used these same questions or slightly revised versions of them, always finding a positive bias toward the whiteness of the dolls and a negative one toward blackness (Naughton and Davis "Discourses of "Race" in Early Childhood: From Cognition to Power" 25).[3]

The Clarks' experiment was replicated over the following decades in other countries, including New Zealand, South Africa, Australia, Germany, France, and Italy, always showing similar results regardless of the place, the context, or the year in which the test was made (Naughton and Davis "Race" and Early Childhood Education: An International Approach to Identity, Politics, and Pedagogy 25). In 2011, the experiment was replicated in Mexico by the National Council to Prevent Discrimination, and recorded in a video that went viral worldwide. The children, as in the original test, were confronted with a white and a black doll and asked to point out the good and the pretty one, selecting, in the vast majority of cases, the white doll. Next, they were asked to indicate which doll looked like them. A child, a dark-skinned 'mestizo,' points to the white doll, and when the interviewer asks him for the features in which he believes he looks similar to the doll he—seemingly puzzled—utters: "in the ears."[4] This was only the most recent of such tests meant to demonstrate how children are socialized into deep-seated prejudices, acquiring notions of racial hierarchies from very early ages.

In this work, I inquire into discourses on 'race' and ethnicity in children's literature published in Europe, where the research on the social constructions on these topics is much less developed than in the United States and other Anglo-Saxon-settled societies. I focus the study on a specific country, Spain, which has been the main destination for Latin American and African migration into Europe over the past two decades. As in other European countries, the Spanish debate on multiculturalism, 'races,' and ethnicities often overlaps with that regarding immigration. Immigration and cultural diversities have gained important social attention in Spanish society, yet most research has centered on the representation of racial/cultural difference in the media, especially in political speeches (Burchianti and Zapata-Barrero 403), or on public educational policies specifically concerned with the challenges posed by the task of schooling an influx of foreign children (Del Olmo 187–89). Research into books specifically recommended to educate children on cultural diversities appears to be crucial to understanding how notions of 'race' and ethnicity are instilled and borders are socially reproduced.

In this project, I explore these constructs in books that are recommended to children up to 11 years old by a prestigious institution in reading promotion, the Fundación Germán Sanchez Ruiperez. I focus on a sample of 60 books that includes not only books originally published in Spanish, but also translations from other European languages; all of these books have been endorsed within the Fundación's Servicio de Orientación a la Lectura Infantil y Juvenil (S.O.L., Children's and Youth Readership Orientation Service), which recommended titles under different topics to assist mediators and teachers in their literary selections.

Transnational Flow of Children

Migration includes not only the movement of adults usually drawn by a potential for improvement in their work, social, or political conditions, and/or of asylum seekers and exiles 'pushed' by political conflicts, but also incorporates other forms of movement. One specific form of note is known as "quiet migration" (Weil)—that is, internationally adopted children. Even if the number of adopted children is notably smaller than that of immigrant children, inter-country adoption has become increasingly visible (and practiced) in contemporary societies and has had a significant impact on everyday discourses about 'race,' belonging, and ethnicity. More than 400,000 children were adopted internationally in the last decade (2000–10) from non-Western into Western countries (Selman "Global Trends in Intercountry Adoption: 2001–2010" 4). Spain presents an interesting case study of these global flows at the turn of the millennium. Coinciding with the boom of economic immigration in the country, Spain was also the top destination for international adoptions in Europe, and Catalonia had the highest percentage of adoptions per live birth in the world (Marre 74).

International adoption became very visible in Spain, and this visibility was translated into the market for children's books, where we can identify a niche of books that aims to assist in the socializing of this new form of family reproduction. These books reflect new discourses circulating in relation to the Global North/Global South divide and to the construction of international adoption as a humanitarian practice (Vich-Bertran 329, 336). Research on adoption cultures in the United States shows that adoptive families increasingly describe themselves as 'interracial' and transnational. The origin is today not only acknowledged, but pivotal in the construction of the adoptee's life narrative. In different Western countries, adoptive parents engage in what psychologists call practices of 'racial/ethnic socialization." These include, but are not limited to, giving their children ethnic names, talking to them about the culture of their country of origin, buying 'ethnic' books or toys, enrolling them in language lessons, and traveling for holidays to the countries where they were born. Providing adoptees with specially tailored stories appears to be key in these socialization processes regarding adopted children's origins.

The flow of economic migration and international adoption into Spain coincide quite extraordinarily. Between 1990 and 2010, Spain was also presumably the European country receiving the largest number of non-EU immigrants (Eurostat).[5] Ricard Zapata-Barrero argues that the speed of the migratory flows (the number of new immigrants) has also played a key role in the development of public discourses about immigration. In Spain, migratory speed increased spectacularly between 2000 and 2005 (Zapata-Barrero "Policies and Public Opinion Towards Immigrants: The Spanish Case" 1115), coinciding with the peak of international adoptions; in 2004, more than 5,000 children were adopted by Spanish couples (Selman "Global Trends in Intercountry Adoption: 2001–2010" 33–35). Interestingly, before the 1990s both immigration and international adoption were statistically irrelevant. Despite the intra-national differences among the so-considered historical communities (Catalans, Basques, Galicians), Spanish society had regarded itself as a homogenous society until well into the 1990s; if there were 'racial' differences to be acknowledged, they were those tracing the division between natives and the fairly numerous Roma communities that were—and are—largely marginalized. At the turn of the millennium, integration, multi- and inter-cultural became buzzwords in rapidly changing public discourses. Nevertheless, this debate has been criticized for referring predominantly to the new immigration, often ignoring the evolving challenges posed by new socio-cultural formations within national borders (Zapata-Barrero "Managing Diversity in Spanish Society: A Practical Approach" 384).

The comparison of immigration and adoption narratives in children's books reveals how certain ideologies regarding 'race,' ethnicity, and national belonging are reproduced and resisted.[6] Adoptees and children from migrant backgrounds face similar—yet also often antagonistic—processes of racialization in a society that still self-represents as homogenous and 'White.' A large number of internationally adopted children—some 70%, according to a recent study—report suffering from discrimination, racism, or xenophobia at schools[7] (cf. Tobella-Mayans). The media, nevertheless, most often refers to a society that welcomes international adoptees and celebrates the diversity resulting from adoption, a diversity that is not only related to an emerging multiculturalism, but also to a new landscape of family formations. It is only in recent years, with the coming of age of the first generation of international adoptees—most often girls adopted from China in the mid-1990s—that this celebratory self-presentation is starting to be questioned[8] (cf. Hierro). Anthropological research on Spanish adoptive families has shown that adoptive parents appear to be unaware of the racism their children experience, yet they do engage in some practices of 'culture keeping' or 'ethnic racial socialization' like the ones described above (San Román and Marre 131–33). The books surveyed here are related to such practices and reveal strategies for resisting processes of racialization and hegemonic views on family formation.

Despite the possibilities opened up by a comparison of discourses on international adoption and immigration, very few research projects approach both, and, perhaps coincidentally, very few children's books present migrants and transnational adoptees in the same story. Throughout this book, I explore the differences and similarities in these discourses by focusing on the narratives of origin and belonging. This comparison also sheds light on the role that books recommended for children are meant to play in instilling certain values of Western democracies in times of emerging cultural diversities.

Books for Future Generations

Throughout their history, children's books have been used by adults to encourage readers to think or behave in particular ways. Academic research in this field has become more and more aware of the need to deconstruct our ideas of childhood and the adult-child relationship shaping our preconceptions about what the most appropriate books and stories for children are. Barbara Wall claims that authors are forced to appeal to a "double address" (Wall 35): not only the child but also all those adults who mediate, such as the publisher, parents, librarians, experts, etc. Hans Heino Ewers calls those adults the "gatekeepers" (Ewers 28), emphasizing how they define what can be labeled as children's literature in the first place. Even writers and publishers who attempt to resist dominant social values are part of a system that is under ideological pressure; as John Stephens argues, "writing for children is usually purposeful" (Stephens "Language and Ideology in Children's Fiction" 3). Authors attempt to instill the positive perception of socio-cultural values informed by what is esteemed in the culture's past, as well as certain aspirations for its present and future. As Stephens notes, "Since a culture's future is, to put it crudely, invested in its children, children's writers often take upon themselves the task of trying to mould audience attitudes into a 'desirable' form, which can mean either an attempt to perpetuate certain values or to resist socially dominant values which particular writers oppose" (Stephens "Language and Ideology in Children's Fiction" 3).

Children's literature takes place in a battlefield or at least in a field patrolled by adults who may have different conceptions about what a child is and which books make better reads yet, nevertheless, share a belief in the need of keeping an eye on these books and the reading practices. Books from the literary canon are continuously revised by adult gatekeepers that become aware of how they render sexist or racist messages. Some of these books, such as *Tintin au Congo*, have been removed from library shelves in the United States (Singer 30); others, like Die Hexe in Germany, have had sections rephrased in newer editions (cf. Kuzmany). The reflections and debates on the values reproduced in children's literature frequently also relate to how teachers and parents may mediate and foster critical readings of ideologies that today are rejected. Most often in these approaches, ideology is considered unmistakably negative, which ignores the premise that cultural practices are always ideologically informed and, more importantly, neglects the ways current educative models may also be criticized as ideology driven in the future. As historian Philippe Ariès remarked, 'family' and 'childhood' are ideas that function within cultural and social frameworks as carriers of changeable social, moral, and ethical values that shift very rapidly and in close relationship with social discursive transformations (Lesnik-Oberstein "Defining Children's Literature and Childhood" 17).

A look into children's books about immigration and international adoption sheds light over current and predominant ideologies about 'race' and cultural origin. We often associate ideology with the form in which a dominant power legitimates itself, naturalizing or universalizing beliefs so as to render them self-evident and excluding other forms of thought. We often say, for instance, that something or someone is 'too ideological' when conflicts are suppressed or masked to favor a determined agenda. The phrasing 'too ideological' implies a notion of falsehood or, at least, of being dazzled by a particular illusion. I understand ideology in a much broader way, as informing all of our cultural practices. In his *Ideology, an Introduction*, Terry Eagleton provides six possible definitions for what ideology is, ranging from a comprehensive concept of ideology as involving all signifying practices and symbolic processes in a determined society, to a much more reduced meaning in which ideology would be those ideas and beliefs that help to legitimate the interests of a ruling group or class by distortion and/or dissimulation. I find myself closer to the first definition, and appeal to what Eagleton describes as:

> Ideas and beliefs (whether true or false) which symbolize the conditions and life-experiences of a specific, socially significant group or class. The qualification "socially significant" is needed here, since it would seem odd to speak of the ideas and beliefs of four regular drinking companions or the Sixth Form at Manchester Grammar School as an ideology all of its own. "Ideology" is here very close to the idea of a "world view."
>
> (Eagleton 29)

In this definition, ideology is not necessarily negative; it emphasizes the promotion or legitimation neither of sectorial interests nor of social power. I am interested in inquiring into how dominant social discourses reproduce their conditions, but I do not understand ideologies as necessarily engaged with the promotion and legitimation of groups in the face of opposing interests.

Moreover, I believe that narrations constitute ideology rather than solely express it. This emphasis may be understood by looking to the claims of the 'narrative paradigm' elaborated by Walter Fisher. Fisher argued that people understand the world and make decisions by following narratives—credible stories—rather than logic and that communication is mainly done by storytelling (Fisher 63). In recent decades, scholars from various fields have come to claim the importance of stories and narratives in creating meaning, modeling identities, and gaining social recognition (cf. Bruner "Self-Making and World-Making"; Bruner "Life as Narrative"; Somers; Andrews et al.; McAdams et al.).

In this context, a critical inquiry into depictions of so-called cultural diversities in children's literature turns out to be a privileged form of unveiling discourses on belonging and exclusion, and of showing how stories are instrumental in the performance and reproduction of the nation. I believe that books written and recommended for children can provide us with a microcosmic look at how discourses emerge and are subject to continuous change as they are informed by those values that shall be passed on to the next generation. An inquiry into ideologies in texts for children would be not only engaged, as Stephen Thomson phrases it, with identifying "the flagrant instances of prejudice or authoritarianism, but rather to confront in itself the baggage of habits and structures, the very décor of the little world it carries about with itself, and which orders its own critical narratives" (Thomson 146). Moreover, the critical reading of books labeled for children opens up new understandings of how narrative texts are ideological in their interpellation—that is, in their construction of the reader as a subject. I am in this inspired by Althusser's conceptualization of ideology as that reproduction of submission that can only take place when the individual is turned into a subject. Individuals must be equipped to respond to the needs of society, an end that is achieved by constituting the social subject and, we could say, construction of the reader as a subject, the process that Althusser calls "interpellation" (Medina 169). Children's books, as texts that are targeted, recommended, and often also read out loud to children, constitute and conceive this child/reader as a subject expected to respond/engage in certain ways. Throughout this book, I take a look at how this specificity of 'children's literature' performs and constitutes social relationships of subordination organized around the categories of 'race' and ethnicity.

Black and White Fictions

I write 'race' in inverted commas to resist the idea that 'races' are biologically funded. I do believe in the need of using this category because as Smedley and Smedley indicate, "race indeed exists" (Smedley and Smedley 4) as a cultural creation with a great "symbolic and social effectuality"(Donald and Rattansi 3). Ethnicity is, needless to say, also a problematic category, especially when used to categorize people in different social groups without acknowledging the multiplicity and dynamism of belonging, but I do not put ethnicity in quotations because it is assumed to be a term that describes a cultural category, and it is not to be related to a long history of scientific 'evidences'

The idea of biologically founded racial hierarchies stems from the time of European expansionism and colonization, and lasted until well into the 20th century. Later, in the long shadow cast by the atrocities committed in the name of race during the Second World War, the scientific consensus was to dismantle the concept, arguing that the differences within the so-called 'racial' groups themselves were bigger than those to be found between groups ('races'). Today, it is often assumed in Western societies—and especially in Europe—that 'racial' categories are notions of the past and that affirmative actions in favor of minorities are no longer necessary. Moreover, the argument goes, these actions should be dismissed all together as a form of what has been called "reverse racism" (Bonilla-Silva 3–4). But if we assume that both 'race' and ethnicity are social constructs (Appiah "Race, Culture, Identity: Misunderstood Connections" 55), we become aware of how the latter construct has gained ground as the politically correct form for addressing the former. Both terms establish differences between the hegemonic White-Western and those of non-Western, non-White backgrounds following a deeply ingrained assumption of White and Western as the 'normal,' non-coloured, non-marked ethnic group (Dyer 12). As mentioned before, I refer to Black and White with capital letters, following Richard Dyer's insistence on the need to understand whiteness as an ethnic category, too. In his view, 'racializing' whiteness helps to reveal white privilege and the processes of racialization. In other words, Dyer proposes to look at racism not only as effecting the disadvantaged positions of certain groups of people, but also as leading to the unearned privilege of others. Here, Black and White are not simple descriptors of skin tone, but terms that acknowledge the politics that generate these colors in classificatory systems over time (Bernstein 4).

The replacement of 'race' with ethnicity also sidelines the idea of a power structure, and suggests that the social formation operates with pluralistic groups rather than along hierarchies (Barker 250). In his lengthy study "Racism and Discourse in Spain and in Latin America," Teun van Dijk coins the term 'ethnicism' (2) to refer to how contemporary racism in Europe stresses the cultural and linguistic differences. Nevertheless, Van Dijk goes back to 'racism' as the best term for describing the dynamics of exclusion and subordination, arguing that "implicitly—and though often denied—appearance often remains part of the criteria by which the Others are defined as being 'different' from 'us'" (2).

A term also used by van Dijk and other authors is "new cultural racism." The British scholar Martin Baker was the first to call attention to how discrimination against African, Caribbean and South Asian communities in the United Kingdom differed from earlier racism in that it had no reference to notions of inferiority, no need for negative stereotyping, and no interest in blaming the minorities for the country's problems, yet discrimination persisted on the base of a 'tribal' behavior among political and cultural elites. This new or cultural racism is the one that—when explained by British scholars—poses the mythic British/English way of life as challenged by the intrusion of 'foreign influences.'

The claim of an emergent new or cultural racism has been backed by scholars from different research contexts (Räthzel; Balibar; Rattansi "Racism: A Very Short Introduction"; Giroux; van Dijk "New(S) Racism: A Discourse Analytical Approach"; González Alcantud; Anthias and Yuval-Davis; van Dijk "Ideology: A Multidisciplinary Approach" 278). These new racisms stress the idea of cultural gaps between groups, implying that they are more or less immutable. Physical traits are no longer mentioned, as they would be quickly associated with racist attitudes, especially references to differences in skin color (Solomos and Back 20). Yet the ideology of indisputable essential difference is preserved when notions of unchangeable, essential cultural traits are remarked as in those echoing stereotypes such as the supposed avariciousness of the Jews, the alleged aggressiveness of Africans and African-Americans, the criminality of Afro-Caribbeans, or the slyness of 'Orientals' (Rattansi "Racism: A Very Short Introduction" 105). The focus, therefore, on the analysis of ideas of 'race' and ethnicity aims to provide an access to the understanding of the dynamics that produce (national) borders.

This book is divided into seven chapters. In the first chapter, I explain how the Fundación Germán Sánchez Ruiperez reviewed new children's books and elaborated lists of recommended readings through a reading promotion program called Servicio de Orientación a la Lectura infantil y juvenil (the S.O.L., Children's and Youth Readership Orientation Service). The S.O.L. was a paradigmatic program in reading promotion because it aimed to survey the entire production of children's books in Spain, organizing the endorsed materials according to themes that provided teachers and mediators with lists of books to deal with different social issues. I describe how resident experts at the Fundación explain their work, inquiring into how the ideas we have about childhood and the importance of reading shape what is written, published, and recommended to children. I especially inquire into the experts' ideas and experiences with immigration and international adoption that illuminate understandings about how books are supposed to promote a respect for cultural diversity. In the second chapter, I make explicit my own cultural studies approach to the question of how 'race' and ethnicity are narrated to children. I reference previous research on the representation of minorities and ethnic groups in children's books, while also keeping a distance from questions focused on representation, to instead focus on the preferred narratives for dealing with cultural difference. I explain why narrative analysis and critical theories related to identities guide my exploration of the stories told to explain migration and transnational adoption. Finally, I describe how I selected case-study materials to be analyzed, and how these books may be related to a broader publishing market.

The other five chapters make up the core of this work, which is organized as a narrative analysis of a sample of 60 children's books and their peritextual material—blurbs, covers, pedagogical guides, and the S.O.L. recommendations written for each of them.

Chapter 3 is focused on books about international adoption that share a 'master plot' in which a recurrent story focused on the difficulties faced by the adoptive parents is repeated with some variations. After reviewing this recurrent skeletal plot and how it functions as a narrative to be opposed to that in which families are formed by blood relationships, I inquire into the point of view and focalizers in these books arguing that they have a performative aim in the sense of Austin's performative acts of language 'making' the adoptive family while narrating it.

In Chapter 4, I review tropes and recurrent plots in books about immigration to uncover how stereotypes are reproduced even when they appear to be contested. I inquire into the agency of the various characters sketching how locals very often take the role of the helpers and rescuers of foreign people and how the latter only feel integrated when they learn to self-present themselves as exotic performing an "authentic" ethnotype to please the group.

Chapter 5 tackles the cases in which 'race' and racism are acknowledged rather explicitly. A first section is devoted to those books in which racial differences are explicitly set forth: these are usually books that classify people in different groups—very often simplified as having different skin colors—conveying the idea that we are all the same on the inside. Some books refer to an emerging landscape of diversity in which immigration is thematized alongside international adoption. In a second subsection, I survey episodes of explicit racism in these books. Strikingly, racism is most often sidelined, and racist characters disappear quickly from the stories; moreover, those who are discriminated against do not react to the attacks, and the privileged white characters appear to be unable even to identify the racist behaviors they witness. Finally, I explore the interplay of the visual and the verbal in the production of meaning inquiring into the visual depiction of 'races' and racism while analyzing praised picturebooks recommended to educate on the topic of diversity in different countries.

In Chapter 6, I delve into how 'race' intersects with other cultural and social signifiers with the focus on analyzing how through the telling of certain stories 'race' is 'made' and 'unmade.' I examine the intersection of gender and ethnic/racial discourses, the link between whiteness and (female) beauty, and how social stratification or class intersects with 'race' differently in adoption and immigration narratives. Finally, I explore the intersection of 'race' with (dis)ability discourses—analyzing with special attention to portrayals of the adopted child (as if) disabled and the adoptive parents as figures that have access to the technologies to mind the gap. Throughout the analysis of different intersections of 'race' with other signifiers of social power, in argumentation, it becomes clearer how adoption makes us rethink the parent-child bond as central to the reproduction of the nation.

Finally, in Chapter 7, I focus on the intersections of kin and nation narratives. I open by surveying the portrayal of immigrant and local families, focusing on the figures of mothers—native and foreign—as secondary characters in the books where ideas about cultural background become clearly stereotypical. This chapter operates as a closing text for the entire argumentation, examining the overarching metaphor of the Nation as Family and the way this root metaphor structures politics of belonging and exclusion. In this organization, foreign children are turned into redemptive figures for world inequalities and are often portrayed as resilient orphans who are flexible and eager to be cared for/adopted by the new nation as a family that thrives.

The final conclusions are woven around a biographical account written by an adult migrant, *Bully, Yo vengo de Doubirou*, by Bully Jangana, published as a children's book to educate on diversity. This chapter addresses certain topics that emerge when critically reading Jangana's book, bringing closure to some key aspects of the discourses on immigration, international adoption, belonging, and 'race' discussed throughout the book.

Notes

1 Posted on the Facebook account of Miss Representation.
2 The speech was recorded some weeks before the Oscar awards at an event organized by a magazine that features Black women, the Essence Black Women in Hollywood luncheon.
3 These tests have often been used to argue that Black children grow in self-hatred, yet as Robin Bernstein argues, we have to be careful of not drawing overly simple conclusions from this study. Bernstein claims that these tests only indicate a preference for white dolls following a cultural script in toy culture in which white dolls have the main roles and black or dark ones are subordinated; moreover, she argues that we can read the selection of the white doll as an act of resistance against processes of racialization (Bernstein 194–96).
4 This video can be viewed with English subtitles on YouTube https://www.youtube.com/watch?v=kXq27eASXoo. The *Los Angeles Times* published an article regarding it cf. http://latimesblogs.latimes.com/world_now/2011/12/mexico-racism-video-children-debate-race.html#sthash.VQQ4Jr8A.dpuf. Retrieved Apr. 10, 2015.
5 I say presumably because the statistics are difficult to compare. Spain has historically reported a high number of irregular migrants because, until 2013, migrants would benefit from registering in the local councils, gaining access to healthcare and schooling.
6 I follow the long-standing convention of writing 'race' in inverted commas to highlight the resistance towards the idea that 'races' correspond to existing biological differences. In this book, I also write both White and Black with capital letters as part of an effort to make visible whiteness and deconstruct the categories based on color.
7 According to a study conducted by the association of adoptive parents "Ume Alaia" in Viscaya, Basque Country, described in the article "¿Cómo vas a ser del Atleti si eres negro?" published by Alba Tobella Mayans in El País Jan. 6, 2014.
8 An ethnographic documentary was released in 2014 under the title "Generación Mei Ming: miradas desde la adolescencia" and reviewed by Lola Hierro en El País in the article "La adolescencia de las niñas Mei Ming" May 20, 2014.

1 The Books We Recommend to Children

Ideologies and Politics in Reading Promotion

In its quotidian use, 'children's literature' is an unproblematic term: it refers, simply, to the literature aimed at children, published by specialized editors and placed in determined shelves in bookshops and libraries. But as soon as we use the term within an academic context, the questions begin to arise: what is 'children' in children's literature? And its inverted version: what is 'literature' in children's literature? I will not delve into the depths opened by these questions, but will adhere to Hans Heino Ewers' claim that children's literature is an 'action system' (Handlungssystem) (Ewers 53) in which different actions form a stable chain—production, distribution, evaluation, and consumption—and in which adults act constantly as "co-readers" (Ewers 43) of the books, although they are presented as if addressed exclusively to children. Hans Heino Ewers calls our attention to the power of this "mediator circle" (25) formed by teachers, librarians, and other specialists in determining what children read and what we praise as good examples of children's books.

In this book, I inquire into a sample of books recommended by a prestigious institution in reading promotion in Spain, the Fundación Germán Sánchez Ruiperez, which led the most extensive program in recommending readings in the country, the Servicio de Orientación a la Lectura infantil y juvenil (S.O.L., Children's and Youth Readership Orientation Service). This program was first promoted and supported by the Spanish Publisher's Association and the Spanish government through its Books, Archives, and Libraries Direction.[1] It presented an overview of all new publications, reviewing up to 500 books annually. Their recommendations are all accessible on their website where they also upload different publications for teachers and mediators of children's literature. The S.O.L. was a singular and paradigmatic program in reading promotion because it organized the recommendations according to themes, thus providing teachers and mediators with endorsed materials to approach diverse social issues.

In March 2013, I visited the headquarters of Fundación Germán Sánchez Ruipérez in Salamanca, where I had the opportunity to explore their book depository, interview reviewers, and participate as an observer in the team meeting in which new publications were discussed. Previous to this stay, I had already read more than 100 books recommended by S.O.L. in relation to the themes of immigration, adoption, and cultural diversities, and I also had a preliminary conversation with Luis Vásquez, the S.O.L. director based in Madrid. I went to Salamanca with the aim of better understanding what went on "behind the scenes" of the book recommendations, since I was—and am—very curious on how the ideas we have on childhood and the importance of reading model why certain stories get written, published, and read, while others are silenced.

In all interviews with the reviewers, I first let the interlocutors explain their work, with as little interference from me as possible.[2] I did however start by explaining that I was researching discourses on 'race,' ethnicity, immigration, and international adoption in children's literature and that these interviews were meant to provide some context of the books' circulation that referred to these topics. In one instance, this first explanation led us immediately to a number of books on cultural diversities and to the educational material that the S.O.L. had produced on ethnic diversity. In all other cases, the reviewers first introduced their own work for approximately 10 to 25 minutes, and then I posed questions that were mostly related to the way in which they would praise a certain book or a group of books for dealing with the topics at hand.

At times, my questions puzzled the interviewees. It appeared to me as if our conversations could be divided in two halves: during the first half, they told a story they could narrate without difficulties. During the second half, they were confronted with questions on which they had not reflected—or not at length—and were occasionally unsure how to answer. I took care to insure that these conversations did not seem a test that they could fail. Nevertheless, a reluctance to reflect further on their thematic recommendations persisted among the interviewees.

To attempt to understand this reluctance, I must reflect on the context of these conversations. On the one hand, it might be the case that the position of the expert-researcher somehow set against the interviewee hindered the exchange. Yet, I am tempted to downplay this factor mainly because the S.O.L. reviewers and, moreover, the S.O.L. selection team are themselves positioned as experts in their field. They are all mediators who participate frequently in congresses and seminars at which both university scholars and researchers affiliated with other institutions (state-funded bodies, nongovernmental organizations [NGOs], publishing houses, foundations) gather. Rather, I am tempted to explain this reluctance as one generated by the topic at stake. During the years in which I have been working in this project, I have realized that phrasing the project as one about 'narratives of ethnicity and 'race'' tended to create resistance on the part of the interlocutor. Whenever I phrased it as one about inter- and multiculturalism, people would relate to it much more easily. The resistance toward the concept of 'race,' and the particularities of the European approach to the term—in contrast to the United

States, Europeans are not accustomed to classifying themselves in racial groups—is explored in different sections throughout this book and more extensively in Chapter 5. I learned to describe my project as one that explores the representations of diversity that result from migration (and international adoption), yet some references to 'race' during these interviews might have made some interviewees uncomfortable.

I should also acknowledge here my own position as an ethnically marked researcher. My Chilean origin appears to have motivated a number of Latin American examples; the representation of Latino immigrants in Spanish children's literature is actually rare when compared with the prevalent figure of African migrants, but the interviewees frequently mentioned the very few books that feature characters from Latin America as examples of a much more inclusive children's literature.

The Production of Readers

The S.O.L. website ranked on the top positions when terms such as 'lectura infantil y juvenil' (children's and youth literature), 'biblioteca familiar' (family library), 'orientación lectura' (reading orientation), or 'lectura infantil' (child reading) were searched in Google.[3] Children's literature mediators in Spain and in Spanish-speaking countries often consulted this depository, and many bibliographic resources take the S.O.L.'s recommendations as a starting point (cf. García Alonso). As the S.O.L. directives point out, there was no other program on reading promotion doing something similar, and a key to their success was that each book was carefully catalogued according to its genre, the age of its ideal reader, and the list of possible topics to which it referred. In contrast, all other initiatives of recommended readings either praise literary quality with awards—such as the White Ravens honors given by the International Youth Library in Munich to the best picturebooks—or publish selections of endorsed materials on particular subjects—such as the project Kolibri, in Switzerland, which endorses cultural pluralism in children's literature.

Each book recommended by S.O.L. had a review addressed to adults and another for the intended young readers. As such, these reviews offer rich material for the analysis of social discourses on childhood, reading, and diversities. Interestingly, when the S.O.L. website was replicated on the follow-up program Canal Lector, only the reviews for adults were transferred. A reviewer explained the decision by saying that the site was, nevertheless, mostly used by adults even if it was originally meant to be also a tool for children and young readers. We may wonder why the young readers did not use the platform as much as intended. It may be explained by the design of the website's interface and its appeal, or lack thereof, to young readers, but it may be also taken as an indication of how children's books circulate differently among adults and children.

For example, Barbara Wall differentiates situations in which a book might have a "single audience" (Wall 35)—when it is directed to children without caring about the adults, a minority of the books in her opinion—a "dual audience"—what we often call 'crossover literature' in which both children and adults are equally addressed—or a "double audience," in which the authors write down to the children and take good care of being on the level of adults, the strategy that most books follow. This practice of double reviewing reflected the ambivalent position of children's literature between the adult and the child and art and pedagogy that many authors have seen as constitutive of the field (cf. Weinreich; Lesnik-Oberstein "Defining Children's Literature and Childhood" 21). The reviews for adults highlighted the educative values of the book, while those for children tried to promote the reading of the books by giving some hints about their plots.

In the conversations with the S.O.L. reviewers, I inquired about possible tensions between the aesthetic and the use-value of the books recommended; that is, I questioned the weight given to the imagined pedagogical benefits of reading a certain book when they would not necessarily agree on its literary quality. The mediators all agreed that they were guided by a principle in which reading promotion was meant to find appropriate books for children that would facilitate their access to more complex aesthetic forms, and that, therefore, they disregarded other purposes, those "plain" pedagogical purposes. This claim can be related to a tradition in which the question of the (moral) values of children's books is left in abeyance, an approach that began to be contested in the 1970s when scholars and educators became more concerned about the ideologies present in literature for children (Pinsent 5). Nevertheless, deciding to promote and praise aesthetic quality over other values does not solve the problem, as the aesthetic quality in children's literature is most often related to imagined needs and capacities of the ideal reader, the child. Pablo Barrena, from the Selection Team in Madrid, summarized this quest for aesthetic quality:

"Si admitimos que existe una pirámide de lectores donde en la punta tenemos los lectores más maduros y sofisticados, los mejores lectores, y abajo tenemos una base mucho más amplia de lectores más mediocres o muy regulares o de poca lectura, esa base es mucho más amplia y es la base social donde hay un lector incipiente. Ahí es donde era más confusa y más difícil (la selección) puesto que tienes que seleccionar obra mediocre de una calidad baja, que también había que admitir, pero se hacía muy difícil porque hay mucha más producción (mediocre)."

[If we admit that readers form a pyramid where the most sophisticated, the most mature, the best readers are at the top, at its base we would have a broadened out number of readers, a social base of incipient readers. (The selection of books for) this base was more difficult and unclear because you had to select second-rate works of low quality, which must be admitted, but it became more difficult (to decide) amongst these books as there are many more of them] (Barrena).

This figure of the pyramid was repeated on other interviews and illustrates transparently the idea of a highbrow/lowbrow cultural divide in which sophistication is opposed to mass consumption, an idea that has informed cultural policies in the past century with the creation of lists of canonical classic books that would educate the "masses" in moral and civic values (a principle associated with the tradition of Leavisism). A children's literature mediator would then play the role that Pierre Bourdieu described as that of "specific authorities of selection and consecration" reproducing "cultural legitimacy" (90), the legitimated 'taste' that reproduces itself in interrelation with the dynamics of social stratification. A (guided) consumption of so-called popular/mass/low culture, which in this case would be that 'second-rate' children's books, would increase the chances for developing a desire and appreciation for more sophisticated manifestations. This idea informs various practices in reading promotion, such as the creation of book clubs where readers could 'read their way up' as numerous changes in the curricula in which best sellers have been included with the hope of getting children into reading. John Storey recognizes two main strategies for introducing popular culture and popular literature into schools: one in which the "popular" is condemned as second-rate culture and another inspired by the hope of eventually leading the students to appreciate "higher" art (Storey 52). The latter appears to be a guiding principle in the practice of the reading promotion of this institution, which associates the benefits of the early exposition of children to literature. The Catalan scholar Teresa Colomer has conducted extensive studies on the children's literature offer in Spain showing that books targeted to older readers are usually those having more complex narrative structures and using a larger array of literary techniques, yet she also points out to how thematic innovation is more visible precisely in the books for early readers (Colomer 112–15).

Even if the Selection Team in Madrid appealed to the idea that they only considered what they described as "literary values" when recommending a book, the reviewers in Salamanca who were hands-on in mediation argued that they also took into account other possible outcomes a book could bring. Apart from "getting children into reading," they mentioned: "to facilitate talking about certain topics" and "to reinforce certain skills worked on at school" (S.O.L. reviewers). During a team meeting of reviewers in which I was present, they praised mostly the books that were being recommended for their aesthetic elements— considering the importance not only of the verbal narration, but also of the visual realm and lay-out of the book—they even mentioned some external factors that made them useful, such as the "letra ligada" (hand-writing), a feature schoolteachers kept looking for.

Interestingly, none of the mediators would recall rejecting a book on ideological grounds. Books were dismissed in most cases because they did not provide a suitable aesthetic experience: they had plain unattractive illustrations, unconvincing characters, or a poorly resolved plot. I asked a reviewer what happened if a book had a sexist or racist message that might have been overlooked by the Selection Team in Madrid, and she replied that it may occur, as the people doing the first selection did not have time to read carefully all books, but that she could not recall a case in which something like that had happened. When I asked the reviewers how they deal with (ideological) differences between them while deciding whether a book should be recommended or not, they dismissed the possible discrepancies: "We are always reading articles... We keep ourselves updated. Maybe someone had once difficulties understanding something, but in general we have a common vision" [Aquí estamos siempre leyendo artículos... Nos mantenemos al día. Quizá alguna vez a alguno le ha costado entender algo, pero en general tenemos una visión común] (S.O.L. reviewer, my emphasis). Interestingly, this 'common vision' is related to being updated by reading articles; knowledge would, thus, give us access to a single and truthful interpretation of the world; education would facilitate a common understanding of the world by distinguishing the right from the wrong and suppressing differences.

As someone working on academic research, I was expected to naturally agree with them on the books that would be helpful for socializing children in a society that has been changing after migration. Yet after reading more than 100 books recommended by them, I had become quite skeptical about the possibilities these books gave to resist narratives of exclusion. It was not only that I had encountered numerous stereotypes reproduced in them, but also that these books did not resist or subverted those notions of culture and identity as fixed categories to be tightly linked to geographic origin. Moreover, the approach to cultural diversities appeared to be more informed by a certain political-correctness than by a cultural awareness aiming to be power-sensitive; in this way, the stories ended up reproducing the status quo and the relationships of subordination between White-western and non-White 'foreign' characters.

During the days spent in Salamanca, I became more aware of how this approach toward diversity was influenced by the discursive specificity about children's literature. If the reviewers had worked with adult literature, they may have been keener to acknowledge their own subjectivities. They would have probably been more pressed to reflect on how their own preferences and socio-cultural constructs determined the ways they praised one or another book. Contrastingly, this idea of them having a 'common vision' recalled to me Clifford Geertz's ideas on a 'common sense' in which local cultural constructions are presented as universal and total (Geertz 77). Dismissing differences and believing that it was desirable and achievable to have a common view on what made a book endorsable appears to be specific to this field in which adults may be versed on what would make better readings for children.

The Production of Diversity

The S.O.L. reviewers appeared not to be aware of the fairly big number of books about adoptees that have been published in the last years, yet most of them knew families that have adopted internationally and were or had been seeking children's books in which similar experiences were portrayed. Contrastingly, they were fairly well documented about books tackling what they often phrased as the 'problem' of immigration. They would refer to these books as reflecting the new society and would prefer those that did not aim to put a strong message through "as those published by Oxfam that are quite instructive" [cómo los que publica Oxfam, que son muy instructivos] (S.O.L. reviewer). In general, they referred to immigration as a phenomenon that posed new challenges rather than as a constitutive feature of modern societies and did not mention, for instance, how the long history of Spanish emigration could also be a topic explored in literature.

As mentioned before, the reviewers preferred to speak of interculturalism and multiculturalism rather than of 'races' or racism. These two first concepts had fairly clear definitions: they used 'interculturalism' to label books in which people from different ethnic backgrounds interact, while they preferred 'multiculturalism' for those set in Africa, Asia, or Latin America where a determined ethnic group would be presented. One of the reviewers explained to me that by 'multiculturalism' they included books "about how does a Chinese, an Indian, or a Black in an African tribe live" [acerca de cómo vive un chino, un indio, o un negro en una tribu en África] (S.O.L. reviewer). This explanation reflects that widespread take on ethnicity as bound to geography and opposed to the image of Western Civilization that informs most stories set in Southern or Eastern countries. Indeed, most of the books about that rest of the world would be set in Africa and in most cases the characters would live in very small and underdeveloped villages or would just take place in natural landscapes.

One reviewer confessed that first they were all confused about how to differentiate between the books that would be labeled as multiculturalism and those about interculturalism, but that now they all can clearly distinguish when a story portrays "distintas culturas" [different cultures] being 'multicultural' or presents them "en diálogo" [in dialogue] (S.O.L. reviewer), being intercultural. It is often remarked how multiculturalism has been so differently constructed in the settler countries and in Europe (cf. Welsch 247–248; Joppke), if only because in the

United States, Canada, and Australia it forms part of a national project, whereas in Europe it is connected to emigration.

We should also consider the particularities of the Spanish context. Spain became a country of destination for work migrants only in the 1990s, rather late in the European context. By then, the European stakeholders were already replacing the idea of 'multiculturalism'—a term coined in the wake of identity politics movements—by new phrasings such as intercultural dialogue and intercultural education which are more connected to diversity related to immigration and to the discussion of integration policies (cf. Abdallah-Pretceille). Spanish institutions picked up the new term rather quickly, and today we find 'interculturalidad' as a leading principle in different national and local programs. Yet, as Catalan scholar Ricard Zapata-Barrero argues, interculturalism may be the aim, but the policies rather seek the assimilation of newcomers: "Even though cultural diversity is perceived as an opportunity for enrichment of Spanish and Catalan schools (and society), the management of language and religious diversity highlights the limits of this intercultural approach in practice. Although interculturalism is the declared goal, in essence, integration is still pursued through assimilatory practices" (Zapata-Barrero "Managing Diversity in Spanish Society: A Practical Approach" 394).

Wolfgang Welsch claims that both concepts reinforce the traditional conception of single cultures as islands or spheres and proposes to rephrase the cultural exchanges as transculturality: "Cultures de facto no longer have the insinuated form of homogeneity and separateness. They have instead assumed a new form, which is to be called transcultural insofar that it passes through classical cultural boundaries. Cultural conditions today are largely characterized by mixes and permeations" (Welsch 3–4). This concept can be related to Homi Bhabha's "hybridity" (294) and to what Mary Louise Pratt introduced to the English-speaking academia as "transculturation" (7), a concept taken from Cuban author Fernando Ortiz; even if with different emphases, they all claim that cultures are fluid and in continuous exchange, a patchwork with different layers. Yet, these approaches have had little impact beyond academia; if transferred to the children's books production and circulation, they would probably show up in more characters with multiple affiliations and with an emphasis on routes (journeys) instead of roots (origin).

By using 'interculturalism' instead of 'multiculturalism,' the S.O.L. reviewers emphasize the importance of the exchange. One of them defines it as the "the integration of the one who comes with the one who is here" [la integración del que viene con el que está acá], a definition in which we may nevertheless trace that practical philosophy of 'assimilation' that Zapata-Barrero points out: the exchange appears to be something the newcomer does to integrate with the locals. Moreover, as this construction reveals, interculturalism is related to immigration and, more specifically, to the influx of new immigration, that is, with those new people arriving rather than to the existence of 'foreigners' in the everyday life in plural and complex societies.

Notably, when referring to multi- and interculturalism, none of the S.O.L. reviewers mentioned religion as a flank of cultural difference. In the books recommended, indeed, religious differences are rarely thematized; such themes appear almost exclusively in translated books originally published in other European countries. Religion appears to be the most sensitive topic related to pluralism, and as such is kept out of publications for children. Interestingly, religions are much more frequent in informative books that present people with different creeds with very simple explanations; these books praise a desirable spectrum of differences while avoiding references to possible conflicts.

In the Global North, the word *multicultural* has come to refer to the existence of distinguishable foreign communities. A multicultural neighborhood will offer kebabs, Indian food, and bazaars and will include racially marked people dressed differently, most probably in tunics or long cotton shirts. Multiculturalism is mosques, spices, and djembe drums. Stanley Fish distinguishes between what he calls 'weak' or 'boutique multiculturalism' characterized by a superficial appraisal of foreign cultures, usually mobilized around food and festivities as opposed to "strong multiculturalism," which recognizes how some differences are irreconcilable, but says one must put up with them anyway (Fish 378–80).

After the civil rights movements achieved an erasure of 'racial' categorization from everyday phrasings, *multicultural* has also become an adjective to refer to 'racially marked' people, more predominantly in Europe where African descendants can be easily connected to rather recent migratory movements. Most of the books portraying discrimination against racially marked people recommended by the S.O.L. were not labeled as being about 'racism' but only as about 'immigration,' 'multiculturalism,' 'interculturalism,' and/or 'social integration.' When I asked a reviewer about this, she explained: "there is no racism, because it does not have that connotation of discrimination to a Black, Chinese or Japanese person. I believe that today it does not have that much to do with physical characteristics" (no hay racismo porque no tiene esa connotación de discriminación a una persona negra o china o japonesa. Porque creo que hoy no tiene que ver tanto con características físicas) (S.O.L. reviewer). In this answer, we may trace the widely extended idea that we live in a post-racist society in which prejudices based on physical appearance no longer exist. While speaking of physical characteristics she nevertheless mentions national affiliations, Japanese and Chinese. Racism in Spain, as in other European countries, has for a long time meant the discrimination suffered by the Roma communities, who are also considered to be of a different 'race.' In the catalog of the S.O.L. recommendations, "racism" leads us to a number of books about its history in the United States—such as texts about Rosa Parks or about the history of slavery—as well as to stories in which some animals—in most cases black or dark animals discriminated by those with lighter fur/skin/plumage.

In this first chapter, I have attempted to sketch some features of the context in which the books analyzed below were recommended. The interviews with the S.O.L. mediators provide insights not only into the values and ideas that inform this selection but also on circulating meanings of diversity, culture, and interculturalism that influence the practice of reading mediation. In contrast to some other initiatives, these recommendations are not meant to advance the recognition of minorities. On the contrary, the recommendations are informed by a traditional discourse on the importance of literature and the book as media for fostering aesthetic appreciation, which is considered to be a value in itself. Nevertheless, this opposition of the use-value (pedagogy) against the art-value (literature) in the mediation of children's books becomes blurry when situated within the descriptions and explanations given by the S.O.L. experts. In their answers, we may trace how the recommendation of children's books becomes a site for ideological battles even when ideology is disregarded. These interviews may reveal a widespread approach to children's literature mediation and diversity in which books are mainly recommended because they refer to certain topics—in this case, immigrants, adoption, multiculturalism—but without further consideration of what meanings of culture and diversity lie underneath or of how (hegemonic) power is represented and narrated. While closing this chapter, we may also note here that the diversity deriving from migration is not only disconnected from that of transnational adoption, but it is, in general, unrelated to other possible issues of subordination and exclusion. As has been evident throughout, there is very little reflection on the role of stories in the reproduction and resistance of power structures.

Notes

1 In 2013, hindered by the financial cuts provoked by the Spanish financial crisis, it was closed down yet replaced by a similar initiative, Canal Lector, that involved Latin American counterparts—Ibby Mexico and the CRA libraries in Chile—to make up for the lack of Spanish institutional support.

2 I first met the chair of the reviewers, Luis Miguel Cencerrado, who selected four other colleagues—Marisa (María Isabel) Pata, Teresa Corchete, Lorenzo Soto and Vega Villar—whom I interviewed during the following days. All of them were by then employees at the FGRS and wrote weekly book reviews. I do not individualize their answers here, but rather refer to them as a group, since they emphasized how they have developed a "common view" in the years working together. In contrast, I do individualize the answers of the two members of the Selection Team in Madrid—Luis Vásquez and Pablo Barrera—who worked to create a first list of recommended books that were then delivered to Salamanca.

3 After the end of the program in 2013, all this content was transferred to the follow-up project, http://www.canallector.com, which also ranks on the top positions in the search engines.

2 Framing the Questions
Previous Research, Theoretical Frameworks, and Case-Study Materials

In this chapter, I unfold the references and theoretical stances that inform my position: a cultural studies perspective on children's books that seeks to identify recurrent narratives about 'race' and ethnicity. I move away from distinguishing rights from wrongs and from the need of identifying those 'good' books about cultural diversity to focus instead on how certain theoretical developments allow us to understand better what texts do or attempt to do. The question of why children's literature underrepresents minorities or 'different' ethnical origins has been there for a long time; I attempt to comment on this not so much from the paradigm of representation but thinking about how narrative and identity are intertwined concepts, how identity is constituted in narratives, a perspective that guides us in the plot analysis of the next chapter. Finally, I explain the selection of the case study materials, 60 children's books recommended to educate on cultural diversity.

The Very-White World of Children's Literature?

Children's books published in Western countries have been slowly including a number of non-White characters in their pages since the 1960s. Since Nancy Larrick's groundbreaking "The All-White World of Children's Literature" in 1965, the representation of 'race' also became a matter of scholarly interest (cf. Nieto "Foreword" ix). Larrick's article unveiled how children's literature was a racist domain and resounded during the wake of the Civil Rights Movement and the first developments of multicultural policies in the United States. Yet, even if today we may identify a growing number of books and picturebooks aiming to depict a diverse society, recent research shows that non-White characters are still strikingly underrepresented (Horning et al.), and that characters from foreign backgrounds are most often portrayed according to stereotypes (Naidoo 24). Most of the research on the representation of minorities has been conducted in the United States, Canada, and Australia. In those countries, children's literary criticism responds not only to a children's book market that takes up the social changes derived from migration movements but also to the particularities of the formation of settler societies with the consequent marginalization of autochthonous, native populations. Scholars working in the United States, Canada, and Australia have articulated debates on what multicultural or antiracist children's literature criticism may be and how it can impact children's book mediation (cf. MacCann; Botelho and Rudman; Short; Richter; Cai; Lowery). One of the most debated questions has been how to create "true multicultural children literature" (Cai xiv)—that is, authentic and culturally conscious representations and whether these stories may also be written and/or illustrated by authors who do not belong to the depicted minorities (Yokota "Issues in Selecting Multicultural Children's Literature" xviii; Fox and Short; Martin). This question was predominant during the 1990s when scholars took up Sonia Nieto's claim for more "realistic literature that asks even young readers to grapple with sometimes wrenching issues" (Nieto "We Have Stories to Tell: A Case Study of Puerto Ricans in Children's Books" 188). In the following years, the conversation evolved to question how books presented as informed by multicultural values would, nevertheless, be written by authors of White backgrounds, few of whom were of the demographic areas, 'races,' or classes represented in their books (Stephens "Advocating Multiculturalism: Migrants in Australian Children's Literature after 1972"; Pearce 238). When revisiting this topic some years later, the Australian children's literature researcher John Stephens noted the tendency to include more characters from minorities in the position of the focalizers—that is, as characters that render a point of view—yet he still remarked how this new insight onto marginalized subjectivities was conducted by authors that could be classified as British-Australian (Stephens "Multiculturalism in Recent Australian Children's Fiction:(Re) Connecting Selves through Personal and National Histories"; Pearce 238). Clare Bradford warns us that the so-called multicultural children's literature reproduces a "weak multiculturalism" which Stephens argues derives not just from naïve optimism but also from the representational strategies in which the perspective is always that of the dominant culture (Stephens "Schemas and Scripts: Cognitive Instruments and the Representation of Cultural Diversity in Children's Literature" 18).

Postcolonial theory informs these approaches onto the so-called multicultural children's literature, and it has also inspired further explorations of children's literature as related to a (post)colonial practice in which children are the subaltern and talked down (Nodelman "The Other: Orientalism, Colonialism, and Children's Literature"; McGillis; Bradford). The representation of otherness and cultural difference is, therefore, to be related with implications on pedagogical practices and whether they are adult or child centered. Concepts stemming from postcolonial theory are also instrumental for Yulisa Amadu Maddy and Donnarae MacCann's claim regarding an emerging "neo-imperialism" in children's books about Africa, in which the alleged African need for White humanitarianism would be repurposed for new audiences (Maddy and MacCann).

The scope of the research and the sharpness of these claims are reduced when we look at the research in continental Europe, where fewer children books about cultural backgrounds and minorities are published in the first place. The depiction of minorities in children's literature has rarely been the focus of comprehensive studies.[1] We do find numerous articles on the representation of ethnicities, immigration, and how they are related to the construction of national identities, yet it is not possible to identify an articulated debate similar to the one held by American, Australian, and some British scholars.[2]

The most articulated debate on immigration, diversity, and children's literature in Europe has focused on pedagogical practices. Here we may highlight the international project Visual Journeys, led by Evelyn Arizpe at the University of Glasgow—including partners in the United States, Australia, and Barcelona—that investigated immigrant children's responses to wordless picturebooks and had an impact in the practice of literacy training for schoolchildren who cannot yet master the local language (Arizpe et al. "Visualizing Intercultural Literacy"; Arizpe et al. "Visual Journeys through Wordless Narratives"). In Spain, the Grupo Gretel led by Teresa Colomer edited a collection of essays on children's literature and language didactics that also deals with migration within the classroom and conducted research on the response to picturebooks by immigrant children (Colomer and Fittipaldi). Yet we find very few studies devoted to the analysis of narratives in these books; we may here mention Xavier Minguez López's study on interculturalism in Catalan children's books for children, in which he explores recent books revealing how "foreign" characters are underrepresented and subjected to stereotypes (Minguez López), as Jaana Pesonen's dissertation on multiculturalism in Finnish children's literature that illuminates how whiteness is connected to the national project (Pesonen).

Research on children's books and adoption is, as might be expected, a much less developed field on both sides of the Atlantic. Up to now the big majority of articles and the few books on the matter have been published in the United States and Canada, and deal with children's books available in those countries (cf. Park; Nelson; Mattix and Crawford). However, it is beginning to be a much more salient topic, since adoption studies have been expanding out of the field of developmental psychology to include a wider range of questions about identity, belonging, and origin and a number of essays dealing with adoption narratives have been published in the United States (Novy Reading Adoption: Family and Difference in Fiction and Drama; Novy Imagining Adoption: Essays on Literature and Culture; Callahan; Homans; Jerng). In 2015, a special issue on adoption and foster care in young adult literature was edited by an American and Dutch duo—Sarah Park Dahlen and Lies Wesseling—for the *Children's*

Literature Association Quarterly. This issue included an article of mine in which I explored orphan narratives in books for pre-adolescents about immigration and adoption. In their introduction, Dahlen and Wesseling assert that this article reveals a novel, fruitful line of inquiry and call for new research into the relations between adoption narratives and diaspora as adoptees increasingly tend to be equated with migrants rather than with orphans (Dahlen and Wesseling 320). Despite the interest in how transnational adoption raises a whole new set of questions about nationality, 'race,' and heritages, no previous study has compared the discourses on immigration and adoption in children's and young adult's literature.[3]

The Narrative Core of Identities

Children's literature and media appear to be privileged sites for cultural studies and for the analysis of discursive constructions, since these are highly monitored fields informed by consensus in a society. This study inquires into the stories we tell children to explain immigration, the international adoption of children, and 'race.' My exploration of these stories, of what meanings may be lying underneath them, and of what their aims may be is primarily informed by concepts stemming from two main theoretical developments: narrative discourse analysis and critical theory approaches to identity. Narrative and identity are intertwined concepts if we understand identity as performed through narration (cf. Bruner "Self-Making and World-Making").

Perhaps the most structured set of concepts that I rely upon is narratology, the theory and study of how narrative structures affect our perception. The concept of master plot developed by Herman Porter Abbott from which individual narratives draw to assimilate particularities to more generic models for understanding the world helps me to identify recurrences in the storytelling and to suggest that they unveil shared worldviews; in other words, certain stories get repeated while others are silenced or marginalized because those repeated conform to more accepted and persuasive explanations of a referential reality (Porter Abbott 40–46). I sketch masterplots for international adoption and for immigration inquiring also into the role these stories play or aim to play. The analysis of plots also profits from Nöel Carroll's ideas on how certain stories have a "narrative closure," that is, an ending that brings a feeling of completeness with the promise that the characters will not be bothered again with the same problem (Carroll). The idea of narrative closure appears to be very helpful to understand children's books, which are often characterized by their happy endings. An exploration of causality sheds light on suggestions of morality: the outcome of actions in a story passes on the implicit message that if one acts in a certain way, one gets certain consequences. The exploration of causality also profits from the distinction between "constituent events" of a plot that are to be told apart from those "supplementary events," which do not have major consequences for the story (Porter Abbott 20–22).

A question I seek to answer is what are the 'tell-able' stories about immigration and international adoption. Molly Andrews introduced the notion of 'tell-ability' to analyze recurrences and preferences in the creation of life narratives—that is, as a useful tool to apply narrative methods to social sciences (Andrews). It is, nevertheless, a very helpful concept to question why certain stories circulate (are published, recommended, read, etc.) in the highly monitored field of children's literature.

Another very relevant narratological concept of use here is that of the existing layers of 'focalization.' The idea of focalization as the 'point of view' of a narration was first elaborated by Gérard Genette and later developed by Mieke Bal (Bal Narratology: Introduction to the Theory of Narrative) as an important tool to analyze ideology and subjectivity beyond the figure of the narrator. I draw upon Bal's categories (33), since she also includes the notion of delegation of the focalization (162); I propose to understand this delegation, in certain cases, as a transference and as a colonization of the point of view. These ideas on transferences and colonization assist my reflections on how the perspective from which a certain story is told may also reveal features of (the imposition of) power structures.

I connect the analysis of focalization in these stories with the adult/ child divide that structures the production of books for children in the first place. This adult/child divide has motivated extensive debates among children's literature scholars starting from Jacqueline Rose's seminal essay *The Case of Peter Pan or the Impossibility of Children's Literature* (Rose). Rose claims that children's literature is as impossible as it is contradictive in its terms: it claims to be about children while is in fact about those adults who figure the child for their own purposes and fantasies. This idea has been seconded, among others, by Karin Lesnik-Oberstein, who argues that the criticism of children's literature always pretends "to find the good book for the child," disregarding how our concepts of childhood are linked to socioeconomic, political, and cultural divisions that affect society at large (Lesnik-Oberstein *Children's Literature: Criticism and the Fictional Child* 3). Children's literature would stem, therefore, from adult fantasies about who the child is, fantasies informed by the illustration of ideas by Rosseau and Locke regarding the purity and innocence of children (Baaz 55). Rose's much-debated text raised awareness about the socio-cultural construction of childhood as a universalistic and natural stage and removed the innocence from children's literature criticism by stressing how children's books are instrumental in this cultural construction of childhood. Rose and Lesnik-Oberstein's claims inform my approach to these books and their paratexts as texts about childhood in the first place. Nevertheless, I do not follow their claims regarding the impossibility of children's literature if only because, as David Rudd argues, the child is not only constructed by the adults, but is also a constructive and creative force that does exist. In Rudd's view, children's literature also refers to a broader field of creation and negotiation rather than solely to adults' fantasies about the child (Rudd 39). The reflections on how this adult/child divide pervades books addressed to children gives us insights into the analysis of how these stories are focalized—that is, on which points of view are rendered through the narrations. This may also be connected to Maria Nikolajeva's concept to aetonormativity (Lat. aeto- pertaining to age) that indicates an "adult normativity that governs the way children's literature has been patterned from its emergence until the present day" (Nikolajeva "Theory, Post-Theory, and Aetonormative Theory" 16). Nikolajeva argues that the most tangible form the power imbalance between the child/adult takes is that of an ostensibly adult narrative voice and the child focalizing character. In the following chapters, I explore adult views that are transferred or colonized to these child focalizing characters.

Another concept that is very helpful in this study is that of conceptual metaphors elaborated by George Lakoff and Mark Johnson in the groundbreaking *Metaphors We Live By* (Lakoff and Johnson). Lakoff and Johnson argue that metaphors not only reflect the way we perceive the world but also govern our everyday functioning. They identify root metaphors from which other metaphors spring, which are so embedded in language and culture that they are not to be taken as metaphors. Lakoff and Johnson illustrate this with examples such as money is time, life is a journey, and nation is family—metaphors used recurrently and from which a number of other metaphors stem. I identify conceptual root metaphors in these stories and analyze their implications in the creating of narratives that naturalize cultural constructs.

The narrative analysis includes not only verbal texts but also visual narrations, especially since three-quarters of the books considered in this analysis may be labeled as picturebooks, following a definition in which the verbal and the visual have equal importance (Moebius 169). The remaining books also include illustrations. Reviewing the debate about the need for a theory specific to children's literature, Maria Nikolajeva argues that "the closest we have come to an independent, specific theory is in picturebook criticism, a rapidly emerging academic field" (2009, 15). I rely on a number of studies published in this evolving area in the last 15 years (Colomer et al.; Nodelman "Decoding the Images: Illustration and Picturebooks"; Nodelman "The Eye and the I: Identification and First-Person Narratives in Picture Books"; Nikolajeva and Scott; D. Lewis; Sipe; Happonen; Thiele). These works help to understand the interplay of the visual, the verbal, and the material in books for children and are complemented by more general theories on visual semiotics, most prominently in Gunter Kress and Theo van Leeuwen's

The Grammar of Visual Design (Kress and Van Leeuwen). I also integrate insights from an emerging visual narratology (Bal "Introduction: Another Kind of Image"; Horskotte) to explore the concept of visual focalization.

This theoretical framework of concepts and theories stemming from literary studies is complemented by studies and reflections on identity, difference, and representation. Among the most prominent bodies of work informing my perspective, I highlight Postcolonial Theory, Imagology, Critical Race Theory, and Intersectionality.

Both immigration and international adoption discourses are very productively analyzed with postcolonial perspectives. From Edward Said's reflections on the West's patronizing depictions of the Orient and its tendency to create binary oppositions such as civilized/wild, culture/nature, reason/body, to Homi Bhabha's further ideas on 'ambivalence,' 'third space,' and 'hybridity,' postcolonial theory illuminates and identifies the conflicting forces that shape stereotypes. As Homi Bhabha claims, difference is performed and created through representations, and multiculturalism is more a desire for distinguishing cultural boundaries than a product of those differences. Bhabha's concepts are helpful for understanding the difficult (de)construction of origin in adoption narratives; as adoption scholar Tobias Hübinette argues, the 'third space' finds in the internationally adopted children a very pertinent example, since in them categories such as kinship, territory, culture, religion, and memory are estranged (Hübinette "Disembedded and Free-Floating Bodies out-of-Place and out-of-Control: Examining the Borderline Existence of Adopted Koreans" 155).

Imagology is a neighbor discipline to Postcolonial Studies even if it is not so much concerned with power imbalances, but with the crystallization of certain stereotypes in national discourses. As Postcolonial Theory, Imagology has been most productive in studying literary texts, which theorists regard as a "privileged genre for the dissemination of stereotypes, because it often works on the presupposition of a 'suspension of disbelief' and some (at least aesthetic) appreciative credit among the audience" (Derksen 26). Imagologists introduced concepts such as 'hetero-image' (the image of the Other), 'auto-image' (the domestic identity), 'spected' (referring to the national culture represented as Other), 'spectant' (the national culture as a point of view of others), and 'ethnotype' (the stereotypical representation of a character according to ethnic features), which help to identify the production of otherness in these texts. Emer O'Sullivan notes that children's literature is a particularly valuable source for studying the various schemata, conventional national attributes, and their counter-stereotypes, since all these are clearly reflected in the texts meant to assist early stages of socialization (O'Sullivan 1–2).

Critical Race Theory calls for the recognition of power relationships embedded in the socio-cultural construction of 'race.' Various texts more or less explicitly related to this line of thinking are fundamental to unveil what is at stake in the representations of 'race' and ethnicity in these books (Appiah "Race, Culture, Identity: Misunderstood Connections"; Delgado and Stefancic; Zamudio et al.). Stuart Hall's ideas on the racialized regime of representation shed light on the reproduction of verbal and visual stereotypes (Hall "New Ethnicities"; Hall *Representation: Cultural Representations and Signifying Practices*). Richard Dyer's interrogations on whiteness and his claim for identifying 'White' as an ethnic category have been fundamental for the understanding of 'auto-images' and for an exploration of the production of national ethnicity in books meant to educate about cultural difference (Dyer).

Last, Intersectionality (cf. Crenshaw; Prins; K. Davis; Yuval-Davis "Intersectionality and Feminist Politics"; Yuval-Davis *The Politics of Belonging: Intersectional Contestations*) provides an overarching approach to explore the interplay of 'race' and ethnicity and how these categories intersect with politics of belonging. Intersectionality claims that the divisions of class, gender, ethnicity, nationality, stage of the life cycle, and religion, among others, are deeply intermeshed and continually co-defining each other. Originally a contribution from the Gender Studies field, Intersectionality cautions us against traditional, one-dimensional analytical conceptualizations of identity and assists us in the identification of the axes of social power (Yuval-Davis "Intersectionality and Feminist Politics" 198). Intersectionality argues that the classical conceptualizations of oppression within a society—such as racism, sexism, or homophobia—do not act independently from one another but intersect. Despite its popularity among gender scholars, there has been considerable confusion concerning how it can or should be applied (K. Davis 67). Here I draw inspiration from the approach sketched by Baujke Prins, in which she differentiates a systemic intersectionality (mostly U.S. based) from a constructionist one (mostly UK based); the latter refuses to assume that the subject is primarily constituted by systems of domination and marginalization. Prins emphasizes how identity cannot be grasped by a list of characteristics, which would inform us about the 'what' of a person, but that the 'who' can only be shown through the construction of storytelling and life narratives. Prins builds upon Stuart Hall's claim that we are simultaneously less and more than the sum of social categories with which we are identified. She illustrates her point in an article in which she analyzes the social positioning exercised by her former schoolmates—Dutch and Moluccan—when explaining their lives. In her approach, the subject negotiates its position across the axes of social difference, a negotiation that takes place through storytelling. This constructionist approach underpins how different social categories become complicated and are even contradicted in the narration. It allowed me to think further about how the representation of ethnicity may be understood as a presentation, a performance, in which senses of belonging and affiliations are made rather than reflected.

The S.O.L. Recommendations: A Case Study

This study is based on the books recommended by the prestigious Fundación Germán Sánchez Ruiperez (FGSR) from 2001 to 2013, the years in which they ran the Servicio de Orientación a la Lectura infantil y juvenil program (S.O.L.). The sample is formed by 60 children books endorsed for children younger than 11 years old focusing on those that presented what Temple, Martínez, and Yokota describe as "contemporary realistic fiction" set in Western societies presenting racially marked characters (cited in Yokota "Realism in Picture Books for Children: Representations of Our Diverse World " 65). This filter excluded a number of animal metaphors, in which the references to otherness, immigration, or adoptions were looser, as well as a large number of informative books in which cultural differences and ethnicities are simply explained or defined.[4] I looked through hundreds of books endorsed by the S.O.L., selecting those that include characters that were presented as having an ethnicity or 'race' marked—in the visual and or the verbal narration—as different.[5]

The books that constitute this sample were published between 1998 and 2011. One third of them are translations from other European languages originally published in the United States or in other European countries. In this work, I touch only superficially issues of translation referring to how—and why—some texts may travel to other contexts; European books seems to be preferred to American, despite the vast offer of the later. Three quarters of the sample are picturebooks, considering that these are those in "which words and pictures are treated as semi-autonomous and mutually attractive chains of meanings, rather than as fixed images serving as a supplement to meanings fixed in words" (Moebius 169). This can be explained by the age span we here consider—up to 11 years old—and to the growing number of picturebooks and illustrated books published in the last two decades.

In our sample we can clearly distinguish two groups of books: those about adoption that are rather explicitly addressed to adoptees, their siblings, and friends, and a broader group of books about migration and people with migrant backgrounds. We find very few books in which adopted and migrant characters coincide. In *Teo Aprende a Convivir*, Teo—a very popular Spanish character—meets people from different backgrounds in a 'multicultural' party held in his neighborhood. Among children from migrant couples, there is also a Russian adoptee, and an entire page is devoted to an explanation of what international adoption is. We find a similar plot in *Una fiesta sin igual*, where the neighbors get together, each of them contributing a dish from their original countries, and a Spanish mother brings a Chinese plate she learned to cook while visiting China to pick up her daughter. In *Todos los colores del arco iris*, a child explains how in his classroom they have 'all the colors.' The group includes children who immigrated with their parents as well as children who were adopted internationally. (The adoptees come from Russia, China, and Ethiopia, and the immigrant characters from Ecuador and Morocco, reflecting the major trends of adoption and immigration into Spain.) In these three books, international adoption and immigration are presented as different, parallel practices that result in a new ethnic/'racial' social landscape. It is quite transparent in them a pedagogic aim of using children's books as a means to manage and negotiate identities in a changing scenario.

Apart from these, we find a couple of books in which references to ('transracial') adoption and immigration coincide with no explicit aim to establish parallels. Very interestingly, the coincidences occur in stories that may be related to rescue narratives in which we could infer a past of forced displacements even if not explicitly acknowledged. This appears to be quite relevant if we take that there is no such thing as a third group of stories that we could identify as dealing with refugees. Despite the fact that Europe and Spain have been receiving refugees since World War II, exiles, and asylum seekers are seldom depicted in children's literature published in Spanish. Most of the stories about forced displacements refer to World War II or to more recent conflicts in regions afar from Spain such as Nepal, the Middle East, or Afghanistan without referring to the journey to Europe. Some Spanish books deal with Sahrawi refugees from the former Spanish colony in the Western Sahara, but they are all targeted to young adult readers. (Note that exceptions include *Los Gigantes de la Luna* and *Palabras de Caramelo* by Gonzalo Moure, both recommended to readers between 9 and 11 years, which we did not consider as part of the sample of this study as those stories take place in Africa.) In our sample, we have only one book identified by the reviewers as about refugees, *Ziba vino en barco*—which recounts the journey to the 'Western' land of a girl with her mother. Nevertheless, we may identify a number of books in which forced displacements appear to blend in with immigration/adoption stories. This may be the case, for example, in *Caja de cartón*, a book that tells the story of a baby girl who travels with her mother to Europe because there—the narrator tells us—girls do not sleep in cardboard boxes and mothers do not cry. The boat carrying them sinks into the sea, but the girl and her mother survive. They live with other marginalized immigrant/refugees in houses made of cardboard boxes that one day are set on fire. After that atrocious day, the girl does not see her mother again but is (happily) adopted. It is unclear—and it appears to be irrelevant—whether they were immigrating into Spain because of some economic conditions or fleeing from persecutors. Interestingly, the happy ending is not to become protected by the state under an asylum program, but having the young girl adopted. Something similar happens in *Blanca y Viernes*, a book that will be analyzed in detail in the last chapter. In it, a boy who could easily be described as a refugee, if we follow certain clues given in the story, is nevertheless presented as an immigrant and becomes adopted at the very end. Interestingly, these two books are not meant to circulate as other adoption books: they were not written and published with transnational adoptees as ideal imagined readers, and the adoption is rather a happy ending for a story of misfortunes than a condition thematized. If we close read the reviews by the S.O.L. mediators, we conclude that books about adoption would apparently be appealing only to adoptees, their siblings, and playmates, whereas books about immigration are meant to educate a wider audience about social diversity. This sketches a binarism of books about/for which can be connected to that pedagogical aim of children's literature mediators explored more in the next chapters. As we will explore throughout this book, adoption and immigration narratives communicate in various ways speaking out needs to negotiate national identity and belonging in new and heterogenous environments. In this work, we focus the analysis on the modes in which discourses on transnational adoption and migration are related to narratives of 'race' and diversity exploring how agency and the capacity for self-fashioning is opened or limited through storytelling.

Notes

1 Perhaps this is with the sole exception of Nazli Hodaie's *Der Orient in der Deutschen Kinder und Jugendliteratur* on the German representation of the Arab and Oriental world in children's and young adult literature.
2 A list of such articles would include but is not limited to Weinkauff, Gina. "Between Village Mentality and Cultural Hybridity: Mapping the Immigrant Self." *Bookbird. A Journal of International Children's Literature* 49.4 (2001): 17–25. Weinkauff, Gina. "How Far Is It to Elsewhere? On the Awareness of the Alien in German Children's and Youth Literature." *Anuario de investigación en literatura infant y juvenil. Universidad de Vigo, Facultad de Filología y Traducción* 9 (2011): 211–26. O'Sullivan, E. "Repräsentationen Eigener Und Fremder Kulturen in Der (Kinder)Literatur." *Dialoge Zwischen Den Kulturen: Interkulturelle Literatur Und Ihre Didaktik.* Ed. Honnef-Becker, I.: Schneider Verlag Hohengehren, 2007. Gomes, Jose Antonio and Ana Margarida Ramos *Literatura Portuguesa Para La Infancia Y Promoción De La Multiculturalidad.* El libro infantil y juvenil desde la diversidad cultural. 2011. Ommundsen, Åse Marie. "Childhood in a Multicultural Society?: Globalization, Childhood, and Cultural Diversity in Norwegian Children's Literature." *Bookbird: A Journal of International Children's Literature* 49.1 (2011): 31–40. Pesonen, Jaana. "Anti-Racist Strategies in Finnish Children's Literature: Physical Appearance and Language as Signifiers of National Belonging." *Children's Literature in Education* 44.3 (2013): 238–50. Ramos, Ana Margarida. "Crossing Borders: Migrations in Portuguese Contemporary Children's Literature." *New Review of Children's Literature and Librarianship* 20.1 (2014): 26–39.

3 These topics have only been briefly referenced in Sarah Park Dahlen's research on Asian Americans adoptees (Dahlen).

4 This selection followed the possibilities given by the S.O.L. search-engine itself: I decided to include only those books that were labeled as about 'Vida Real' and 'Mundo en Sociedad,' which resulted in a sample composed of fictional stories that could be labeled as realistic.

5 Defining what is an ethnically or 'racially' marked character is certainly problematic as it reproduces the idea of existing racial classifications that this text contends and the very hegemonic idea that whiteness is unmarked. Nevertheless, I had to commit myself to reproduce these classifications in order to have a reduced number of books in which to explore race narratives. I may note here that I looked for marks in relation to the idea of a foreign origin—usually acknowledged in the verbal text—as well as to visual marks in the illustrations in which racial contrasts were created.

3 I Came by Plane
The Masterplan of International Adoptions

Adopted characters used to be—particularly in the fiction of the nineteenth and early twentieth centuries—orphans who by the end of a story were adopted (think of Dickens' characters, Anne of Green Gables, or Orphan Annie); today, though, we find a growing number of books in which the adoption is not just a happy ending, but rather the story itself. Children's books about adoption are books for adoptees that are written, recommended, and bought with the aim of providing adopted children with mirror-narratives to be used as building blocks in the construction of their identities. The growing frequency of international adoption and the new approaches to their socialization—today, adoption is acknowledged and placed at the center of a life narrative rather than glossed over—are keys to understanding the emergence and importance of this topic in children's literature. This new approach shall also be framed within a broader social and cultural context in which personal stories and biographies are emphasized; children who do not resemble their parents are often asked to explain this difference, and these books present stories in which to rework their own narrative explanations.

Interestingly, most of the books about adoption recommended by the Fundación Germán Sánchez Ruipérez are structured upon a recurrent skeletal story, a "master plot" (47) as conceptualized by Herman Porter Abbott. The analysis of this plot not only reveals features of the discourse on international adoption, but also sheds light onto how books and cultural production play a role in the making of the family, or, borrowing a concept by Norwegian anthropologist Signe Howell, in the 'kinning of foreigners' (Howell 2). It can be argued that these stories, rather than targeting children cater to a need of their adoptive parents to turn those into one of kin.

Books about adoption assist adoptive families in their struggle with what American anthropologist Sara K. Dorow phrases as the "impossible contradictions" of international adoption. Dorow argues that the identity and belonging of the adoptees will be always haunted by (1) how the child is at once both a commodity to be exchanged and an object of care and compassion, (2) the contradiction between the biological origin and the artificial kinship, and (3) how adoptees are both citizens and foreigners in the countries where they grow up (Dorow *Transnational Adoption: A Cultural Economy of Race, Gender, and Kinship* 16–23).

To better understand the socio-cultural and geopolitical context of transnational adoptions today, I first review in the current debates on contemporary international adoption with a close look at anthropological research on Western adoptive families. Next, I outline the structure of this master plot of international adoption, dividing it into the three moments of the Aristotelian plot and arguing that in these narrations the adoption is told relating to the biological process of having a child—that is, mirroring the processes of conceiving, expecting, and delivering a child. Finally, I analyze the narrative voice and "focalization" (Bal *Narratology: Introduction to the Theory of Narrative* 160) to explain how the points of view employed enable the performance of kinship justifying international adoption in times when the practice is becoming increasingly contested.

The Controversies of International Adoption

Most researchers in adoption studies point out the international humanitarian campaign for fostering children who were abandoned after the Korean War (1950–53)—children born to Korean mothers and fathered by American soldiers—as the starting moment for transnational adoption (Oh). This chronology could be debated if we trace previous institutionalized experiences of children's circulation, such as during the Spanish Civil War (1936–39) or in various countries during World War II (1939–45). The origin of transnational adoption could be even traced back to the European colonial times, when children of the Empire were moved into Western settings in the belief that it was in their best interests. However, researchers stress the importance of recent decades—from the mid-1990s onwards—in the institutionalization and unprecedented expansion of transnational adoption transferring a growing number of children from the so-called Third World to Western families. The so-called boom of inter-country adoption has been explained by pointing to the increased number of children to be adopted that was largely triggered by the new geopolitical order after the fall of the Berlin Wall and the Iron Curtain. This led to a first (short) spate of adoptions from Romania, soon followed by a massive number of adoptions from China and Russia. The entrance of these two countries greatly changed the numbers of transnational adoptions, which more than doubled between 1995 and 2005 (Selman "From Bucharest to Beijing: Changes in Countries Sending Children for International Adoption 1990 to 2006" 42). During the last 15 years, China has maintained an indisputable first place in the list of originating countries with more than 10,000 children undergoing foreign adoptions annually.

Nevertheless, due to new domestic policies, the number of children sent by these countries has diminished. Rather than cooling off the adoption boom, this decline has heated up the debate on adoption's pros and cons (M. A. Davis 150–59).

The unprecedented magnitude of the transnational adoption wave cannot be purely explained by the reframing of the world geopolitical order, but is rather the result of intersecting social changes, medical advances, and family legislation. In his history of North American adoption, E. Wayne Carp (Carp 196) emphasizes how the changes in contraceptive technology, cultural values, and Constitutional law during the 1960s and 1970s transformed the institution of adoption, provoking a drastic decrease in the number of infants available for internal adoption. In the United States and Northern European countries, this coincides with the beginning of the steady practice of international adoption, backed by the liberalism and racial integration efforts of the 1960s (Kim 141). The legalization of abortion in the 1970s and 1980s also had an impact, reducing the number of children available for internal, national adoption (Thompson 441). As domestic adoptions became harder to obtain, international adoption emerged as the best alternative not only for childless couples, but also for those who wanted to extend their family without going through the process of pregnancy—from Hollywood actresses to single mothers, single fathers, and same-sex couples.

The movement of children from developing to Western countries has been largely explained within the discourse of Global North-Global South charity, and was largely regarded as a beneficial practice for all involved: the children, the adoptive parents, and the biological parents. A 1986 UN declaration saw international adoption as: "an alternative means of providing the child with a family" (cited in Bergquist 626), but it could be argued that it is just the opposite: an alternative means of providing a family with a child. In the past decade, researchers have studied how international adoption advocates have constructed an image of abandoned third-world children as 'waiting children' (Cartwright 86), labeled as children at-risk to be rescued through adoption: "(They) are seen as victimized by a poverty that can be remedied through transformation of the state, modernization, education, technology, and science" (Ortiz and Briggs 41).

Today, the international adoption of children is mainly regulated by an international convention, the 1993 Hague Convention that has been ratified by 85 countries and demands certain regulation of adoptions in the origin countries. Nevertheless, this convention has been criticized for lacking definitions of key terms like "adoptable," "orphan," or "best interests of the child" (Thompson 463–64), and, overall, for being insufficient to protect the rights of the children. Anthropologist Barbara Yngvesson ("Placing the 'Gift Child' in Transnational Adoption") argues

that the countries end up being accomplices in a process of child commodification that takes place in international adoption:

> Reconfigured as a 'legal orphan' that is 'available' for adoption, this
> child becomes a particular kind of 'natural resource' for the state
> that has produced it. The role of the state in this form of production
> is both more subtle and more powerful than its role in producing
> identity rights. (11)

The major claims against international adoption are funded in the
charges of children's trafficking and commodification, and in the close
relationship between legal and illegal practices (Yngvesson "Going
'Home': Adoption, Loss of Bearings, and the Mythology of Roots"
10–11). Coinciding with the emergence of this debate, the number of
children today available for inter-country adoptions has diminished because the principal countries of origin are deliberately bringing down the
numbers of international adoptions in an attempt to improve their image
and contradict the impression that they cannot take care of their children. Meanwhile, demand for adoptable children has increased: more
and more Western couples are delaying parenthood, with the result that
when they do decide to have a family of their own, their fertility has
decreased considerably. The more adoption is 'needed,' the more heated
the dispute of its pros and cons becomes.

The voices of adult Korean adoptees who criticize their experiences
and accuse their parents and adoption agencies of color-blind racism has
been instrumental to the debate. Through all kinds of autobiographical
texts, Korean adoptees have told their stories of failed assimilation and
the impossibility of belonging to either their destination country or their
origin country (cf. Hübinette "International Adoption Is Harmful and
Exploitive"; Eng; Trenka). The Korean (failed) adoption experience has
motivated a completely new approach to the question of how 'race' and
physical differences impact the practice of international adoption:

> In an earlier era, adoption across borders was assumed to be straight-
> forward: A child traveled to a new country and stayed there. A child
> born in Korea and adopted in Minnesota was expected to grow up,
> and remain, simply a (white) American. Parents and adoption orga-
> nizations did not question that their acts were good deeds.
> (Volkman "Introduction: Transnational Adoption" 1–2)

Contemporary international adoptees are no longer raised as simple
(White) children. "Today, adopted people—children or adults—are expected, or at least invited, to explore their multiple identities: to retain a
name, to imagine their birth families, to learn about 'birth cultures,' perhaps to visit the birth country" (Volkman "Introduction: Transnational

Adoption" 2). The interest in the country of provenance and the efforts to provide adoptees with a (racialized) origin story is perhaps the most prominent feature of twenty-first-century international adoption.

Spain, Top Destination Country for International Adoption

Excepting some isolated cases, international adoption began in Spain in the mid-1990s, which was rather late compared to other European countries. Despite its delayed start, Spain was the European country where international adoption had its most spectacular growth in the boom period that ran from 1995 to 2005. Peter Selman explains it as the result of "the sharp decline in fertility during the 1990s because of deferred childbearing and the consequent increase in infecundity" (Selman "The Movement of Children in International Adoption. Development and Trends in Receiving States and States of Origin 1998–2004" 34). Spain entered the twenty-first century as the European country with the highest number of adoptions in Europe, and second only to the United States on the list of the top receiving countries. Moreover, the Autonomous Community of Catalonia in Spain had the highest rate of adoptions per population in the world (Howell and Marre 294).

What makes Spain such an internationally "adoption-inclined" country? Researcher Diana Marre, from the Autonomous University of Barcelona, explains it as a result of several social changes and new laws that were approved after the end of dictatorship in 1975. Marre remarks the rapid legalization of contraception, divorce and, under certain circumstances, abortion. Spanish feminists promoted the right of women to delay childbirth or to remain childless and what took decades in other countries to develop happened in less than one decade. Spain had the highest European birth rate in 1975 (2.8 per woman) but the lowest in 1995 (1.17 per woman). It also favors Spaniards' international adoptions that the local law preserves genitors' rights almost until they themselves renounce them. This last reason is crucial to explain the appeal of adopting a child in another country, since that child is first labeled as an 'orphan' and would start a new life from scratch. In the Spanish national adoption system, one can adopt a child who will preserve— and, in certain cases, even be obliged to maintain—bonds with his or her original family. This, and the time it takes to adopt through the national procedure, made international adoption the best alternative for those willing to extend their families but unable to do so. We must also consider that while international adoption is almost always labeled as 'transracial,' domestic adoption could fall under the same category. Adoptive parents opting for the Spanish system are often white middle or upper-class couples who are paired with children born to unwed migrant mothers.

A Masterplot of International Adoption

If we look into the list of books recommended about adoption, we note that half of the titles are structured upon a similar skeletal story. A great number of these books have been written either by adoptive parents or by their close friends, and even if they are not explicitly labeled as biographical many of them have a clear testimonial inspiration.

This masterplot of international adoption starts with the presentation of a heterosexual couple. (There are very few examples depicting monoparental families and none presenting same-sex partners.) The story first tells us about their strong desire to parent and the long and difficult process they face before being able to travel to pick up the child. If we divide this masterplot in the three moments of the Aristotelian plot, we may understand that presentation of the characters is that of the expecting parents, and the action of the plot is the adoption that ends in that journey to the origin country. The climax, therefore, is the encounter with the child, lived as if giving birth; a final denouement comes once they are all back 'home.' This narrative is also biblical in structure—Jesus's parents traveled to a foreign place to "get" him, although he was born from Maria, he was in a sense adopted too (at least by Joseph), since his father was technically the Holy Spirit. After the birth, the family of three journeys together through many dangers to return home.

In the following pages, I inquire into the plots and point of view in twelve books recommended about adoption; all but two of them were originally published in Spanish or Catalan. I include in this group *Tell Me Again About the Night I Was Born*, a book that recounts a national adoption in the United States, but that shares the same plot structure and narrative strategies as books about parents adopting internationally. This book, written by the actress Jamie Lee Curtis, is frequently mistaken in Spain as depicting an international adoption, and it is often mentioned as one of the favorite books about adoption.

The Desire to Parent

The adoption masterplot begins constructing a powerful desire to parent that takes the form of an immeasurable love for that imagined child to be adopted. The expecting parents get prepared and overcome different hitches as if enduring a (difficult) pregnancy. The child, on the other side, is also portrayed as expecting, but lacking agency and individualization.

I Love You Like Crazy Cakes, a children's bestseller about adoption translated into Spanish as *Te quiero, niña bonita*, and *En algún lugar de China*, a book written by a Spanish adoptive mother, recount the experience of adopting a Chinese girl. Both stories begin with the mother handling the bureaucracy and preparing the trip and end after they arrive 'back' home with the child. *En algún lugar de China* includes fantasy elements with a bird character that triggers the adoption announcing the parents that a girl is waiting for them in China and indicating to them that they must follow a red thread to meet the girl. This image also recalls the Annunciation paintings in which the Holy Spirit appears as a dove announcing to the Virgin Mary that she will have a child.

The first pages in these two books (Figure 3.1) give us good insight into the organization of agency. As stressed by scholars working on picturebooks' semiotics, images often have the role of 'saying' what the verbal text will not (Nikolajeva and Scott 12). *I Love You Crazy Cakes* and *En algún lugar de China* begin featuring the waiting child with double-spread illustrations of orphanage rooms (Figure 3.1), while the mothers are taking actions. Those images denote the family-less existence in orphanages and speak of the lack of identity of this child, who is only transformed into an individual when encountered by the new parents. The beds in a row may also recall images of industrialized production. Strikingly, both books describe adoption from China, the principal origin country of adoptees and, as we know, main producer of commercial goods for a globalized market. However, the textual account in these books avoids referring to orphanages or to any of the geopolitical issues that favor overseas adoption—the texts only mention that a child is 'waiting' for them in China.

La Galera—a Catalan publisher specialized in dealing with diversity—has published a collection about adoption with six titles targeted to the most common origin countries of Spanish-adopted children: China, Russia, Ethiopia, Nepal, Ukraine, and Colombia. They were all written by

Figure 3.1 The first pages of *I Love You Like Crazy Cakes* and *En Algún Lugar de China* contrast the waiting of the children with the active preparation of the mothers. Illustrations by Jane Dyer and Emilio Amade.

different authors but follow very closely this master plot of international adoption by first presenting the couple, then continuing by describing the journey to pick up the child and ending happily at 'home.' Remarkably, the verbal text does not say the word "adoption" but makes a reference to it by stressing how much they wanted and longed for that baby born far away. In the book about adoption in Russia, the father-narrator explains that they wanted to have a second child and that after a lot of discussion they decided that "lo tendríamos e iríamos a buscarlo a Rusia" [We will have him and we will go pick him up in Russia] (second double spread) as if getting children in other countries would be a common proceeding.

Couples and singles wanting to adopt have to choose a country at the very beginning of the process and to do so they weigh different factors such as the transparency of the adoption process, the length of the waiting period for that country, and various details of the regulations such as whether single parents are accepted, the required length of the stay in the country before taking the child, or if they need to demonstrate a certain income. Along with these variables, the ideas associated with different countries play a significant role and also imply a most often non-spoken selection of the desired physical traits of the baby (Dorow "Racialized Choices: Chinese Adoption and the 'White Noise' of Blackness" 364; Marre 77).

Researchers have noted, for instance, that Russia and Eastern Europe were preferred by parents who do not want to deal with a so-called transracial family, whereas China used to be chosen by those who desired to have a daughter rather than a son, since most adoptees from China were girls due to the one-child policy (Jacobson 15–19). These books avoid delving into the reasons to choose one specific country with the exception perhaps of *Llegué... de Colombia*, where the parents explain "nosotros queríamos que nuestro hijo fuese de Colombia, un país de clima suave y de gente amable. Por eso, Carlos, fuimos a buscarte allí" [We wanted to have a child from Colombia, a country of mild weather and kind people. That's why, Carlos, we went to pick you up there] (second double spread). In this quote, we may not only trace certain preconceived ideas about Colombia but also how the desire to parent moves the narration forward, and, as this quote already announces, it is a desire that confers a subject position to the adoptee. Butler's reading of Althusser's concept of 'interpellation' would understand this as the constitution of the pre-existing subject in the 'interpellative hail' (Salih 78). The adoptive parents' desire constitutes the son, Carlos, who is asked to respond to this call assuming that he comes from a land of kind people.

The Journey to the Child

The main event of the adoption masterplot is the trip to pick up the adoptee; books often include drawings of airplanes or suitcases and describe this journey as very long. In *Llegué de... Colombia*, the narrator explains that "el viaje fue largo, muy largo y muy emocionante. Tuvimos que coger tres aviones y volamos sobre pueblos, montañas y ciudades; incluso sobre el inmenso océano Atlántico" [the trip was long, very long and very touching. We had to take three planes and flew over towns, mountains, and cities; we even flew over the huge Atlantic Ocean] (fourth double spread). *Llegué de... Rusia* uses the same resource: "tuvimos que coger dos aviones y atravesar toda Europa" [(we had to) take two planes and travel throughout the whole of Europe] (and an illustrated world map shows how far away Siberia is from Spain) (third double spread). The geographical distances are stressed as one more proof of how adopting is not an easy way to get a baby but a process to be compared to the biological process of having a child. The adoptive mother in *Isha, nacida del corazón* is afraid to fly but manages to travel twice to India—a trip that requires two connecting flights, she explains—before being able to bring her daughter home. In some cases, the books also include an account of the hitches faced at home when applying for the adoptions. The narrator of *Llegué de... Rusia* tells that they had to marry in order to adopt him: "¡Qué jaleo! (...) Lo hicimos por ti, ¡y fue un día muy feliz!" [What a hassle! (...) We did it for you, and it was a very happy day!] (second double spread).

The difficulties do not fade out after landing in the country where the child was born. These difficulties are shaped by the cultural differences that are treated, nevertheless, as minor problems. In *Llegué de... Ucrania*, the narrator tells: "De nuestra estancia en Ucrania recordamos mucho los platos típicos: el kéfir, la smetana, el borsh y unos pasteles muy dulces. Pero costaba encontrar la comida, y siempre teníamos que caminar mucho para ir a comprar" [From our stay in Ukraine we remember a lot the typical dishes: the kefir, the smetana, the borsh and some very sweet pies. But it was very difficult to find food, and we always had to walk a lot to buy it] (eleventh double spread). It is unclear to the reader whether it was also difficult for Ukrainians or if it is a problem uniquely faced by Western tourists, unaccustomed to the local food. In any case, this account stresses the parents' ability to get by in that country as well as their respect for the local culture, while remarking how the cultural differences imposed difficulties on them.

The origin country is often presented as an exotic land, especially in the visual depictions. Each of the books of La Galera collection, for instance, includes a double spread with data on the country of origin and also a short dictionary of words and phrases that speaks that desire of the adoptive parents to get through in the country of their child while resembling the lists of ready-made sentences for adventurous tourists who believe they give them real access to a foreign culture.

The insensitive exoticization in the visual depictions may be explained by attending to how picturebooks are created when a finished text is sent by the publisher to the illustrator, who does not have the same authorial involvement in the final product, the most common practice in the publishing industry (and remarkably common in Spain). The illustrator's quest for pictorial solutions might, therefore, be much more influenced by circulating stereotypes than the verbal text that goes through more filters and may be more power-sensitive to the production of otherness through representation.

The illustrations in *Isha, nacida del corazón* are a case in point. In them, the girl waits for her parents in a Persian palace, probably inspired by the Taj Mahal, an unlikely landscape for any Indian child, let alone children living in orphanages. On the front cover, the girl in the palace raises her arms to the moon which may evoke that global connection of international adoption as well that non-Western connected-to-nature spirituality that appears to be recurrent in depictions of some world regions. These illustrations construct the origin as a place from where the adoptee can convey a story of proud differentiation. Poverty and abandonment are overwritten with exoticism.

The (Happy) Encounter

The difficulties are left behind in the very moment in which they meet their child. The climax of these stories is the encounter with the adoptee, a moment that is usually told by emphasizing the uniqueness and singularity of the child and how they were compatible from the very first moment. In *En algún lugar de China*, the couple meets the Chinese girl sitting outside the orphanage and the three are united in a hug: "Madre mía ¡qué alegría!" (22) [Oh my God, what a joy!] (eleventh double spread); The parents adopting in Ukraine tell the girl that "enseguida nos robaste el corazón" [you stole our hearts right away] (fourth double spread), and those in Nepal that "en tus ojos brillaba una luz muy especial" [a very special light shone in your eyes] (fourth double spread). The mothers in both *Tell Me Again About the Night I Was Born* and *I Love You Like Crazy Cakes* drop tears of joy when holding the baby for the first time.

The first meeting—which often coincides with the handing over of the baby, as in the most usual procedure of international adoptions—is rendered as a happy encounter in all of these books. The narrators—with focalization on the adoptive parents—recount that moment as a magical moment that signalizes a new start in life. Interestingly, some testimonies also suggest that this may not have been so smooth for the child. But that initial uneasiness is quickly overcome: "tu ponías cara de tímido y no te atrevías a abrir la boca. Apoyabas la cabeza sobre tu mano como si tuvieses vergüenza, pero por debajo de la nariz se te escapaba una sonrisita que nos decía que estabas a gusto" [you had a shy look and didn't dare open your mouth. You were leaning your head against your hand as if you were ashamed, but you were letting out a little smile that told us you were at ease] (*Llegué de... Rusia*, fifth double spread).

If there is a driving force behind the masterplot of international adoption, it is the force of love. The infinite love of the adoptive parents is put forward not only to explain how it is that children born to a foreign mother can be parented by a Western couple, but also to weave the family together: the love of the parents creates that indissoluble parent-child tie. Perhaps implicitly in opposition to the relinquishing progenitors, the adoptive parents are presented as loving the child unconditionally. That powerful tie of love is born in the desire and illusion of having a child—it is, therefore, born from the power of imagination. The narrator in *Llegué de... Ucrania* opens up telling the adopted children: "Mientras imaginábamos como seríais, ya os queríamos mucho" (first double spread) [While we were imagining how you were going to be, we already loved you a lot]. This vast love of the parents is in consonance with contemporary discourses on the family as described by sociologists Ulrich Beck and Elisabeth Beck-Gernsheim in *The Normal Chaos of Love*. Beck and Beck-Gernsheim make the point that the transformations of sexual life, domestic labors, and equal rights for women in the last half of the past century have had a huge impact on the narratives of family. Among other effects, the instability of the couple's love turns the child into the "unique, primary love object" (Beck and Beck-Gernsheim 37), a bastion against the vanishing chances of loving and being loved. These love narratives inform the cultural construction of parenthood at the turn of the twentieth century. The absence of the undeniable blood tie makes this performance of love even more necessary, and in the encounter with the child this love is first materialized as if having a magical force: parents are surprised by the uniqueness of their children and tell a story in which the children respond accepting their promises of love. The journey home and the child's successful adaptation—represented with a good night's sleep—reassure the reader that what had begun as presumably fragile infatuation will last forever.

Figure 3.2 The mother reads a book that has a similar elongated format to the book we are reading. Illustration by Emilio Amade.

After that first encounter, the story is quickly closed with a trip back 'home,' a trip that may resemble the coming back from the hospital and the baby's first time at what will be his or her home. A sense of belonging is sealed in occasions with references to a broader group of people that celebrates the arrival of this adopted child as in *Te quiero niña bonita* when all relatives and friends come to visit the new mother and her baby. Many of these stories end referring to the first night the child spends at the new home and most include images of the parents at the bedside or under the door's threshold. Some of these last illustrations function as meta-narratives showing the parents reading a book that closely resembles the one the reader has in his or her hands. In *Tell Me Again About the Night I Was Born*, the adopted girl falls asleep under a book with the title "I" open over her chest. The same title had appeared at the very beginning when the girl first asks her father to read again her story. *Tell Me Again About the Night I Was Born* tells us about the origin story of the adopted girl, a story she has read tons of times already and that, we are told at the end, was first read the very first night the girl was at home. In a similar way, the last page of *En algún lugar de China*—Picture 2—features the mother sitting by the bed of the adoptee with an elongated book similar in shape to the one the reader would have in hands suggesting that this mother reads the same story. In these metanarrative references we may trace how the fictionalized account of the adoption is meant to be performative, to have a real impact in the adoptee's context.

We may read these stories as having a therapeutic aim: by telling the right story of the adoption, the emotional well-being of the adoptee can be secured, and he or she can have a good night's sleep. This therapeutic aim is to be related with the idea that abandonment and adoption inflict a "primal wound" upon the adoptees that would jeopardize their future affective relationships. In these books, therefore, the rather traumatic past is only obliquely evoked in the illustrations, which largely avoid delving into it. Interestingly, in all but one of 20 recommended books about adoption, the word "orphanage" is avoided; euphemisms such as "casa de los niños" [house of the children] (in *Llegué de... Ucrania*, third double spread) are used. While the visual depictions of orphanage rooms convey a life of hardships, the textual account emphasizes how the children spent happy days there even if they missed having parents. Perhaps to counter these unfortunate images, the rooms of the adoptees in their new homes are always portrayed in detail, proving their individualized existences and how they have gained an identity. *En algún lugar de China* was inspired, precisely, by the parents' bedtime storytelling and their efforts for creating a properly decorated room for the adoptee. It all started when Emilio Amade, the illustrator of the book and the uncle of the adopted girl, painted an airplane on one of the walls of the girl's future room while the couple waited for the adoption to be confirmed. Ana Folgueira, the author and mother, referred to that plane when putting forward an origin story during the girl's bedtime routine. From that practice of domestic storytelling the book *En algún lugar de China* was born,[1]

Adultism, Perspective, and Memory

Children's books about adoption very often take the form of testimonial accounts of the adoptive parents that address an extra-diegetic narratee, the adopted child supposedly reading the book. In some other cases, they are narrated by the adoptee, yet very interestingly, this adoptee appears to lack his or her own point of view, and, in an inverted way, this adoptee addresses the adopted parents asking for this origin story to be told. In comparison with books about immigration, it is remarkable that those about adoption are in most cases told from the point of view of a character within the adoptive family—parents, adoptee, or a sibling—and, as previous research on books about adoptions in China shows, are meant to assist the familial storytelling (cf. García González and Wesseling 260–63). Kristin Langellier and Eric Peterson argue that families are small cultures in which certain ways of telling are passed through generations and this passing over depends on the retelling and performance of those stories over time (Langellier and Peterson 40–43). These books may be read as devices to perform these stories, and these stories are seen as building bricks of the narrative identity of the adoptee and of the adoptive families.

International adoption—whatever precautions are pursued in international conventions—is part of a global market, and parents become aware of it during the process: "The anxiety that the child might be a commodity is aroused by the incontrovertible fact that as the child moves from one site of nurture to another, money has to change hands; agencies are established, 'baby flights' are chartered; tour packages are assembled" (Anagnost cited in Dorow *Transnational Adoption: A Cultural Economy of Race, Gender, and Kinship* 115). These origin narratives try to counteract this anxiety, to divert this awareness, and to achieve this, it is not enough just to tell determined stories. These must be performed too. By performing, I refer to J.L. Austin's speech act theory and his categorization of "performative utterances" (Stainton 239) to the situations where saying something is doing something, rather than simply reporting or describing it. In the next pages, I trace the performative function of these adoption books in the points of views used to render the stories as well as in how they reflect and give cues for a repetitive domestic storytelling. These books may be read as presenting origin stories that are inspired and at the same time aim to inspire familial narrations.

Transferring Perspective and Voice

Mieke Bal's elaboration on Gérard Genette's concepts of 'focalization' and 'focalizors' (163), which are to be distinguished in function, not identity, from the narrator, is useful to understand point of view. The focal character 'sees' the narration, and, even if it may coincide with the narrator, it needs to be differentiated. Bal emphasizes that even in supposedly objective third-person narrations, events are presented from within a certain vision, so she proposes to complement the question of 'who is speaking' with 'whose vision is presented,' a question uttered in the awareness that language shapes vision and worldview rather than the other way around (Bal *Narratology: Introduction to the Theory of Narrative* 17). Answering the question of who speaks in a text does not necessarily explain whose eyes are lent to the reader to understand the events and the story's world. An inquiry into the focalization of a narration is, therefore, crucial for an understanding of how the text projects subject positions onto the readers.

Where most differentiate between first- and third-person narrators, Bal suggests that narration is necessarily always done in a first-person voice, since there is always an "I" seeing the story and speaking from a determined viewpoint, whether or not that "I" is an actual character in the story. She proposes, therefore, to distinguish between an "external narrator (EN)" (22), in the cases in which this voice does not refer to itself as a character and a "character-bound narrator (CN)" (22) when it is identified with a center of consciousness that plays a role. Bal further differentiates between "character-bound focalization (CF)" (148) when the story is seen through the eyes of a character (it may shift from one to another even if the narrator remains the same) and the "external focalization (EF)" (149), when an anonymous agent functions as the focalizor. Bal suggests that the EF may delegate or yield focalization to the characters. Bal's categories help me not only to identify the points of view from which the stories are rendered but also when this point of view is transferred passing over ideological positions within the story. I examine these transferences to illuminate how these books function as justifications of international adoption naturalizing the adoptive bond and neutralizing other possible narrations.

I prefer to speak of a transfer of the focalization rather than of a delegation—as conceptualized by Mieke Bal—since the latter implies a movement toward an intimate and personal point of view from one of the characters. By transfer, I aim to stress how the point of view wants to be replicated; transfer recalls the process in fine arts by which a design or image is transferred from one surface to another, as by ironing a printed design onto cloth, ending up in a copy that loses certain properties. This movement from origin to copy also recalls the act of translation as it never produces an exact copy and something is always lost in the process even if not acknowledged as such. These adoption books aim to translate the experience of the parents to the children's point of view elaborating origin stories that are as if images ironed and copied onto another surface.

The outset of the six books about international adoption published by La Galera reveal this effort of transferring a story and inscribing a memory on the adoptees. Each of these books uses the imagined voice of the adoptee in the title: *Llegué de... (country). Cuéntame mi historia* [I Came From... (country), Tell me my story], while the story inside is narrated by one or both parents. The title, therefore, suggests that the children are asking for this story to be told and promises that they will take it as a foundational block in their biographical constructions. In these books, we may identify from cover to cover four different voices: (1) the first-person voice of the adoptee in the title, (2) the parent who narrates the story, (3) an external narrator who gives information about the origin country in a first annex, and (4) a psychologist who provides guidelines for the parents in a second annex. These other three voices wrap up the account by the adoptive parents, legitimating their point of view and suggesting the benefit of transferring it to the adoptee.

The voice of the specialized psychologist, Mercé Villaseca, is crucial in this legitimation. She explains that many of the adopted children are curious about their origins and that it does not mean that they do not recognize their parents as authentic. She adds that they often want to travel to the place where they were born but that they will necessarily feel identified with the culture in which they have been socialized: "nuestra cultura, la que le hemos transmitido, la que ha vivido desde que era un niño" (our culture, the one we have transmitted, the one he/she has experienced as a child) (fourteenth double spread). Villaseca uses the second-person plural to refer to the upbringing of the adopted children as a stylistic device to empathize with the parents, but also denoting that the upbringing of the adopted children involves a broader group of people, a society that goes beyond the specific family. Villaseca's words, therefore, aim to integrate the search for the origins into a narrative in which the adoptive family is, nevertheless, stronger than any blood bond, 'racial' identification, or feeling of displacement that the adoptees may feel.

Children's books about adoption appear to be instrumental to what the Norwegian anthropologist Signe Howell calls the 'kinning of foreigners' (Howell 2)—that is, the cultural processes and narratives involved in making the adopted child one of kin. As claimed before, these books are not presented as the parents' testimonies but as stories foundational to the adoptees' (auto)biography. The possible tensions and disruptions between these two points of view or life stories are dismissed. Yet, strikingly, one of the main points of debate today for researchers on international adoption is the power imbalances in what is called the 'adoption triad' formed by the biological parents, the adoptive parents, and the adoptee. Critics of the legislation and policies on international adoption claim that it has been crafted to fulfill the expectations of the adoptive parents, the most powerful end of the adoptive triangle, while leaving the voiceless, poor, uneducated biological parents out of the picture. Discussions regarding whether adoptions are done with the 'best interests' of the children in mind help to obscure how adoption actually follows the interests and needs of the adoptive parents and turn the adopted children into objects of protection rather than considering them subjects of rights (Marre and San Román; Fonseca et al.). These discussions have become more notorious when celebrities are involved such as when Madonna's or the Jolie-Pitt's adopted children have been claimed by their biological mothers (cf. Jacey).

The titles of the Llegué de... collection may have been inspired by Jamie Lee Curtis's *Tell me again...*, a book that also emulates the voice of the adopted child as if asking for her story to be told:

> Tell me again about the night I was born ... Tell me again how you would adopt me and be my parents... Tell me again about the first time you held me in your arms ... (2–3)

Every page starts with a "tell me again," indicating that the character narrator (CN) quotes from a previous narration and that the story told by the parents will be appropriated by the child. Pulling from Mieke Bal's classifications, we could say that this CN—the adopted girl—narrates with a focalization in the parents, who are the ultimate viewers/tellers of the origin story. In this book, and to a certain extent in most of the children's literature about adoption, the operation to provide the adoptee with an origin story veils the desire of the adoptive parents to inscribe their own story as the foundational, origin story of/for the adopted child.

The visual narration is very often also mobilized to convey a child's viewpoint in picturebooks. In the *Tell me again...*'s first double spread, we see the parents from the girl's perspective. The father holds a toothbrush and the mother a pajama; we do not get to see their faces but we know as a child knows what this means: it is bedtime. Obviously, this perspective cannot be maintained throughout the book. In the next double spread we have a top-view of the parents' bedroom even as the first-person voice carries on: "Tell me again how you and Daddy were curled up like spoons and Daddy was snoring. Tell me again how the phone rang in the middle of the night and they told you I was born. Tell me again how you screamed" (3–4). We know that the image rendered cannot have been seen by the adoptee, but she may imagine it with all details. By telling her complete story while asking for it to be told, she reassures the parents that the point of view has been transferred and that she understands her life as they have projected it.

The ending in *Llegué de...Colombia* illustrates how these books are meant to found a life story. On the left page, a dark-skinned Colombian boy kisses his white parents while on the right page we read: "Encontrarnos y convertirnos en tus padres ha sido un regalo maravilloso. Nosotros solo hemos escrito el inicio de tu historia. Lo demás aún lo has de vivir." [To meet you and to become your parents has been a marvelous gift. We have only written the beginning of your story. You'll live out the rest of it] (22–23). We may read this ending as establishing a beginning that would remain unaltered: the adopted child would then complete his biography with his further experiences without modifying this beginning, which the parents have so kindly written down.

In *Isha nacida del corazón*, the story of how the parents adopted a girl in India, the story that reflects this described masterplot of adventurous parents finding a child meant to be theirs, is told as an embedded story. The frame-plot of the novel fleshes out the new questions and anxieties haunting Isha as she grows up and has to deal with being different from her classmates. We do find in this narration plenty of references to how the origin story she has heard since she was young has been fundamental in her identity formation and how the repetition of this story throughout the years has facilitated this appropriation. The novel recounts how Isha listens once more to this origin story and shows that the girl is able to complete the father's account with her own memories. However, they are not 'real' memories but constructed upon those of the parents. This recalls Marianne Hirsch's concept of "postmemory" (Hirsch), used to characterize the creation of memories when being socialized in determined (post-trauma) narratives without having the direct experience, a concept developed in relation to the children of Holocaust survivors. Hirsch introduced this term to analyze the construction of the past and trauma in the artistic and literary production of the children of the survivors, yet I find it useful to understand what appears to be pursued in these books: the inscription and inheritance of the memories of the parents by the children.

Isha nacida del corazón is narrated by an external narrator that alternates the focalization on the mother, the father, and the girl. The story begins after a classmate, Marta, tells Isha that her mother cannot be her real mother because she is Black, a comment that triggers a crisis on the adopted child who does not want to be different. Once home she tells her mother about this, and the mother tries to comfort her. The following fragment illuminates how in their dialogue the focalization shifts from one to the other. This quote begins with a dialogue between the mother, Sara, and the adopted girl and, after a full stop, continues with an external narrator who delegates the focalization on the girl. To clarify this further, I marked out the types of focalization and further context of the conversation in parentheses:

> "—¡Pero yo no quiero ir allí! (Isha says that she doesn't want to go to where her biological mother is)
> —¿Y quién te ha dicho a ti que yo lo iba a permitir? —Sara se estremecía, como si le arrancaran los brazos, sólo con imaginárselo. (CF in Sara, the mother)
> Hace ya tiempo que Isha está preocupada por sus orígenes. Hoy no ha sido, precisamente, un buen día. El comentario de Marta negando la autenticidad de su madre ha provocado un nuevo desasosiego.
> Ahora ya con el pijama puesto, aguarda a que su padre entre en la habitación para poder reclamarle: «¡Papá, cuéntame mi cuento!» (CF in Isha, the adopted daughter)." (21–22)

> [—But I don't want to go there! (Isha says that she doesn't want to go to where her biological mother is)
> —And who told you that I was going to allow that?—Sara shuddered, as if her arms were pulled off only by imagining it. (CF in Sara, the mother)
> Isha has been worried about her origins for a while now. Today hasn't been a good day. Marta's comment about her mother's lack of authenticity has provoked a new feeling of uneasiness.
> Now with her pajamas on, she waits for her father to come in to claim him: «Papa, tell me my story!» (CF in Isha, the adopted daughter)

The fragment opens with Isha saying that she doesn't want to go to India. Then, the focalization is on Isha's mother and her fear of having her daughter drawn away, which would feel as is her "arms were pulled off," as if her daughter was part of her own body. In the next paragraph, the focalization seems to be taken from the mother to the girl without any clear indication of it. Nevertheless, in the last paragraph quoted, the focalization is clearly on the girl who waits eagerly for her father to come to tell her a story, the origin story. The father will then recount how they went to India and will give details of all the difficulties they faced in the adoption process using a third-person voice; Isha listens to this story of love, desire, and adventure and becomes reassured that she is a very special and chosen child, not just one who was there for the taking. The focalization in this embedded story remains mostly in Cesar, the father, who takes the voice of an external narrator. This voice also gives some glimpses of what Isha is thinking:

> "La señora Khan apareció con Isha de la mano. ¡Estaba preciosa! Una tela de una sola pieza envolvía su cuerpo de señorita de casi cinco años.

—Se llama sari, papá.

—¿Y a ti quién te lo ha dicho, marisabidilla? ¿Quién te ha hablado del hombre que lo inventó al tejer una tela muy larga por quedarse atontado mirando a una hermosa mujer?

—Tú...

Isha apareció envuelta en un sari, como un regalo de los dioses (...) César sacó del bolsillo siete pulseras de colores y un collar de bolitas. Sabía que no lo entendería, pero pensó que bastaría con el gesto.

—Toma— le dijo—, son para ti.

Isha dejó caer todo al suelo y se agarró con fuerza a la falda de la señora Khan. Todo estaba siendo más difícil de lo que habían imaginado.

—Pero si yo deseaba tanto que me fuerais a buscar." (123)

[Mrs. Khan appeared holding Isha's hand. She was so pretty! A single piece of fabric wrapped around the body of a little five-year-old lady.

—It's called a sari, Dad.

—And who has told you that, know-it-all lady? Who has told you about the man who invented it knitting a very long piece of fabric dazed by the sight of a beautiful woman?

—You...

Isha appeared wrapped in a sari, as a gift from the gods (...) César took out from his pocket seven colorful bracelets and a necklace. He knew that she wouldn't understand, but thought that the gesture would be enough.

—Take them—he said—they are for you.

Isha threw them all to the floor and held tightly the skirt of Mrs. Khan. Everything was turning out to be much more difficult than what they had imagined.

—But I was desiring so much that you pick me up]

The nature of Isha's interruptions gives close account of how this point of view aims to be transferred. In the first paragraph, the adopted girl interrupts her father's account to complete it showing how versed she is in the Indian traditions. Isha knows what a 'sari' is, and we are told that it is precisely the father who is the one to thank for transmitting that cultural heritage to her. This dialogue also remarks how culture travels with a reference to the tale of the man who invented the saris. The character of César reassures, therefore, that adopters are people who grow in cultural awareness and respect for local traditions and that they can do remarkably well in transferring them. The focalization on him would give better insight into the difficulties and efforts adopters go through. This focalization is strategically complemented with one that sometimes is on Isha, who is not only grateful for what her father has done and does not only assimilate his own views as hers, but who also contributes to this narration sharing her own memories that reassure her father's. "Pero sí yo deseaba tanto que me fuerais a buscar!" [But I desired so much that you pick me up!] says the girl, as if recalling that very moment in which she meet her parents. The repeated and ritualized telling of that origin story in which the child has been waiting for those parents has finally constructed a memory about the encounter to be taken as real.

The Implied (Adopted) Reader

In *Language and Ideology in Children's Fiction*, John Stephens argues that any analysis about ideology and point of view must address the distinctions between 'author,' 'implied author,' and 'narrator,' as well as the one between 'narratee,' 'implied reader,' and the 'reader' in the actual world (23). The pair of the 'implied author' and the 'implied reader' would have no narrative function but operates as the bearer of implicit social practices and ideological positions, since certain ideas and values are taken for granted in the communicative act of the narration. The implied author—a term first coined by Wayne Booth—differentiates from the author in that he is not the real author of the book, but the one we can infer from the narration; the implied reader is the reader to which the book is targeted. This reader obviously differs from the flesh and bone reader, but in these books about adoption, he or she becomes a quite clear figure: an adopted child.

As I have sketched out here, in many of the adoption books the narratee is made explicit when the narrator addresses a 'you' to whom the story is told. This 'you' coincides with the figure with whom the implied reader should identify—that is, the adopted child who will be reading the book. In many of these books, this narratee coincides with the adopted child, while the narrator and the implied author appear to coincide with the figure of the adoptive parent. All these books would therefore share what Philip Lejeune distinguishes as the quintessential feature of autobiographical narratives: the coincidence of narrator, author, and principal character. Even if not overtly presented as testimonial accounts in the paratexts—the cover, front matter, or back matter—we learn through reviews or press material that these books have been written by adoptive parents inspired in their own domestic practices of storytelling who also aim to fill in a gap in the publishing market. The parents aim to pass down the adoption experience to the offspring and believe that other children in similar positions may also benefit from this. These books may be not overtly presented as testimonials, since the stories have been remediated according to what the authors think would make an appropriate children's book. Events are modified according to what would make a better story and details that might be too personal about each process are avoided, perhaps to facilitate the reading and identification of other ideal (adopted) readers. *En algún lugar de China*, the book in which events are more clearly fictionalized, introduces a magical element to explain the beginning of the adoption process. In this way it avoids recounting the rather mundane process of filling in papers and adoption applications. This story starts when a bird asks a woman if she would like to parent a girl, indicating a red thread that the couple has to follow until meeting the girl who is waiting for them in China. The story is narrated by this woman, the mother, while addressing the narratee, the adopted girl.

Studying adoption narratives in the United States, Margaret Homans claims that adoption is a "fiction-generating machine" (Homans 5) in which the question of origin motivates and inspires the familial storytelling and the creation of the past for the needs of a present. *Usoa, llegaste por el aire* [Usoa, you came by air] written by Patxi Zubizarreta Dorronsoro, a well-known children's book author, does not follow the adoption masterplot but uses similar narrative strategies and focalization transferences to target that ideal (adopted) reader, thus providing a narrative with which to identify. The story is told by an anonymous witness addressing a narratee, the adopted girl: "Te llaman Usoa, Paloma, la niña que llegó por el aire. Y puede que por eso te guste tanto mirar el cielo, porque de allí viniste, de allí te trajeron" (first double spread) [They call you Usoa, Paloma, the girl that came by air. And maybe that explains why you enjoy watching the sky so much; you came from there, from there you were brought]. This narrator shares with the previous one the use of interpellation, yet in this case, there is an external narrator instead of a character narrator in the figure of the adoptive parents. Usoa is a girl who reflects on the reasons her biological mother had to give her away, and the narrator responds by reorganizing that origin as one that begins in the journey to the Western country. The narrator mentions that she came 'from the sky,' which may on the one hand underline a privileged origin to be opposed to that of immigrants—she came by plane rather than on a packed open boat—and on the other hand may de-essentialize the origin as located in the journey rather than in the origin land. The narrator projects onto the girl this longing for an origin that is not there anymore: the sky as a no-place. The narration later includes a letter written by the biological mother in which she explains her decision to give her away to keep her safe from the famine and wars suffered in her African country. This letter is not addressed to the girl, but to the ones who would find her on an airplane to a country "donde haya comida y paz" (18) [where food and peace may be found]. After including this letter, the narrator adds: "Tu madre de aquí también es muy buena y ahora mismo te está llamando para cenar. Además sabes que este año no faltará el dinero en vuestra casa" [Your mother here is also very good-hearted, and she is calling you for dinner right now. You also know that this year you won't lack money at home]. The EN focalizes again in the adoptee and asks her to acknowledge that her adoptive family has material means, as if that will dispel her feeling of uneasiness. This narrator addresses the adoptee, urging her to stop questioning her origin to instead focus on the benefits of being adopted—to have food on the table and to be safe from wars and famine.

Silenced Biological Mothers

Interestingly, in *Usoa llegaste por el aire*, the only book in which the voice of a biological mother is heard, this mother does not address the narratee in the letter there included yet gives the child a name—Kasai. This name, we know from the title already, has not been kept by the adoptive parents who have chosen the Basque name Usoa.[2] This letter written by the biological mother and included in the narration has not been able to transfer identity to the child. We may wonder why this piece is included. This letter allows us to imagine the figure of a biological mother, a figure excluded from most of the stories about adoptions perhaps of how it may complicate the univocal narrative of the Western parents. Yet, at the same time, it may be argued that the way her perspective is included may be instrumental to counteract the haunting stories about child trafficking by reassuring that this mother has given her baby away not only voluntarily but as part of a strategic plan for the child's future.

Usoa llegaste por el aire also departs from the adoption masterplot because, in her origin story, the adopted child is not to look back to her origin country as an asset that makes her part of a diaspora, but rather as a place from which to flee. The imaginary figure of the rescued orphan surfaces quite transparently. This trope may be traced in some other books that do not follow the adoption masterplot described above such as *Caja de cartón*, in which a girl migrates with her mother to a place where "las niñas no duermen en cajas y las madres no lloran" [where girls don't sleep in boxes and mothers don't cry] (second double spread). In the new country, the girl of *Caja de cartón* ends up losing her mother and is adopted by a local family: this adoption rescues her not only from the terrible past in the origin land, but also from the hopeless present they were having in the destination land. In *Caja de cartón*, the biological mother is not only evoked—as in *Usoa llegaste por el aire*—but becomes a character visually depicted as a dark-skinned woman wearing a head scarf. The new mother has a fairer skin tone, and we are told that she loves the child and that the child loves her. More importantly, as in the other stories reviewed above, the adoptee tells us proudly about her new house where she has "mi habitación, mi cama, mi armario" [my room, my bed, my closet]. Having an own room appears to be a key improvement in an adoptee's life, the guarantee of a right to an individual identity as well as a way to show off the material means of the new family in contrast to those of her origin. These books coincide in how they pass over the message of how fortunate the adopted child is. The children need only be thankful and love those parents who love them so much.

In *Reading Adoption*, the American literary scholar Marianne Novy explores adoption plots in plays uncovering how most of them end up reproducing the idea that only one set of parents can count as the "real" one (185–86). We may read these books, addressed to children, as avoiding dealing with the idea of two sets of parents in the first place by stressing how they have to trace their origin in the place where they have received care and nurture. Usoa needs to understand that she 'came by air' as the adoptees portrayed waiting have to understand how special they are to be bond to those Western parents before they reach them at those waiting houses for children. Biological parents are to be kept out of the picture to make sure that they do not threaten the figure of the 'real' set of parents.

In the Place of Conclusions: *Yuyuba*, a White Baby in the Jungle

In this chapter, I review how the recommended books about adoption form a homogenous group in which similar strategies are used to provide adoptive families with stories in which the images of child trafficking that surround international adoption are dispelled. The described masterplot of international adoption focuses on the enormous love of the adoptive couple and how this love—coupled with the material means of these families—may be taken as ample justification of adoption and as proof of how the child will be provided for in the new family and new country. In some cases, the material means of the adoptive family are directly or indirectly mentioned as a warranty for that happy life, too.

One book, though, presents a possible adoption from a very different perspective. *Yuyuba*—originally published in French as *Jujube*—tells the story of a White baby abandoned in an African country, an ironic inversion of the global flow of children from non-Western to Western countries. A girl, Farafina, finds the baby in the jungle and takes her home, but she is discouraged to discover that her mother wants to give the child to a woman of the village who has long desired to have children but who is also known for her very bad temper. The story describes how Farafina, manages to get her mother so attached to this baby that she finally decides to make her part of the family. The story, therefore, takes an ironic approach toward the idea that the desire to parent may be followed by a right to parent.

Yuyuba may be the only recommended book about adoption that appears not to be meant to help adoptees in their identity formation, but rather uses transnational adoption as the inspiration for an ironic tale. The rest of the books function as mirror narratives with characters that have the same age of the implied readers and similar biographies and are in most cases also tailored according to the country of origin. These mirror narratives never address a collectivity, that is, a group of adopted children who would share a position—such as the generation of girls adopted from China—since the notion of uniqueness appears to be fundamental for the narrative of being adopted. David L. Eng questions the paradoxical position of the adoptive parents, who need to deal with this 'otherness' of the children that has been provoked by their own decisions to adopt transnationally (cf. Eng 1). In these books, we may trace an effort of the parents to overcome this difference by naturalizing the adoptive bond as if it were a biological bond. In this move, transnational adoption has also to be stripped of any relation to geopolitical imbalances or broader social contexts, while at the same time it is narrated as a magical event that brought a unique family together.

This review of focalization reveals how these stories are meant to pass down the perspectives of the adoptive parents to the adoptees. The parents' stories are told as if proudly appropriated by the adoptees; the parent's desire to parent is paralleled with a narrative about the adoptee's desire to be parented. Often addressed in second-person voices, these desires and feelings are projected and inscribed onto the adoptive characters. These transferences speak of the performative aim of these books: they are meant to weave the family together as instruments of what anthropologist Signe Howell describes as the 'kinning of foreigners' in transnational adoption. The assertive narration of the parents does what biology could not do: transform that child into one of kin to whom they will be bound forever.

Notes

1 An interview with the author, originally broadcast by the news program of channel Tele 5, is available as a YouTube video: http://www.youtube.com/watch?v=YQbUG4W2pWU.
2 This book was originally published in Basque. The first Spanish translation keeps the Basque name, Usoa, while the second translates it into Spanish, Paloma.

4 They Came from the Desert
Immigration Plots and Tropes

Within the subset of books having migrant characters, we do not find a single masterplot as the one sketched for those about adoption, yet we still find some similar plots and repeated tropes, which appear in different books.

In a large majority of these books, immigration is thematized in the figure of the child with migrant background whose journey is decided by adults, a fate that may recall that of young adoptees even if this forced displacement is precisely an issue avoided in the books about adoption. We also find a handful of books that take other approaches: a few present young men who immigrate illegally and face difficulties, while others coincide quite surprisingly in using the figure of The Three Kings to weave allegories about immigration and exclusion. In this chapter, I first review the stories of successful integration of young migrants to continue analyzing what the stories about irregular immigration and the allegory of The Three Kings tells us about the narratives of belonging and exclusion.

Books depicting migrants differ from those depicting adoptees in that most of the latter are recommend to adopted children as helpful reads. The books about immigration are not—at least not by the reviewers— recommended to immigrants. Rather, they are endorsed as educational material to familiarize local children with the difficulties newcomers face. We find rare examples in which migration is connected to the production of cultural diversity and minorities: as the analysis shows, it is rather presented as something coming with people that arrive as if they would not stay avoiding in this way to deal with the formation of multiculturalities. As in the previous chapter, I first briefly introduce immigration as a social phenomenon with attention to its particularities in Spain. Also mirroring the structure of Chapter 3, I first explore the cultural construction of the migrant by inquiring into recurrent tropes and plots and then analyzing focalization as a salient feature of the texts' ideological stances.

Human Migration at the Turn of the Millennium

Even if it is not a new phenomenon, the world is undergoing its largest human migration in history. The International Organization for Migration (IOM) states that there are more than 200-million migrants around the world today, which corresponds to more than 3% of world's total population, a percentage that is expected to increase in the future. Today, the greatest number of migrants travel from less to more developed countries and from rural to urban areas as a way to improve their living conditions and pushed and pulled by the market forces of late capitalism. Migration is framed by globalization; just as goods and services are being traded more freely across borders, more and more people are looking to live and work overseas, even if freedom of movement is not necessarily increasing (cf. Keeley).

In the last decades, human migration has become a hot topic, coupled as it often is with a complex debate on the perceived burdens of so-called multiculturalism. Migration is very often constructed as threatening (cf. Ibrahim; Verkuyten; Triandafyllidou; Lentin and Titley), a discursive construction that has been sharpened after the 9/11 attacks; the tension between native and non-native citizens, in which cultural differences— usually seen in the form of religious differences—are stressed, has been increasingly growing (Yuval-Davis *The Politics of Belonging: Intersectional Contestations* 1–2). After the 2005 terrorist attacks in London were attributed to British citizens from non-Western backgrounds the debate on the 'integration' of ethnic minorities—usually phrased as the reluctance of them to integrate—has been strongly intensified (Minkenberg 44–45).

Europe has been experiencing a backlash of multicultural policies in the last fifteen years. Steven Vertovec and Susanne Wessendorf trace this change in an insightful collection of essays that unveils how the discourse of immigration as a threatening force to the nation has propagated in different European welfare societies beyond the boundaries of fearful right-wing parties (Vertovec and Wessendorf). In the introductory chapter to *Europe's New Racism*, Nora Räthzel claims that in the age of globalization and neoliberalism the patriarchal attitude of civilizing natives has been replaced by a defensive attitude toward threatening intruders (21). She argues that foreigners today are today not so much pictured as closer to nature—even if these images persist—but rather as understanding modern society so well that they take advantage of its institutions. In 2010, Chancellor Angela Merkel stated that Germany's approach to multiculturalism had "absolut gescheitert" [utterly failed] and that new policies were needed to make sure that people immigrating to Germany would make the effort to fully participate in the host society. Merkel did not provide a definition of what she understood under multiculturalism or participation, neither did then prime ministers David Cameron and Nicholas Sarkozy, who seconded Merkel in the following weeks. Yet, in all three cases, the 'failure' of multiculturalism was perceived as related to the growth of Islamic communities in European states. Nicholas Sarkozy appealed to the idea of a national identity, which would be opposed to those of the newcomers: "We have been too concerned about the identity of the person who was arriving and not enough about the identity of the country that was receiving him" (*Daily Mail*).

Even though multiculturalism is elusive to definitions and its meaning mutates from context to context, we may argue that the term emerged to refer to the ethnic/cultural diversity created by immigration into Western countries in the last half of the twentieth century. The term "multiculturalism" was first coined in the 1950s, but it did not have a relevant public use until the 1970s and 1980s, when the approach to minorities shifted from that of assimilation to a quest for recognition in different Western countries. Multiculturalists would plead for societies in which no culture would be imposed upon another, and in the Anglo-Saxon settler countries—Canada, Australia, United States—this debate evolved to include the question of how to protect native minorities and organize group rights (Abbey). As Merkel's, Cameron's, and Sarkozy's statements show, the so-called multiculturalism has fallen out of favor, but it is still unclear what changes does this brings. Keith Banting and Will Kymlicka argue that we should not read it as a backlash, since most of the policies created in previous years are still maintained and new ones are created even if new terms such as 'diversity policies' are now preferred.

Multiculturalism today is often replaced by interculturalism, which would denote the need for different cultures to interact and negotiate or, in its most flexible variations, would claim a recognition of "common human needs across cultures and dissonance and critical dialogue within cultures" (Nussbaum 62). Advocates of interculturalism promote the interaction between cultures as a means to save the so-called 'cultural gap,' which would lead to the formation of ghettos and ethnic enclaves. Interculturalism is connected to the ideology of integration as opposed to assimilation (Schneider and Crul 1144), a paradigm shift that aims to acknowledge how identities are multiple and in continuous change. The emergence of identity politics in the second half of the twentieth century promoted self-identification and led to the formation of minority-oriented interest groups. New technologies and advances in communication have had an important impact for these groups. Arjun Appadurai notes the emergence of "diasporic public spaces" (4) facilitated by the media. These would create new forms of belonging, such as youngsters of Turkish origin watching Turkish TV in Germany or Pakistani taxi drivers in the United Kingdom listening to Muslim sermons recorded in Iran. Appadurai notes how electronic media—especially television—has modified cultural spaces to construct identities that are no longer tightly territorialized (48). The Internet multiplies the possibilities of forming and connecting communities, not only beyond national borders, but also across them in segmented ways that do not necessarily match with the traditional categories of identity related to class, gender, and 'race.' Social scientists have introduced new concepts to approach this changing scenario. The term 'transmigrant,' for instance, is used to describe how the daily lives of contemporary migrants depend on constant interconnections across international borders and may not be structured around the idea of origin and destination (cf. Schiller et al.; Smith and Guarnizo). Transmigration is a concept that aims to acknowledge how culture is always hybrid, fluid, and porous.

Spain, Top Immigration Country 1990–2010

The influx of immigrants into Spain resembles that of international adoptees described in the previous chapter, even if the number of new immigrants exceeds that of the adoptees by at least 100 times (cf. Eurostat; Selman "Global Trends in Intercountry Adoption: 2001–2010"). Spain began to be a destination for work immigrants only in the 1990s, rather late compared with the most prosperous countries of Western Europe. Spain—like Ireland and Italy—has a large tradition as an emigration country. Yet, from the mid-1990s the figures for immigration into Spain rocketed and continued to increase until the Spanish financial crisis led to their decline. Spain was the European country with the largest number of immigrants in 2005; yet, five years later, in 2010, it led the list of the European country with the highest emigration rate, even though it still received one of the highest quotas of immigrants (Eurostat; Lanzieri and Corsini).

When compared to that of other European countries, immigration into Spain reveals certain distinctive features: a very high percentage of irregular (or 'illegal') immigrants (González-Enríquez 247), a public policy focused on the control of immigration rather than in providing means for the integration and inclusion of foreign-born populations (Zapata-Barrero "Policies and Public Opinion Towards Immigrants: The Spanish Case" 1007–1008), and a particularly marked professional over-qualification of foreign citizens when compared to nationals (Eurostat 41). In the following pages, I provide some explanations and consequences of each of these three features.

At the turn of the millennium, Spain was considered to be the European country with the highest number of undocumented citizens. Carmen González-Enríquez explains this by attending to different factors: "firstly, [Spain has] a strong and relatively vibrant informal economy in which irregular migrants could find employment; secondly, the relatively positive social attitude towards migrants when compared to other European countries; thirdly, the traditional tolerance towards illegality embedded in Southern European political culture; and, finally, the provision of social rights for irregular immigrants in Spanish law" (González-Enríquez 247). Regarding the latter, she referred to the access migrants had to public health and schooling after registering in the City Hall.[1] Yet, in the political and media debate, the elevated number of 'illegals,' as they are often—if controversially—called, is usually presented as the result of a weak control of immigration that would have a "efecto llamada" [literally a 'calling effect'] that would motivate new migration presenting Spain as attractive for prospective undocumented migrants (García Castaño et al. 120). The role the 'boom' of irregular immigration played in the emergent economy of the 1990s supplying cheap workers is most often dismissed or minimized.

As in other countries, immigration in Spain is often described as a threat to a nation that needs to control its borders (Kleiner-Liebau 159–61; van Dijk Racism and Discourse in Spain and Latin America 47). In the Spanish case, public policy on immigration appears to mirror this rather restricted media debate, focusing mainly on controlling irregular immigration yet dismissing the need of a means for social inclusion, which is mainly delegated from the national to the regional (Autonomous Regions) and local levels (provinces and municipalities). At the national level, we find the GRECO (Programa Global de Regulación y Coordinación de la Extranjería y la Inmigración), which states as a goal "the integration of the foreign population who contribute actively to the economic growth of Spain" (translation by Geiger 223). As Martin Geiger remarks, the principles of this national program for immigration already make evident that 'integration' is restricted to those 'good migrants' who contribute to the Spanish economy while dismissing the existence of their non-economically-active relatives and of older and/or retired immigrants (Geiger 223–25).

Another distinctive feature of immigration into Spain when compared to other European countries is the high over-qualification of immigrants—that is, the number of immigrants who have higher education and/or experience than is required for their jobs. The European statistics show that this inequality between foreign citizens and nationals could be observed in all countries—except Switzerland—and was particularly marked in Greece, Italy, Portugal, Cyprus, Spain, and Estonia (Eurostat 41). In the OECD (Organisation for Economic Co-operation and Development) measurements, 42.9 percent of the immigrants are overqualified for their jobs compared to 'just' 24.2 percent of the nationals (Sanz 170).[2]

The period in question here—1990–2010—may mark the first, precarious stage of development of a discourse about immigration and interculturalism in Spain. Immigration into Spain was rare before the 1990s, yet it sky-rocketed by the end of the decade due to the booming economy at the time. Ricard Zapata-Barrero points out that "it is surprising that there is no discourse policy on identity nor on multiculturality in Spain" (384). The Catalan scholar claims that this is especially clear when parliamentary and political parties' discourses are analyzed: "it seems as if there was a common tacit fear of talking about immigration in identity terms (. ...) The words 'multicultural-ism' or 'interculturalism' were not pronounced once in a debate that revolved around security and socio-economic issues" (Zapata-Barrero "Managing Diversity in Spanish Society: A Practical Approach" 384). Zapata-Barrero goes on to argue that in Spain diversity is not man-aged according to a set of ideas, as the French republicanism—which defends an assimilation approach—or the British multiculturalism, but rather takes the form of a 'practical philosophy.' This 'practical philos-ophy' may be quite racist as the case of Rosalind Williams showed. In 1992, Williams, with an Afro-American background, was stopped by the police in Spain and asked to show her identity documents, some-thing no other person at that place—a railway station—was asked to do. Williams refused and ended up taking the case to court, demonstrat-ing that the police had been instructed to control the identity credentials of non-White people (see Report on Human Rights by United Nations 297). Latterly, the police have denied the continuity of these controls based on racial phenotypes, but a report from Amnesty International shows that in 2011 they were still performed.

As in other European countries, immigrants are perceived as being divided into two big groups: those immigrating from within Western Europe, or from North America and Australia, are mainly considered to be 'foreigners' or 'ex-pats,' while those from the rest of the world are labeled as 'immigrants' (Santamaría 62). This division speaks of a class divide, but also of how it is coupled with the perception of racial differ-ences. A similar division is found in research about so-called 'same race' adoptions when they refer to children coming from Russia and Eastern Europe and 'transracial'—those adopted elsewhere (Reinoso et al. 2). In an article about transnational adoption, Beatriz San Román points out how Spanish population considers itself White, even if they would not be labeled as such in other cultural contexts: "From self-perception, the non-white phenotypical diversity of the Spanish society is new and comes as a result of the immigration that took place at the dawn of the millennium" (San Román 232).

Teun van Dijk claims that the overtly racist discourse is rare in the Spanish political discourse when compared to that of other European countries such as France, Austria, Italy, Denmark, and the Netherlands (van Dijk *Racism and Discourse in Spain and Latin America* 20). He suggests that this may be explained by attending to the explicit democ-ratization process that has taken place after the long authoritarian op-pression under Franco. In Spain, the extreme right wing is associated with Franco and xenophobic parties do not get to resemble those that have gained considerable power in other European countries. Neverthe-less, van Dijk argues that non-explicit racism is similar to that found in other European countries. He traces this 'moderate racism' in the promulgation and further modification of the Ley de Extranjería, in the discourse of the conservative political party (PP), and in the widespread if controversial use of the adjective 'illegal' to refer to undocumented workers, among others.[3] The popular raid against the Arab communities in the Andalusian El Ejido—an episode that uncovered a fierce social and institutional racism—brought to public light the conditions of exploitation under which a poverty-stricken community of irregular immigrants works, especially in the agricultural centers of the Southern coast. The anti-racist response that this event motivated was apparently forgotten some years later when coordinated bombings against the commuter train system killed 191 people and wounded 1,800 in 2004. As soon as the theory of an ETA (the Basque separatist organization) attack was dismissed by one of an al-Qaeda-inspired-cell, the anti-immigrant sentiment grew and a discourse of a 'clash of civilizations' was constructed in the media.

A pro-immigration, anti-racist discourse is relatively new in Spain. Until the 1990s, 'racism' was mostly used to denote prejudice and discrimination against Roma communities, still largely marginalized in the country (Calvo Buezas 432–34). Now it emerges in the frame of increased mobility and global migration, a process that challenges those assumptions in Spain that link modernization with a weakening of parochial loyalties (Corkill 171). The mobility and atomization of society—as well as the emergence of the macro-structure of European Union—has served to make nationalism and regionalism more, not less, appealing. At the turn of the millennium, Spanish society appeared to be disillusioned about its central state, which was perceived as centralized, bureaucratic, and uncaring. The rise of Catalan separatism at the peak of the Spanish economic crisis may be taken as an example of how cultural belonging comes first.

An Overview of Immigration Narratives

The construction of an us versus them divide is fundamental to an understanding of the (re)presentation of migration as a force between those taken to be foreigners and locals. The reviews written by the S.O.L. experts are a first cultural text within which to identify this us-locals against the them-foreigners divide. Imagologists argue the importance of researching the process by which the 'hetero-images' that refer to the Other are projected in opposition to the 'self- or auto-image' used to represent one's own identity (Leerssen).

Even if children's literature mediation usually responds to the paradigm of the reader's identification with the protagonists (Nikolajeva *Power, Voice and Subjectivity in Literature for Young Readers* 85; Stephens *Language and Ideology in Children's Fiction* 68), the books about immigration are not recommended by the S.O.L. experts to children who have gone through experiences similar to those of the protagonists but rather to readers who would not have had any previous contact with migrants. Moreover, the reviews appear to be informed by a binary opposition between locals and others, in which the first are imagined as Spanish children born to Spanish parents and the latter refers to those with migrant backgrounds.

Stuart Hall points out how, even if the epistemology of identity is that of sameness, of being identical, identity is created by highlighting differences ("Introduction. Who Needs Identity?" 8). The 'other,' is constructed to give a sense of cohesiveness to the in-group. In the conceptualization of Imagologists, the 'culture regardante' needs to 'regard' the other culture in order to construct its own self, a collective identity that would define an essential feature of those who are within the limits of the 'us.'

The S.O.L. reviews construct an 'us versus them' divide while dismissing the group of 'them' as possible beneficiaries of this cultural production. The recommendation for *No soy Rubia, ¿y qué?* [I'm not blond. So what?] is revealing: "Las ilustraciones utilizan acuarelas de colores muy vivos que acentúan la expresividad en los rostros de los personajes, inmigrantes que buscan hacerse un hueco entre nosotros," [The illustrations with colorful watercolor stress the expressiveness of the characters, immigrants who try to make for themselves a space among us]. The author and publishers—Kirmen Uribe and Editores Asociados—seem to have had another aim: this book was part of a collection—"y qué" [so what]—in which all protagonists have a condition that makes them in some or another way ashamed: *Mi padre es ama de casa, Estoy gordito, No me gusta el fútbol, No se nadar, among others* [my father is a housewife/I'm a fatty/I don't like football/I don't know how to swim]. In all of them, the story recounts how the protagonist finds a way of dealing with this initial 'problem' and gains self-confidence within a group. Strikingly, in the S.O.L. reviews for the other titles of the collection, the books are recommended to children who may be going through similar situations; as an example I quote from the one about a child who does not know how to swim: "seguro que servirá de catarsis para muchos pequeños que atraviesan situaciones parecidas," [for sure, it will be a catharsis to many other kids who go through similar situations]. The use of the term 'catharsis' may be quite revealing of a circulating idea that books can function as potential therapeutic elements that would trigger the expression of repressed feelings, thus purifying the reader of such emotions.

These books are often recommended because of how they seemingly give us access to immigration, a reality that would be unknown to the group of us readers. In these phrasings, the idea put forward is that this alien point of view will enrich the worldview of the local child with new perspectives. *Luna de Senegal*, about a girl who emigrates with her family from Senegal to Galicia, is presented as an example that gives this access: "abona el terreno a la integración ofreciendo la posibilidad de conocer y comprender las dificultades por las que pasan los emigrantes africanos desde la cercanía que aporta su punto de vista" [prepares the ground for integration, giving the opportunity to know and understand the difficulties African emigrants go through from the closeness that their own point of view provides]. Integration would be facilitated by that emphatic positioning on the foreigner's perspective, a claim that pervades different initiatives in promotion and mediation of books about migrants. At the end of this chapter, I inquire into the meanings that inform this so-called foreign perspective, a key matter when analyzing multicultural or intercultural children's literature to which I also return later in Chapter 6 and in the conclusions of this book.

Most of the books that were labeled as being about immigration have as a protagonist a child who travels to the West with his or her parents and recount this child's adaptation into the new group (a structure followed by *No soy rubia ¿y qué?*, *Luna de Senegal*, *Mehdi y las lunas del zoo*, *Mi nombre es Yoon*, *La Mirada de Ahmed*, and *Mila va al cole*). We do find a few examples in which it is made explicit that the child has already been born in the destination land and is to be considered, therefore, a "second generation migrant" (as in *Mi miel, mi dulzura* and *¿Cuál es mi color?*). As well as some books that deal with the identity of children born from couples with mixed backgrounds—*Noaga y Juana*, *Mi abuela es africana*, *El viaje del Bisabuelo*, *Colores que se aman*, and *Pipocas*.

We may also distinguish a group of books referring to irregular (i.e., "illegal") immigration. The most salient examples feature a character who is undocumented and has to struggle against difficulties. These characters are nevertheless focalized through a local child who meets the immigrant and attempts to help him (very interestingly, all undocumented immigrants are young men of indeterminate age; see *Viruta*, *El Balonazo*, *Blanca y Viernes*, and *Rita Robinson*). Another subset of books thematizes irregular immigration in a more allegoric way using the figures of The Three Kings—*Buscando a Baltasar*, *Noche de Reyes*, *¿Sóis vosotros los Reyes Magos?*, and *El rey negro*—also posing questions about the role color plays in marginalization.

Some books about irregular immigration could also be considered as referring even if very tangentially to stories about forced displacements. We may say that very few stories delve into the reasons the characters may have had to initiate the journey into Europe in the first place. When asked for books about refugees, the reviewers recalled only *Ziba came on a boat*, a book originally published in Australia and inspired by the story of an Afghan girl even if this background is not revealed in the story itself that is focalized through the eyes of this girl. *Ziba came on a boat* ends when the girl and her mother arrive, so it does not bring much to the analysis of ethnicities, 'race,' and origin narratives I focus on here. The S.O.L. reviewers also endorse one of the picturebooks more widely translated to present the drama of asylum seekers throughout Europe, *La isla. Una historia cotidiana* written by Armin Greder, a Swiss author, who coincidently is also based in Australia. Even if other translations of this book are read in primary schools, the S.O.L. only recommends this story for readers over 12 years old, what has left it out of our sample of study. *La isla* shows a naked man who arrives to a shore and is first welcomed and protected by the villagers who then react against him and expel him from town building up a fortress to make sure no one else trespasses the borders again. The illustrations inspired on Edward Munch's expressionism highlight the dramatism of the situation and present the immigrant/refugee as an innocent, vulnerable, and slim individual against a group of taller, fatter, and stronger neighbors who chase him.

We may, nevertheless, identify some stories in which the journey is less triggered by what Migration Theory calls Pull Factors—those that make the destination land attractive—than by Push Factors—those that include conflict, famine, or extreme religious activity as reasons for flight. It is precisely in the group of books about irregular immigration that those Push Factors appear to be sketched out, yet the reasons that have made the characters initiate the journey are rather downplayed in the stories. We do not find a single character that is described in the book as an asylum seeker or a refugee, but we may trace some references to what may have been forced displacements as the case of the boy in *Blanca y Viernes* that comes from land where 'villages disappear.' The European refugee crisis in 2015 has motivated nevertheless the translation and publication of more books that present the migration movement as resulting from war and we may expect more texts to be published in the coming years. *La isla. Una historia cotidiana*, so far, stands out as an exception in the way it problematizes the concept of national borders at the same time that presents the host society as unable to integrate newcomers. *Caja de cartón* depicts a girl who travels with her mother in a boat to the West, which could also be taken to depict refugees, even if the book is recommended as about immigration. The adoption of the girl in the end shows not only how an immigration story converges with one of adoption, but also how they communicate through the evocation of a rescue.

In this chapter, I focus on the analysis of plots about immigration with attention paid to their recurrent tropes and to the ways the stories are led to a solution, specifically analyzing whether or not they achieve narrative closure. In the next chapters, I delve further into how the common narratives and tropes about immigration reproduce, counter, and/or problematize other axes of social power related to the production of belonging and exclusion and how ideas of family and kinship pervade these narrations.

Migrant Children's Journeys into Otherness

Books that have an immigrant child as the main character usually tell the story of how difficult it was for him or her to adapt to the new environment. In most cases, these difficulties are overcome when the characters realize that their (different) origins are assets that their new playmates will value. The narratives of this transformation, in which the child gets to discover the worth of his or her difference, usually take place at the new school, the public space where the children with immigrant backgrounds get to interact with the "locals."

Amira in *No soy Rubia ¿Y qué?* has recently arrived from Tunisia and feels totally isolated from her classmates. The illustrations show her alone at a corner writing down on a piece of paper while the other children play in a group. Amira spends the school breaks writing letters to her aunt, who is back in Tunisia. But Amira's life starts to change when one of her classmates shows interest in what she is writing, more specifically, interest in the Arabic alphabet Amira is using. The classmate asks her whether she can write her name down in Arabic and soon every child in the class comes by with the same request. Having your name written in Arabic and using it as a cover for your school folder becomes fashionable, and only then Amira realizes that she is not isolated anymore. Very interestingly, when this happens, Amira also takes distance from what was meant to be her main psychological complex and accepts her 'difference.' We find a similar storyline in *Mila va al cole*, about the daughter of a couple of Bulgarian immigrants who first goes to school and is not able to follow, because she does not speak the language. Mila wants to make friends but is frustrated to find out that she cannot understand them. In the afternoon, at mealtime, she asks for milk in Bulgarian—"¡Mleko! ¡Mleko!" The very receptive teacher gives her a glass with milk and writes the word down on a piece of paper, draws a cow and a glass of milk and places it on the wall. One of Mila's classmates finds it funny and starts to use the Bulgarian word every day to ask for the milk and soon the entire class adopts it. The Bulgarian word operates, therefore, as a metaphor for Mila's integration and the last sentence in the book rounds the meaning: "A veces una palabra basta para hacer amigos" [sometimes one word is enough to make friends]. Interestingly in this case, the story was not about how Mila learns the local words, but rather about how her classmates are enriched by her presence among them.

Ahmed in *La Mirada de Ahmed* is an Arab child who also feels isolated and does not understand Spanish. His integration takes a bit more time and comes only after he realizes that the rest of the class would be keen to listen to the folk tales he used to listen to in his original town. Soon, this shy and introverted boy becomes a storyteller. The narrator assures us that Ahmed is now integrated but not assimilated, that is, he has not left behind his cultural identity: "Y así, día a día, va aprendiendo a ser uno más del grupo, sin dejar de ser él mismo" [day after day, he learns to be one of the group without giving up his own identity] (20). Following a similar plot structure and resorting to similar tropes, Khoedi, the protagonist of *Luna de Senegal*, manages to reverse a (potential) group hostility against her by standing proudly in front of the class to share a folk tale she used to hear from her grandmother in Senegal. The class praises her with applause. The other students respect her for being able to do something that they could not do and for bringing in a cultural background to which they would otherwise not have access. Similarly, Selva the African immigrant of *La bicicleta de Selva* amuses her classmates with tales of the exotic Saharan desert, which none of them has seen.

In all these books, the immigrant child finds a way in which to communicate the unique features of his or her origin culture to the group, facilitating in this way the immigrant child's integration. In the first two cases reviewed—Mila's and Amira's—the origin language operates as a metonymy of an ethnic difference valued by the group, whereas in the latter three cases—Ahmed's, Khoedi's, and Selva's—the emphasis is on how that cultural background is specifically rendered through their ability to become storytellers. I further analyze how these two motives— language and storytelling—model the (re)presentation of the immigrant child as an ethnotype (Beller and Leerssen xiv), yet first I introduce a story in which the position of the migrant child is not fixed along that divide of 'us' versus 'them' that appears to be so clearly drawn in the stories previously presented.

¿Pipocas? ¿Qué es eso? may be read as a variation from the plot about how valuing one's own difference facilitates integration. Nuno, the main character and narrator, was born in Spain to a Brazilian mother and a German father. (The book was originally published as *Pipocas, Què és això?* in Catalan. Here I will refer to the Spanish translation in which Nuno, the main character, was born in Zaragoza, whereas in the original he was born in Barcelona and, instead of Spanish, he wants to speak Catalan.) Nuno keeps messing up words in different languages and is ashamed that he cannot get any of the three languages correctly. One day a girl from Mozambique moves to his neighborhood and then he realizes that he is the only one who can effectively communicate with her in Portuguese. This discovery opens up a new relationship with his mother tongue and operates as a metaphor of his re-assessment of his origins. Nevertheless, in this case, the focus is not on how the group values this difference and its exoticism but is rather set on Nuno's own and

intimate relationship with his cultural background. In *¿Pipocas? ...,* therefore, the story recounts the individual transformation of the character, rather than a transformation of the group. Significantly, the character is not considered to be an immigrant but rather a child born to a transnational couple who inhabits, simultaneously, different cultural spaces and diasporas. Nuno's senses of belonging are multiple and this appears to be the instructive goal of the story. Coincidently, he is not depicted as marginalized from a group of local classmates, yet he does feel different and was, until his own cultural discovery, ashamed of it. Through Nuno's interaction with the Mozambican girl, he comes to understand the benefits of his trilingualism. At the end of the story, and similarly to Mila's story, his Spanish friend Pablo also adopts some Portuguese words, and Nuno discovers how fashionable his mother tongue can be.

Interestingly, Nuno is at once an immigrant and a local, as remarked by the presence of a real immigrant, the Mozambican girl. In a first page, the boy describes his belonging: "Yo, Nuno, soy de aquí, de Zaragoza, y un poco de Brasil, y también otro poco de Alemania." [I'm from here, Zaragoza, and a bit from Brazil, and another bit from Germany]. If compared to Joana, the girl from Mozambique, he is clearly a local. When he and his friend Pablo take Joana to the amusement park to buy popcorn, Nuno not only translates from Portuguese to Spanish, but also helps Joana to acquire the desired cultural codes:

> "Delante de la churrería Joana me pregunta:
>   —Como é que se diz: meia bolsa de pipocas de cor verde, amarela y rosa em espanhol?
>   Le explico y, con mucha decisión, pide:
>   —¡Una bolsa mediana de palomitas de las de color verde, amarillo y rosa!
>   —¡Por favor!- decimos Pablo y yo al mismo tiempo.
>   —¡Por favor!- repite Joana.
>
> [In front of the 'churrería' Joana asks me:
>   —Como é que se diz: meia bolsa de pipocas de cor verde, amarela y rosa em espanhol?
>   I explain and, very decidedly, she orders:
>   —A medium-sized bag of green, yellow, and pink popcorn!
>   —Please! - Pablo and I add at the same time-
>   Please! - repeats Joana.]

Nuno is trained, as the locals are, to add 'por favor' after any requirement, and proof of this is that he and Pablo—his blond friend—reply at the same time. With his mixed German-Brazilian background, Nuno nevertheless represents Spanish self-image, in opposition to Joana, the newcomer.

Interestingly, in the large majority of books portraying immigrant children, we do not receive further information about how much time they have been living in the Western country; nor are there acknowledgments of where they were born. These books appear to follow the European principle in which citizenship is bound to bloodline heritage—the ius sanguinis model as opposed to ius solis, in which citizens are those born in that land. We may infer that many of the children presented as immigrants in these stories may be second-generation immigrants, but that does not play any role in the form in which they are subjectivized. Interestingly, this registration of difference is slightly less marked when children are born to families with mixed backgrounds. When at least one parent is European/Western, the story might highlight how the child belongs—despite his or her physical appearance—to the country in which he or she has been socialized. Along with Nuno's, this is the case of Eric in *Mi abuela es africana*, Juana in *Noaga y Juana*, and the protagonist of *El viaje del bisabuelo*. They are all portrayed as having certain features that make them different from the others but, nevertheless, as belonging to the place where they have been born and raised up. In these books, the protagonists show that they have a special connection with the foreign place where one of their parents came from, but that, nevertheless, they belong to the country where they are growing up. The so-called "second-generation immigrants" are, contrastingly, presented as ethnotypes. This is the case of *Mi miel, mi dulzura*, a book about an Arab girl who goes back home to Tunisia, or *Cuál es mi color*, which tells how an Arab boy is regarded by the Spaniards as an Arab and by the Arabs as a Spaniard. This last book reveals the power of hetero-images and how they may impact the construction of the self of those who are turned into objects of otherization.

The Language-Integrationist Plot

The language usually plays a key role in the processes of bordering depicted in the books. Even if immigrants from Latin America used to be the most distinctive minority in Spain—they made up 24 percent of the foreign-born population in 1999 (Vicente)—children's books about immigration featuring Latino characters are rather scarce. Among the S.O.L. recommendations we find two that coincide in portraying Caribbean Hispanic characters. *Vamos a ver Papá*, published by the prestigious Ekaré, focuses on a mother and daughter's preparations to immigrate to Spain (the father has already been working there for some years). In contrast, *Lleva un libro en la maleta* presents preparations for the opposite type of trip: a girl will return to her native Dominican Republic for holidays after living in Spain for three years.

Spanish law differentiates between immigrants from former colonies—mainly Latin American—and those from the rest of the world and gives to the former the possibility to acquire citizenship after just two years of residence, much earlier than immigrants from other areas (Kleiner-Liebau 151). This distinction might be partially explained by the conception that learning the local language is the first hurdle to overcome in the integration process. In the case of Catalonia, where most of the books of the sample—32 out of 60—have been published, the question of language is even more urgent, because immigrants are often seen as threats to the hard-won battle of Catalan against Castilian (Kleiner-Liebau 98–101). Many immigrants there just get by with Castilian Spanish, but the Autonomous government—the Generalitat—has insisted on the need for Catalan schooling as a way of securing that the second generations will at least be Catalan-fluent, if not able to speak it as a mother tongue.

The language-integrationist discourse takes different forms. Perhaps the most prominent is equating learning the foreign language with a triumph over integration difficulties. Interestingly, the foreign tongue is also valued as a trait of cultural diversity—in *Mila va al cole* and *No soy rubia ¿Y qué?*—and as a means of connecting with others—in *¿Pipocas?...* Very interestingly, in this valuing of the foreign languages we may trace a discourse on diversity in which the foreigner can contribute and in which the cultural exchange is promised as two-directional.

Taking our cue from Lakoff and Johnson's metaphor theory, we may trace a conceptual metaphor in which the acquisition of language speaks about an acquisition of a society's ways of doing. Lakoff and Johnson claim that we perceive and act in order with conceptual metaphors that link ideas in our minds. In these stories, understanding the language leads to understanding how things are or should be done. Going back to the quoted fragment of *¿Pipocas?...*, we may note how Nuno's translation is not only a translation of words, but also one of ways of doing (with his insistence in the *por favor*, for instance). In Khoedi's house, the father has placed vocabulary lists with each word in four different languages: Wolof, of their ethnic group; French, the official-educated language in Senegal; Spanish; and Galician (161). Khoedi's family is portrayed as a model family, and their multilingualism is a distinctive feature; they maintain a link with their ethnic origin at the same time that they manage to belong to the French-educated minority in Senegal. Once in the destination country, they learn not one, but the two languages spoken in the region, showing their respect for the local cultural group that wants to keep its language. The model immigrants are able to deal with the cultural complexities of locality in a global world; they master the global and locals languages in the same way that they adapt to the global flux of labor economy and to the local particularities. There is no such thing as a Wolof-Galician dictionary. In order to learn Galician, the immigrant has first learned French to be educated in the origin country and then Spanish, the dominant language at the destination country. Their integration thus resembles a practice of continuous translation. As translation scholarship has noted, the very process of translation is not just to transfer texts from one language into another, but it is a process of negotiation between texts and between imagined cultures in which the hegemonic culture imposes meaning when the original is constituted as an Other (Bassnett 6).

The plot in *My name is Yoon* illustrates how the original—as a metaphor of the origin—is culturally adapted to be translated. Yoon is a Korean girl who immigrates to the United States. When she arrives there, her parents teach her how to write her name using the Western alphabet. Yoon feels the Western transcription makes her name lose the richness of meaning of the ideogram and refuses to take it as her own. Each day at school, Yoon chooses different words—from the words she is learning in her fast immersion in that new culture/language—to fill in the prints where she should be writing down her name. The Korean girl writes "cat," "bird," and "cupcake" on those forms aware that, by doing so, she is resisting some dominating cultural force. *My name is Yoon* is, therefore, another story of a girl who comes to a new school and at first feels isolated and marginalized from the group/language/ culture. This conflict is solved when a (blonde) girl invites her to play. After she feels that she is taken into account and welcomed by a classmate, Yoon begins to establish relationships and play with the rest of the kids. After a first happy day at school, she arrives home and sings "in English"—in Spanish in the Spanish version, and in Catalan in the Catalan one—and her parents are proud to see that she has decided to adapt to the new place and that she will bring this new language home. The next day her integration is sealed: she is able to 'translate' her name to the hegemonic language, accepting to write Yoon in Western characters.

In these stories, we may trace an ambivalent discourse that moves between integration and assimilation. Immigrants are expected to enrich the host society with their own cultural backgrounds, and locals are portrayed as eager to learn from foreign cultures. The traditional discourse on assimilation presumed the necessary uprootedness of the migrant to assimilate to the local culture. An emphasis on integration would, at least initially, understand that ethnic backgrounds cannot be erased yet that these differences do not impede foreigners from learning the ways of doing things in their destination country. Yet this exchange between the foreigner and the local appears to be quite superficial: in all these stories the emphasis is placed upon how the newcomer needs to learn the local language and how the native language may be an asset that will nevertheless be left behind. We may also read here the pervasive idea that children who are socialized early enough into a new language are more easily adapted and may acquire those ways of doing that will never be acquired by their parents.

The Storyteller Plot

Despite their difficulties with language—or perhaps to counter the image of the immigrant as an unskilled speaker—immigrant children are frequently portrayed as appealing storytellers. We find many key episodes in which foreign children amuse the local classmates with folktales from their homelands, a moment that marks a new social positioning for them.

In Orientalism, Edward Said claims that Western Orientalists constructed the Orient as a reverse of the Occident as a means to reproduce a Western identity. Said reviews the representations of an exotic Orient produced by Western scholars, writers, travelers, and painters, in which sets of polarities are created in opposition to what they understood as the Western essence. The Orient would be represented as exotic, backward, uncivilized, and at times dangerous to stress the West as a region of progress, civilization, and safety. Moreover, the distorted and exaggerated representation of the Arab World dating from the time of European Enlightenment (or even before) would produce the relationship in which the West is superior to the East, providing a rationalization for colonization. We may regard the representation of migrant characters in the Spanish children's' books as informed by that Western self-image described by Said and understand the role these representations have in producing it. Imagologists introduced the concept of 'ethnotypes' to refer to how ethnicities are coded as opposed to the imagined community of 'us,' which tends to be an ethnocentric community, allegedly unaware of how it is also culturally situated (Leersen and Spiering; Leerssen). The trope of the immigrant as a storyteller sheds light onto how the migrant child is presented as an ethnotype deeply informed by (post) colonial imaginaries.

That migrant storyteller comes from an 'exotic' region where things do not occur as in the Western rational world but rather according to rules of fictive imagination. The differences between this region of origin and the Western city are highlighted: the children do not tell about life in cities, but rather about small villages or the desert, a recurrent trope in these books, where life is structured around very traditional activities as farming and recollection. The children often retell tales they have heard from their grandparents; their ancestors give them access to the core of a pre-modern culture that is to be opposed to the modernity of the European classroom. In *Time and the Other*, Johannes Fabian (Fabian) builds off Said analyzing how discourses are constructed to place non-Westerners in a time that is historically previous to Westerner's contemporary time—the immigrant child could be perceived then not only as having traveled great geographical distances but also as having traveled through time to get to their new, contemporary Western homes.

The character of the storyteller immigrant is not only informed by Western ethnocentrism, but it is also to be connected to the prevalent idea that identity is a single and stable category. The migrant is, therefore, an ambassador of a culture that is reproduced from generation to generation. As Anthony K. Appiah ("Identity, Authenticity, Survival: Multicultural Societies and Social Reproduction") claims, the idea of collective, social identities is connected to expectations of authenticity—that is, it anticipates that someone who is affiliated with the determined minority would have a determined, coherent, and continuous behavior as a representative of this group. Appiah illustrates the point saying that being homosexual presupposes a refusal to stay in the closet, and instead to be a proud homosexual, even if a society would not yet treat homosexual people with equal dignity (162). In these stories, the immigrant children conform that normative behavior of being authentic Others performing that desired exotic difference as if authentic.

The Sheherazade Ethnotype

Very interestingly, in three of these books[4] we find references to Scheherazade, the legendary storyteller of *The Arabian Nights*. In *Mehdi y las lunas del zoo*, the mother of the character represents Scheherazade as a human living statue in the streets of the Western city where they now live. She stays still and only moves when someone gives alms. The figure of Scheherazade is turned, therefore, into an immobile figure who earns a living precisely by skillfully staying quiet. However, in *The Arabian Nights*, Scheherazade was the opposite: a storyteller who, through the act of narration, of talking, saves her life and the lives of other women. The story of the Arabian nights describes an angry king who, after discovering that his first wife had betrayed him, marries a new virgin every day, and sends her to be beheaded the next morning. He had already killed one thousand such women by the time that the vizier's daughter, Scheherazade, offers to marry him. Scheherazade was—as described by Richard Burton, the first translator of the text—"well read and well bred" (Burton 15) and knew enough stories to entertain the king. Every evening she starts a new story, telling it through the long night to stop just before dawn breaks. Because the King is too eager to hear the end, he spares her life for one more day. And the day after, Scheherazade ends this tale but starts another to leave unfinished; in this way Scheherazade entertained the king for one thousand and one nights. When she had no more stories to tell, he had already been transformed into a kinder and wiser man, who decides to make her his queen.

Scheherazade and *The Arabian Nights* are widely recognized, emblematic examples of Western Orientalism. Following Said, Reina Lewis pinpoints how the Orient was characterized as "irrational, exotic, erotic, despotic, and heathen, thereby securing the West in contrast as rational, familiar, moral, just, and Christian" (16). *The Arabian Nights*, also known as *One Thousand and One Nights*, was first published in English in 1704, translated by Sir Richard Burton. In subsequent translations, more folktales of Middle-Eastern provenance were interpolated even if they had not been part of the Arabic original. *The Arabian Nights* has been studied as an example of how Western translators—the Orient experts—modified the text according to what would be expected or attractive to the hegemonic Western reader. Moroccan sociologist Fatima Mernissi claims the figure of Scheherazade has been misinterpreted by the West: she is taken as an Oriental sexual icon whereas in her own tradition she would incarnate a female power that is cerebral rather than physical. Mernissi points out how Scheherazade wins over the kings by her ability to penetrate into his brain by using the right words. Her claim is that the image of Scheherazade has been distorted to match the Western fantasy of the Oriental harem and the submissive Oriental woman.

Said's claim regarding the construction of binary oppositions between East and West—or how the East needs to be constructed as an Other in order to secure a definable Western identity—sheds light on the power relationship behind the production of self- and hetero-images in stories meant to promote integration. Mehdi's mother needs to represent the difference in order to earn a living in the receiving country. In her performance, though, Scheherazade is completely divested from that cerebral power Mernissi describes. Significantly enough, she is a statue. Moreover, the narrator of the story, Mehdi, who at first glance appears to render a first-hand and critical perspective on the conditions in which immigrants live and how the system profits from them, is unaware of the symbolic power that subordinates her mother in this performance of the immobilized stereotype.

I have expanded on the use of the figure of Scheherazade to shed light over the representation of the immigrant as an Other who needs to gain a place among 'us,' the 'culture regardante.' Considering the immigrant as a Scheherazade sheds light on the production of the ethnotype and on how the migrant is expected to perform the desired 'authenticity' to entertain the locals. The journey of Scheherazade, remediated from the Arabic tradition by Western orientalists, is one of the images that no longer promotes the self-identification of the group but is instead imposed as a model of identity. Anthony K. Appiah goes on to claim that collective identities—the identification by gender, race, ethnicity, religion, nationality, or sexual orientation—may not be a form of liberation, but rather a "tyranny" (163).

An exploration of the layers of focalization in these narratives helps to explore further this idea. Who narrates and who sees the immigrant as an ethnotype? The question of who sees and tells, of which eyes are lent to the reader to understand the narrative world is very helpful in the discursive analysis of children's books, where we rarely find unreliable narrators, that is, whose credibility has been seriously compromised. Moreover, as different authors point out, children's literature mediation promotes the identification of the reader with the view the focalizer character renders (Nikolajeva *Power, Voice and Subjectivity in Literature for Young Readers* 85; Stephens *Language and Ideology in Children's Fiction* 68).

The S.O.L. review for *Mehdi y las lunas del zoo* claims that reading this story, focalized on an immigrant child, could give a new perspective to the (local) reader: "la historia nos muestra la dificultad de integración del inmigrante en nuestras sociedades y su deseo de hacerlo, pero desde el reconocimiento de su diferencia" [the story shows us the immigrants' difficult integration and their desire to achieve it, but from the acknowledgment of their difference]. This review also reproduces that image of the group of 'us' to be separated from 'them' and puts hopes on this focalization on the immigrant child, who is able to share his own view and, moreover, his desire to integrate. The review also conveys the idea of an interculturalism in which identitarian traits are kept despite of the integration. A close reading of Mehdi's first-person voice, nevertheless, suggests that his views are informed by that production of the Other as an ethnotype. We may focus on the moment he describes his mother's Scheherazade performance:

> "la gente se paraba delante de la figura de Scherezade y, si se atrevían a cerrar los ojos, por un instante oían el rumor de una voz que explicaba historias antiguas de príncipes crueles, de genios encerrados en lámparas maravillosas, de pescadores, y reyes, y ogros, y halcones. La vieja historia de la serpiente que huía del encantador, la de Simbad el marino y la de Alí Babá...
>
> Pero las historias ya existían en la imaginación de la gente. Ella no decía ni una palabra. Sólo el gesto, solo la mirada despertaban la presencia de aquellos príncipes poderosos, de las serpientes, del pescador y de los ogros." (55–56)

[People stand in front of Scheherazade's figure and, if they dared to close their eyes, they heard the murmur of a voice telling ancient stories of cruel princes, of geniuses trapped in marvelous lamps, of fishermen, and kings, and ogres, and falcons. The old story of the snake escaping from the charmer, the one of Simbad the sailor, and Ali Baba... But the stories were already in people's minds. She didn't say a word. Only the gesture, only the gaze, woke up the presence of those powerful princes, of the snakes, the fishermen, and the ogres]

Mehdi describes his mother's work and puts himself in the place of this audience. He is capable of penetrating the minds of the people staring at his mother and is as amazed as they are by the imaginary that she triggers. Interestingly, Mehdi mentions tales like Ali Baba or Sinbad, which were not part of the original Arabic edition of *The Arabian Nights*, but found in subsequent Western translations. Mehdi's first-person view seems, therefore, to be deeply informed by those stereotypes and Western fantasies about the Arab world that he uncritically renders.

The Colonized Focalization

In Chapter 3, I elaborated upon Mieke Bal's focalization theory to propose a 'transferred' focalization in narrations that would presumably render the point of view of the adopted character who nevertheless was rendered as if repeating the parental domestic storytelling. To understand some recurrent turns and gestures in the focalization in books about migrant characters, I would like to speak of a 'colonized' focalization. Both the colonized and the transferred focalization mark forms in which focalization is delegated from, in most cases, an external narrator/focalizer to the character. I have chosen the term 'colonized' with the aim of making transparent my subject position informed by insights of postcolonial theory.

By speaking of a 'colonized focalization' I aim to suggest that the so-called immigrant perspective in these stories is shaped by the host society's view(s). I am aware of how problematic this claim is. In the first place, because it assumes a realist reading of these stories, in which I am suspicious of the views while aiming to compare them to what a 'real' view of the immigrant would be. In the second place, my proposal may suggest that there is something identifiable as a 'host society view' reproducing in this way the us/them divide that I myself had criticized before. Despite these apparent contradictions, reading the pretension of authentic view of the migrant as shaped by views of the local appears to be very productive.

A number of these books are narrated by what we traditionally call a third-person narrator who provides access to the immigrant character's views and feelings—that is, an external narrator focalized in the immigrant character. *La mirada de Ahmed* [Ahmed's view], a title that promises to render the Arab child's perspective, offers a good example of how such focalizations often work. The story recounts how Ahmed feels alien to the school class and does not understand the language his classmates speak. The illustrations also try to convey the child's point of view using a common device in the illustration of first-person texts: the reproduction of the view of the character including the depiction of his back (cf. Nikolajeva and Scott 125). However, certain 'details' evidence here that the story is not purely focalized through Ahmed; instead, it seems that his point of view has been 'colonized.' The first significant detail is in the first sentence, in which we read: "Cuando Ahmed llegó a *nuestro* país, no quería ir al colegio. ¡Se sentía tan extraño!" [When Ahmed arrived in our country, he did not want to go to school. He felt so alien!] (Emphasis mine, first double spread). Some pages later we read:

> "Sus compañeros le miraban con curiosidad. LES EXTRAÑABA VERLO TAN QUIETO. Ahmed no hablaba, no escribía, no sumaba ni restaba; quizá ni siquiera escuchaba las canciones que tanto les gustaban a ellos" (fourth double spread)
>
> [his classmates looked at him with curiosity. THEY WONDERED WHY HE WAS SO STILL. Ahmed didn't talk, didn't write, didn't add or subtract; perhaps he wasn't even listening to the songs that they liked so much].

Who sees, then, in this story about Ahmed's view? The narrator—which speaks for this collective group of classmates—may tell us how this boy feels and what he thinks about the new city in which he has come to live, but how does this narrator knows? Why do we have to trust this narrative voice when the empathy appears to lie somewhere else? Ahmed's view is rendered as authentic, yet he came to 'our' country, as the narrator states at the very beginning. The story ends up depicting Ahmed as fully integrated, transformed into a storyteller of "fabulous stories" (tenth double spread). A reader may wonder if Ahmed feels as integrated as the narrator assures. *La mirada de Ahmed* appears to be unable to render Ahmed's point of view: if anything it can render what in psychological theories of identity is called the "looking glass self" (Coy and Woehrle 154). The term refers to how self-identity is built upon the expectations of the social context. The theory is often summarized with the saying 'I am not what I think I am. I am not what you think I am. I am what I think you think I am.'

White Saviors and Black Kings: Metaphors of Illegality and Marginality

Another possible approach to immigration is present in books that refer to irregular immigration. These books do not put forward integration plots as those described before and are not examples of an (even if superficial) celebratory multiculturalism, but speak of a more uncomfortable and troubled relationship with human migration, its geopolitical explanations, and its legal framework.

Among these books, we may distinguish one group of stories in which a local child befriends an irregular immigrant and four books that allegorize migration with the figure of The Three Kings. Apart from these, irregular immigration (sans papiers) and undocumented work is also thematized in two other books, *Mehdi y las lunas del zoo* and *Wamba o el viaje de la miel*. The first tells the story from the point of view of a child whose parents work in the informal economy while they wait for their situation to be regularized. The conditions of the irregular workers are referred to in a brief passage:

> "En nuestro barrio, sobre los grandes tejados de las casas, había mucha gente que no tenía papeles. A eso se llama: "en situación irregular". No era fácil conseguir aquellos documentos: los certificados, las declaraciones, el contrato de trabajo... Aquellos papeles se daban con cuentagotas. Y la Administración, sometida a la presión de los que sacaban rendimiento de la situación, toleraba aquella ilegalidad" (58).

> [In our neighborhood, over the top of the roofs, you could find lots of people without documents: that is called "in irregular situation." It wasn't easy to get those papers: certificates, declarations, work contracts... They were very miserly to give those documents. And the Administration, under the pressure of those who were taking advantage of the situation, tolerated the illegality].

Mehdi provides a very direct critique on how immigration is handled by mentioning the figure of the Administration—a reference to the government—that would consciously benefit from the exploitation of irregular immigrants as cheap workers and would then tolerate them. Probably the 6- to 8-year-old child to whom the book is addressed will need some help to decode the critique, but this is as referential as it gets. Mehdi's story later introduces fantastic elements to focus on a narration of how the boy misses a camel that they have left behind in his hometown. I must note here how the selection of the camel as the object of attachment reproduces again the ethnotype of the desert so recurrent in these books. Medhi ultimately finds his camel in the local zoo and liberates him. The story ends when the boy runs from the police entering into a TV set with his pet. As I review in the following pages, many books about irregular immigration include fantastic elements and allegories to refer to the situation of undocumented workers.

Wamba o el viaje de la miel uses an abstract and metaphoric way in a very simple story that is meant to be a song. Wamba travels to Europe to find "pollo y miel" (chicken and honey). Once there he realizes he cannot buy food. He is asked to show his documents and ends up defending a bee who is attacked by an old woman with her stick. Wamba finds out that he will be continuously marginalized in this country, where only some can afford to eat and decides to take the bee back to his homeland, leaving Europe behind. This is a rare children's book, since it was part of a broader project done by graphic designers that also included a song and a video, released by a small-independent house, Demipage, specialized in artistic publishing. The author of the text—Daniel Villanueva—describes it as "una solución poética de la inmigración en nuestras ciudades" [a poetic solution to the immigration in our cities] (Jiménez).

This juxtaposition of 'solution' to 'poetic' may be symptomatic of the aims and shortcomings of this and other books here reviewed. In the following pages, I trace how these books—despite their pro-immigration aims—still reproduce discriminative worldviews. If a solution to immigration is pursued, it is only a 'poetic' solution as if acknowledging how stories cannot battle against a (naturalized) structure of exclusion.

Mafias, Pateras, and Rescues

Four other books deal with irregular immigration in stories that could be considered to be more 'realistic,' or at least, in which events follow rules of the possible in real life: *Viruta*, *El balonazo*, *Blanca y Viernes*. and *Rita Robinson*. They can be further divided into two subsets that each present similar plots: *Viruta* and *El balonazo* tell the story of a young immigrant who struggles to survive working in the Spanish informal economy and gets the help of a Spanish boy who is the focalizer of the story. *Blanca y Viernes* and *Rita Robinson* recast Defoe's *Robinson Crusoe* with a Spanish girl in the role of the White shipwrecked man and an African immigrant playing the part of Friday. All four books were published within pro-diversity agendas and present irregular immigrants as victims of the world's unfairness and its tyrannical economic forces, yet in all of them the status quo prevails in the end. In each case, a 'solution' is only possible when the Spanish characters come to assist the immigrants.

Viruta is narrated by Javi, a Spanish boy who meets Jalal, a Kurdish immigrant who is an illegal resident in Spain and makes a living by rinsing car's windshields at the red lights. *El balonazo* is narrated by Daniel, a Spanish boy who meets Maxama, a Senegalese immigrant who sells illegal copies of films and albums in the street. In both books, it is soon revealed that the immigrants are controlled by the mafias that facilitated their entrance into the country. Both are forced by these mafias to work in the informal economy until they have collected the sum they supposedly owe their masters for their passage to Spain. Afterward, Jalal will continue his journey to Germany and Maxama to Paris, where their respective relatives live. The turning point in both stories, whose plots are strikingly similar, comes when the immigrant gets into trouble because of his or her illegal situation, and, in both cases, it is resolved with the help of the Spanish families. (I return to these stories in the last chapter, Chapter 7.)

Blanca y Viernes and *Rita Robinson* also have similar plots. Both books tell the story of a young girl who, during her holidays, encounters an African immigrant and establishes a relationship with him that makes her recall that of Robinson Crusoe and Friday. In the first case, the girl has been reading Defoe's book during her vacation on the Southern Spanish Coast when a 'patera' unexpectedly arrives on the shore, and a young boy manages to find shelter in the girl's playhouse. Inspired by Defoe, Blanca calls him Viernes [Friday] and tries to instruct him in the way that Robinson did with the 'native' Friday. Very interestingly, this story does not provide any trace of critical awareness as to how one of the emblematic texts embodying European colonial rhetoric is used to refer to new relationships between locals and immigrants. Indeed, Robinson's superiority and capacity to thrive inspires Blanca in her 'White savior' approach to the immigrant, who is bluntly represented along the lines of the stereotype of the black savage.

In *Rita Robinson*, the *Robinson Crusoe* plot is subverted. Rita, a selfish Spanish girl, attempts to help the immigrant but only worsens things by doing so. After a shipwreck during an excursion with her family, Rita arrives on a desert island where she meets Amadou, a Senegalese immigrant who has been left there by a mafia organization that was 'smuggling' immigrants into Spain. Rita tries to help him, but he is the one that ends saving her by carrying her in a small boat back to the southern Spanish coast. Once there, the police rescue Rita and try to persecute and arrest the irregular immigrant. The policemen interrogate the girl, assuring her that they only want to assist the Senegalese; fortunately, she does not know where he is and gives a perfectly innocent answer: "Amadou es muy cabezota; no le gusta que lo ayuden" [Amadou is too stubborn; he doesn't like to be helped] (67). The police fail to detain the immigrant, who was wise enough not to trust the girl with his plans. This book does take critical distance from the *Robinson Crusoe*/ White savior trope by including a note of irony and criticism. Moreover, although the story is focalized on the very naïve character of Rita, the happy ending includes the immigrant's border crossing, even if the focal character fails to acknowledge it. We may trace in this ending a subversion of the narratives that protect the borders, but that narrative is also protected from the innocent child chosen to be the focalizer and figure of identification.

Amadou is the exception to the rule that presents (irregular) immigrants as passive characters. We may relate agency to focalization and understand their passiveness as deriving from the fact that the stories are rendered through the active Spanish characters. The passiveness may also be connected to the rhetoric of White humanitarianism that informs colonial claims and that is subject of an ironic turn in *Rita Robinson*. *Blanca y Viernes* reverses Defoe's tale without criticism; on a leaflet released by the publishing house to provide educational guidelines to schoolteachers, it is argued that the book: "brings Robinson Crusoe up to date, proving that people and places may change, but human relationships do not" (consigue actualizar Robinson Crusoe, demostrando cómo cambian los lugares y las gentes, pero no las relaciones humanas[5]). Blanca—a Spanish name that literally means white—fleshes out the cultural paradigm of the paternalizing European figure. Some of the human relationships may change—female figures now take Robinson's role, for example—while other are maintained: in both cases the White characters believe in their cultural superiority over the non-White "Friday."

These books have been published in a context that debates how to control the borders, how to regularize (or not) undocumented workers, and how such actions may encourage or discourage immigration into Spain. These books present the irregular immigrant as a victim of the mafias. In all them, these mafias take the role of the antagonist that is to be fought by the White protagonists and their families. The happy endings are not achieved when the illegal immigrant is documented and has a right to stay, most probably because the regularization of immigrants is a matter of never-ending controversy, even if it is much more likely to happen in Spain than in other European countries. As these four books have been published by the biggest houses in the country, SM and Anaya, it is not surprising that these controversies have been left to the side. Contrastingly *Mehdi y las lunas del zoo*, published by a smaller house (Edebé), may put forward even if briefly the idea that the country benefits from the arrival of low-wage undocumented workers.

In these other four books, irregular immigration will be never be explained attending to 'pull' factors—how the demand for low-wage workers attracts new immigration—but only the 'push' factors in the origin countries. The immigrants in these stories come from desert lands where they have no food and no hopes for the future. Immigrants are presented as having nothing to lose because they do not leave anything behind: they will never mention, for instance, the families that are left behind or skills that will not be useful any more after immigrating. The powerful mafias take advantage of this situation smuggling immigrants into Europe, a region that is not presented as so marked by financial prosperity perhaps in a tacit comparison with the growing power of the BRIC (Brazil, Russia, India, and China) countries, as it is by its humanitarianism. In this construction, Spain is presented as having an unfortunate geographical position as the entrance door to Europe, and it is put forward as a message that this burden of being the border shall be shared with the rest of Western Europe.

King Balthazar's Exceptional Blackness

The representation of undocumented workers can also be traced in four books that use the figure of The Three Kings to speak about racist discrimination. The Three Kings—Caspar, Melchior, and Balthazar—who separately hear news of Jesus's birth in Nazareth and travel there from the East to bring him gifts by following a star, are very emblematic figures in the Christmas celebration in Spain. In the local tradition, Santa Claus does not bring presents but the Wise Men do on Epiphany every 6th of January. Moreover, Santa Claus, or Papá Noel as he is commonly called in Spain, is mostly seen as an intrusive figure linked to the rise of consumer society (and the viral hashtag #yosoydelosreyesmagos -#IamfortheThreeKings is used every year to promote the local celebration against the global Christmas hype). The Catholic devotion to the figure of The Three Kings has a long tradition and the first written piece of Spanish medieval theater (Anónimo 7) elaborated on the Matthew's Gospel narration about these wise men coming "from the East." The figure of Balthazar, the Black Arabian scholar, has been employed in recent years to thematize racism in Spanish society. Among other actions, African descendants have started a campaign against the practice of having White people in Blackface represent him in the parades that take place every January.

Noche de Reyes, *El rey negro*, and *Buscando a Baltasar* tell the story of King Balthazar court's journey to Europe and depict the discrimination they experience when locals are not aware that he is a king. In the last book, the story is focused on the discrimination one of his young pages faces when he gets lost in the city after the parade. All these books were published during a short span of time between 2002 and 2003 and may be considered among the first stories published in Spain to counter an emergent racism in the years when a high influx of new immigration from Africa was beginning to arrive. We may find in them satirical references to the immigration police—who do not allow the King to cross the border in Noche de Reyes—and to the inhuman working conditions of undocumented (Black) workers in the fields of southern Spain—when a lost page of Balthasar's court is forced to work for a living. The aim of all these stories to bring closer to the reader the experiences of irregular immigrants by using a character—who is also the focalizer of the story— who is a beloved figure associated with a large cultural tradition in Spain.

A fourth example, *¿Sois vosotros los Reyes Magos?*, has a rather inversed plot and tells about a girl who would have mistaken a group of immigrants for being the Magi. This book fits into what Sirke Happonen (59) describes as a growing trend of postmodern picturebooks, which present contradictory information in words and pictures. As is common in these books, the interplay between text and images is satirical, and it is expected that the adult mediator—the parent, the teacher—will assist the child-reader to decode the meaning. The story tells of a seven-year-old girl who on her way to the bakery stops to talk with three men that she recognizes as The Three Kings (Figure 4.1). A second illustration would suggest to a more socially literate reader that they are just foreign men, probably undocumented citizens working in the informal sector. A "close viewing" in the way that Mieke Bal (Bal "Introduction: Another Kind of Image") promotes helps us to understand the story of immigration this image tells. What makes them The Three Kings in the eyes of the girl and (undocumented) migrants for a more literate reader?

Figure 4.1 Alba believes she has encountered The Three Kings in the street. They may just be three immigrants. Illustration by María Luisa Torcida.

The girl is presented as being unaware of the discourse that links 'race' or, more precisely, non-whiteness with ethnicity and, very often, with marginality. The three men the girl encounters wear tunics and carry objects just as the representations of The Three Kings do, but what appears to be the deciding factor for the girl may be that one of them is Black. In the first image quoted above, we see how the girl observes the Black man—the strangest face to her, in the narrator's argument—probably concluding then that these must be The Three Kings. A second image includes a broader picture—which the girl is apparently unable to see—in which an adult viewer/reader would understand that they are just three migrants selling goods in the street.

It is rather complicated to apply the category of focalization to images. The analysis of the levels of focalization in these books is done mainly focusing on the verbal texts, even if most of the books we are dealing with are picturebooks. The discussion of how to analyze visual focalization in visual narration is still unsettled. A line of argumentation says that if a story is told with character-focalization, this character would have to remain unrepresented to convey his or her view on the events in the visual narration (cf. Nikolajeva and Scott 128). Perry Nodelman's essay "The Eye and the I" made a seminal contribution to this discussion, stating that fully first-person picturebooks are impossible as images cannot depict a character's perspective. Nevertheless, further research has shown productive attempts to analyze point of view in pictures identifying "visual focalizers" (Stephens *Language and Ideology in Children's Fiction* 179) and moments when internal visual focalization is pursued (Nikolajeva and Scott 128). I will explore these ideas of an existing or desired visual point of view while bearing in mind that terms like 'narration' and 'focalization' describe distinctly different phenomena in visual and textual narrative (Horskotte 190).

In ¿*Sóis vosotros los Reyes Magos?*, a first image suggests that the book renders the girl's view, whereas a second one zooms out from the character focalization to give us an external focalization that would reposition the characters suggesting that they are foreign migrants rather than the Magi. When the girl arrives home, she tells her mother she has encountered The Three Kings; interestingly, she first tells her about meeting King Balthazar. The narration is focalized on the girl, so the reader has no account of what the mother is thinking, but the visual narrator might suggest that the girl is what Wayne C. Booth calls an "unreliable narrator" (Booth 339). In the adult's eyes, the same features that call the girls' attention have a different interpretation: Balthazar's skin color, the grown beards of the other two, and the outfits—tunics, an African hat, a white turban—mark these men as foreigners and as belonging to different ethnic groups. The fact that they carry objects gives one more hint to the reader with social literacy to decode the meaning: they could be street sellers. The mother reproaches the girl for talking to strangers, but the girl replies: "-Pero, mamá, si no eran unos desconocidos. Eran Melchor, Gaspar y Baltasar, los tres Reyes Magos!" [But, mom, they were not some strangers. They were Melchior, Caspar, and Balthazar, The Three Kings!] (sixth double spread). The book ends there. It can be read as a story of how (innocently) children understand 'race' and ethnicities or, the other way around, of how adults are unable to see the world like children. The review recommends this book due to how it: "permite una reflexión sobre nuestra capacidad para aceptar al diferente y nos plantea algunas preguntas" [invites us to reflect on our capacity to accept those who are different and brings up some questions]. We may wonder which questions it did raise for the reviewer. To me, it suggests that immigrants may be as different from 'us' as the representations The Three Kings. If so, why does this happen and what is the role of 'race' in this positioning?

A subtle message transmitted by this and other books is that people who look different are different. Here the visual-verbal interplay suggests that foreigners resemble the exotic representations of the Oriental Kings. The immigrant's representation is again molded with an ethnotype in mind and this ethnotype is fixed on ancestral traditions. The immigrant is not only represented to highlight his or her ethnicity, but also as a preserved image of pre-modern cultures.

Eth(n)ic Deliberations: *El Balonazo* and the Paradoxes of Pro-Immigration Narratives

Carmen González-Enríquez points out that even when most irregular immigrants enter Spain as 'false tourists,' the media focuses on those who arrive from Africa in open boats (pateras) and on the victims of mafia networks. Presumably, the ideal reader of these books is not expected to befriend or even get acquainted with undocumented workers or their children, but is rather expected to acknowledge their existence in these news reports that repeatedly describe immigration as a 'drama' and 'human tragedy' (Kleiner-Liebau 108). The images of pateras arriving on the Canary Islands or crossing the Strait of Gibraltar show how people risk their lives for the chance to enter Europe and become a second— or third—class citizen: an undocumented worker. How do we explain this to children? These books make an attempt to provide narratives in which the country's right to control its migration is balanced with the right of people to migrate (avoiding dealing, as I explained before, with the reasons that push them to do so). Regardless of this pro-immigration aim, these books appear to perpetuate the narrative of immigration as threatening the development of prosperous Europe.

The plot of *El balonazo* gives us important insight into the complexities and paradoxes of pro-immigration and pro-diversity discourses in literature for children. It was authored by Belén Gopegui, a writer affiliated with the left who publishes adult and children's fiction often labeled as ideological and utopian, and it is focalized on the character of a Spanish child, Daniel.

> "No se ven las estrellas. Cuando a Daniel le dieron un balonazo en pleno ojo, vio un triángulo verde del tamaño de una pelota de tenis, a pesar de que el balón que había chocado contra su ojo era de cuero blanco con hexágonos negros." (1)

> [You don't see stars. When a ball hit Daniel's eye, he saw a green triangle of the size of a tennis ball even if the ball that has crashed into his eye was one of white leather with black hexagons]

This opening paragraph sketches the field. The story starts with this demystification of (comic) books for children: you do not see stars when knocked. This narrator promises, therefore, that he will tell us how things are and not how we fantasize they are. The story begins by telling us about Daniel, who is frustrated because of his lack of football skills, until he meets an irregular immigrant, Maxama, who teaches him some tricks to improve his performance. An underlying plot stresses in many different moments of the story how life is not as easy as it is sketched in books and how children may relate to the fantasy stories with which they grow up. Moreover, the S.O.L. review emphasizes that Maxama not only teaches Daniel football but also "about real life" (cómo es la vida en realidad).

After befriending Maxama, who sells illegal copies of CDs and DVDs in his neighborhood, Daniel starts reflecting upon how bad 'real pirates' are when compared to those depicted in books. He reflects on this in a school composition arguing that pirates in the 'real world' may be Robin Hood-type characters who take from the rich to give to the poor, which in this case are themselves, as people in need who copy and sell films and music albums to earn a living (83–84). His reflection leads to a discussion about "pirates" in real life. The teacher, Marisa, explains that books do not necessarily portray reality, and that even if it is sometimes good to guide your actions by those appearing in books, it is important not to confuse the fictive with the real. This is quite an interesting point to make in the context of the books we are discussing here, since in these books we find numerous examples of embedded narratives that are performative within the book, that is, that affect the events of the frame-plot. In these books, as it is probably the case in a large number of books targeted to children, the stories-within-the-story model the behavior of the character in a way that suggests that the same may happen with the ideal reader. The schoolteacher brings in some ethical deliberations explaining that the good and the bad are not easily distinguishable:

> "Robar está mal- dijo Marisa-, pero también está mal que haya personas que no tienen un sitio donde vivir, ni dinero para comer. A estas situaciones, cuando eres tan pobre que no tienes techo ni comida, y otras parecidas, las leyes lo llaman <estado de necesidad>. Muchos vendedores de top manta se encuentran en ese estado, y entonces, como el daño que hacen vendiendo cedes es más pequeño que el mal que intentan evitar, la propia ley dice que no son culpables" (90).

> [It is not good to rob—Marisa said—but is also not good that people do not have a place where to live or money to eat. To these situations, to be so poor that you don't have a roof or food and other similar, the law gives the name of <necessity >. Many of the top manta sellers may be in that condition; as the harm they make is minor to the one they are trying to elude, the law says that they are not guilty]

El balonazo has been orchestrated to drive a complex debate about the place and rights of illegal immigrants in Spanish society. Maxama crystallizes different levels of illegality: he is undocumented, he works in the informal economy, and, moreover, he sells illegally copied material. Gopegui portrays an immigrant who thrice breaks the law and makes the characters wonder which is the correct response. Marisa calls attention to nuances, making clear that decision making is much more complicated in real life than what is portrayed in books for children.

El balonazo ends by placing Daniel in a very challenging and intricate situation: should he lie to a court in order to prevent his friend Maxama from being deported? The police capture Maxama, seizing the illegal copies he was trying to sell. Daniel wants to help him and decides to lie to the judge saying that Maxama's DVDs were meant to be a present to him, not to be sold. Daniel believes the laws are not fair: "él pensaba que si las reglas no decían que Maxama no tenía la culpa de vivir en un país sin dinero, ni decían que lo importante era no hacer daño a los demás, entonces esas reglas no estaban bien" (168) [He thought that if the rules did not say that Maxama could not be blamed by living in a poor country, and did not say that the important thing was not to harm the rest of the people, then those rules weren't right] (168). This statement may be quite revolutionary for a children's book, as in them those infringing the rules usually get punished, and it may be even more revolutionary because it addresses explicitly the controversies of irregular immigration while also commenting on the very heated topic of digital piracy. (Spain is the European country with the biggest market of illegal copies, and the local and national governments have been trying to educate the population on the concept that copying is stealing.) Moreover, Daniel's view about the law does not only come as his own rebellion but it is supported by his parents and by the schoolteacher. Even the judge also understands its unfairness and ends up setting Maxama free. Let me remark this again: *El balonazo* puts forward the idea that the immigration law is so unfair that it is admissible to break it and, moreover, to lie to the court to get through. I remark elsewhere how we find in children's literature a consensus regarding the values to be passed to the next generation and how this implies that controversial issues are rarely touched upon. This book is one of those rare cases in which the author does step into a polemic topic (or two). Nevertheless, a close reading of *El balonazo* shows how even this revolutionary narrative reproduces the trope of the threatening immigrant and the desire for maintaining a status quo.

Endings are privileged sites in which to inquire for ideologies, since the questions posed during the development of the story are resolved there, and the whole story comes to a point in which all that came before should make sense (cf. Porter Abbott 64; Carroll 2). *El balonazo*'s happy ending uncovers the trap in which this pro-immigration discourse is caught. In the trial, Daniel lies to the judge, saying that Maxama's CDs and DVDs were meant to be gifts for him; the judge does not believe him, but he is impressed to find out that the boy cares to that extent for the fate of the immigrant. The defining proof of innocence comes just after when Maxama's lawyer assures the court that the defendant was preparing a trip to Paris in the next weeks to join a cousin. This ends up convincing the judge, who sets Maxama free after recommending that Daniel and his parents take care in verifying that he travels to France.

As remarked before, *Viruta* has a similar ending: Jalal, the Kurdish immigrant, is sent off to Germany after a local family looks out for him. The message is sound: irregular immigrants cannot stay in Spain and will only be innocent if they take their necessity somewhere else. Gopegui, the author of the book, may be keen to criticize the ways illegal immigrants are treated or how we deal with the controversial topic of copyright infringement, but will nevertheless avoid a happy ending in which the undocumented worker can stay. Sending them off to other European country seems the best possible solution and all characters in both stories coincide in imagining the better life that the immigrants will have in their final destinations.

These endings reveal certain features of the problematic discourse on immigration and belonging in Spain, reinforcing its position as a "semi-peripheral society" that needs northern help to take the burden of the border control (de Sousa Santos 207–10). The Spanish society and administration—represented in the figures of the empathetic judge and the progressive schoolteacher—is not to be blamed for the ways in which immigration is handled. Spaniards are as helpful and welcoming as they can be, but they have this unfortunate geopolitical position that obliges them to exercise exclusion.

If we compare these books about irregular immigrants with those that use the figure of King Balthazar, we may conclude that the discrimination and marginalization faced by irregular immigrants is greater in stories that are more distanced from an identifiable realistic context. Moreover, most of the stories about The Three Kings use the Black characters as focalizers offering in this way a metaphoric point of view for the marginalized. In her article "Exit Children's Literature?", Maria Nikolajeva argues that some contemporary children's novels make use of various narrative devices to question the identification of the reader with the focalized character. This would be achieved by using characters that are "alien in some way." She describes the alien characters as: "unpleasant, physically or mentally handicapped, an immigrant, a homosexual, an animal, even a monster" (Nikolajeva "Exit Children's Literature?" 230). In these cases, she argues, the reader does not easily identify with the point of view rendered. Significantly enough, what Nikolajeva lists as 'alien' is not simply strange or foreign to the child in the sense of the experiences he may have had, but it is alien to what is considered good or desirable for the children. In this line of argumentation, kings may not be as alien to children, as handicapped, immigrants, homosexuals, animals, or monsters. A very effective medium to convey a story of discrimination and racism would be then this figure of the Black king. In the following chapters, I delve into the complex and intersected ideas on 'race' and racism and what may be lying behind these 'royal allegories' claiming that they may be reinforcing racist discourses against their own will.

In the Place of Conclusions: The Obsolete Clash of Civilizations in *Ruby Rogers*

In this chapter, I divide the books about immigration in two subsets: those in which the immigrant gets integrated into the group of locals when he or she proudly assumes an ethnotype, and those attempting to make visible the difficulties irregular immigrants go through. Among the first, I identify the trope of the immigrant as a storyteller who amuses the new group with ethnic perspectives and the trope of the language as a key to integration. I then delve into the construction of the immigrant as an ethnotype and how integration is possible when he or she learns to perform Otherness according to the desires for "authenticity" of a group that behaves like an audience. I relate this to Appiah's ideas on collective identities as a tyranny for subordinated subjects. The immigrant is pushed to behave as an ambassador of a pre-modern culture as opposed to the flexible and dynamic culture of the locals.

I gathered in a second subset those books that portray irregular immigration. Within this group, I position four books using the figure of The Three Kings—and predominantly of King Balthazar—to construct an allegory that criticizes the discrimination and marginalization suffered by irregular immigrants from Africa. I also described a group of books in which the irregular immigrant is saved or nearly saved by a young Spanish protagonist. Through the description of these plots, I recall how the discourse of humanitarian assistance that informs colonial narratives prevails in books that aim to educate on diversity. *El balonazo* served as an example of how even a story that promises to step into controversial matters without giving simplistic solutions only achieves a happy ending when the migrant emigrates.

Ruby Rogers, ¿te lo puedes creer?, originally published in the United Kingdom as *Ruby Rogers, do you believe it?*, provides an exceptional approach to immigration and interculturalism. It is part of a collection featuring the protagonist Ruby, a middle-class British girl, who in this book faces two problems: her mother is ill and her best friend, Yasmin, is going through a difficult period. Yasmin is Muslim and has given a presentation about Islam to the school class, after which she receives an anonymous email telling her that it was awful and that she is conceited. Ruby assists her friend by investigating who might have sent this email; she first suspects a friend of theirs who might be jealous. An adult reader might have had other suspicions and may have related this email to an Islamophobic reaction. At least, this came to the mind of the S.O.L. reviewer:

> "Una novela que trata temas como la familia, la enfermedad de uno de los progenitores y la inseguridad que provoca en los hijos, o la interculturalidad, pues la amiga es árabe y sus ideas no siempre son bien acogidas por los compañeros del colegio. Un libro entretenido y fácil de leer sobre temas actuales." [A novel that deals with topics such as the family, the illness of one of the parents and the insecurities that it provokes in the children, and also interculturalism, because the friend is Arab and her ideas are not always well accepted by her classmates. A delightful and easy reading about actual topics]

Apart from confusing Muslims with Arabs, this review misses the point of the novel: the offender does not care about Yasmin's religious background, but is troubled by her personality and behavior. Ruby ends up finding out that the message was sent by a kid that had a crush on the Muslim girl and reacted out of anger about not being taken into consideration. Yasmin's cultural and religious background does not play any important part in the plot development. In Ruby's focalization, Yasmin is not necessarily more different that the rest. Catholicism is the topic in the next class (we have to keep in mind that the story is set in an British setting and first targeted to British readers), and Ruby lets us know that she knows as little about it as about Islam: "Vale, sé que el Papa vive en Roma o por ahí cerca. Una vez soñé con él, pero su imagen se confundía con la Papá Noel" [Ok. I know that the Pope lives in Rome or somewhere around. Once I dreamt about him, but his image was confused with Santa Claus'] (64).

Ruby Rogers ¿te lo puedes creer? has a different approach to difference. In this book, diversity is the rule rather than the exception, and the similarities rather than the differences between people from different backgrounds are stressed. The plot may play with the idea of intolerant and discriminative classmates only to make to make it pointless in a globalized and multicultural environment. Children's literature often resorts to the possibilities that an innocent point of view opens (Nodelman and Reimer 190), yet in this book the characters are not naïve, even if they may be unaware of the tensions among different beliefs and ethnic groups. The children in *Ruby Rogers...* get organized in groups that battle in the competitive field of the school class. At least to me—in any case an adult reader—this portrayal of children's 'innocence' appears to be much more convincing and less shaped by notions of political correctness than other plain celebrations of diversity. Moreover, *Ruby Rogers, ¿te lo puedes creer?* does not seem to have been written to educate on tolerance or diversity and does not present characters to be taken as models of behavior. It is perhaps this approach, this 'sidelining' of ethnicity, that leads me to believe that this novel achieves what others are pursuing. In *Ruby Rogers, ¿te lo puedes creer?*, identity is not fixed by (geographical) origin, children are not ambassadors of foreign cultures (even if they can explain them), and difference does not have to be performed to achieve integration. Nevertheless, difference is marked, cultural origins are acknowledged, and a happy ending comes when friend helps a friend.

Notes

1 After the budget cuts that followed the Spanish economic crisis, undocumented workers were impeded from receiving health care. To have access to these services, migrants had to register what facilitated the data collection, which may also explain why Spain led the list of European countries with irregular migrants.

2 The data used are from 2006.

3 Van Dijk also refers to how racism in Spain has taken the most "virulent popular forms" as in the emblematic case of the community of El Ejido, often recalled in the Spanish debates on racism. In early 2000, the local population of a small town in Andalusia engaged in a raid against the Algerian and Moroccan community after a mentally disturbed immigrant was accused of murdering a Spanish woman. During two days and two nights the locals looted and burned houses, shops, and mosques with the passive connivance of most inhabitants, the police, and the municipal government (van Dijk *Racism and Discourse in Spain and Latin America* 17).

4 In *Mehdi las lunas del zoo*, *Mi miel mi dulzura* and *Isha nacida del corazón*.

5 From http://www.anayainfantilyjuvenil.com/pdf/proyectos_lectura/IJ0023 9401_1.pdf. Retrieved Aug. 21, 2015.

5 The United Colors of the Rainbow

Explaining Human 'Races' and Racism

As mentioned above, we find very few episodes of overt racism or discrimination in these books about immigration and international adoption. The stories appear to be more engaged in depicting processes through which foreign-born children gain self-confidence and manage to feel integrated into the local group, rather than on delving into experiences and clashes of seemingly hostile social contexts. Discrimination is in most cases a "supplementary" rather than a "constituent" (Porter Abbott 230) event of the plots; that is, if it is portrayed, it has no further importance for the development of the story. This approach might respond to a rather prevalent idea that the best tool against discrimination is to ignore prejudices, an approach widely criticized by anti-racism stakeholders who claim that the idea that we live in a post-racist world is instrumental for maintaining racial hierarchies (Bonilla Silva 1–6). The circumvention of discrimination in these books may also derive from a more general attitude toward children's literature as a tool to safeguard innocence of childhood from the corrupt world of adults (cf. Rose). As such, these narratives would seek to distance themselves from depicting the ills of a society that discriminates people based on color and/or social and geographical origins to focus on more hopeful stories. Moreover, it may also be the case that authors and mediators believe that the depiction of discrimination may instill ideas about hierarchies, as argued by one of the S.O.L. reviewers. It goes beyond the scope of this study to assess the effectiveness of this approach, if only because the effect of reading and cultural consumption on our worldviews can hardly be measured by quantitative means. Yet, we may wonder if this depiction of welcoming societies where racism is presented as a matter of the past facilitates the maintenance of racist worldviews, dismissing the opportunity to understand how 'races' have been and are social constructs.

We may identify two broad strategies to approach 'race' in these books: on the one hand, stories that include—even if very briefly—an episode in which someone is discriminated against and, on the other hand, stories that are focused around the celebration of the diversity in which color becomes a metaphor of difference. In the next pages, I review the forms these two strategies take to continue providing a close reading or, as Mieke Bal suggests, a "close looking" (Bal "Introduction: Another Kind of Image") of the word/image relationship in selected examples. Picturebooks promoted to foster cultural diversity reveal themselves to be rich sites in which to explore the resistance and reproduction of the stereotypes, since the verbal and the visual are often not aligned. The verbal text—perhaps because it is more closely monitored—appears typically to be more power sensitive, while in the visual narration we find—perhaps unwittingly—more stereotypes reproduced.

Racism without Racists

Casting a look at the labels given to the recommended books by the S.O.L. reviewers, I quickly realized that they were reluctant to tag the books featuring discrimination against foreigners as being about racism. Numerous books include episodes of overt verbal discrimination—such as *Luna de Senegal* and *Todos los colores del arco iris*—or brutally racist episodes—*Colores que se aman* and *Susana Ojos Negros*—and even if color is in them explicitly mentioned, these books were not labeled as being about racism but as about "social integration" or "immigration."

Characters are physically attacked on the basis of racial discrimination in very few books. Notably, these episodes appear in stories that are more distanced from realistic fiction, as in those that allegorize immigration with references to the Three Kings. King Balthazar seems to make an appealing character to thematize racism, and four different books focus upon this figure. In *Noche de Reyes*, a group mistakes King Balthazar for a marginalized foreigner and beat him to the floor because they disliked "las personas de piel oscura" [dark-skinned people] (18). This story is told with focalization on the king—recounting his point of view—which allegedly brings the point of view and experiences of Black migrants closer to that imagined Spanish reader of these books. It may be noted that his condition as one of the Magi re-signifies 'race' associating it to class, to the royals: King Balthazar is an exceptional person who needs to be treated as such. The four books that allegorize migration with the figure of the Three Kings play with the idea of what would happen if they would be mistaken for ordinary people or, even worse, for migrants. King Balthazar's exceptionality turns him into a possible protagonist to engage with in a similar operation to that of the Academy-Award-winning film *Twelve Years a Slave*, in which slavery is depicted by telling the misadventures of a Black free man who is kidnapped and sold to a cotton field owner. These supposedly anti-racist media might be passing through the message that 'race' itself does not indicate one's social position.

The debate about racism in Europe, and particularly in Spain, has usually been triggered by episodes of physical violence against migrants. These events appear to motivate these stories, yet they are carefully sidelined in them. *Colores que se aman* [Colors that love each other], for instance, was inspired by the assassination of Lucrecia Pérez, a Dominican brutally murdered in 1992, an act of violence that opened a larger debate on racism in Spain. In a book dedication, which is remarkably included at the end and not at the beginning of the book, we find a reference to the case that inspired the book. The story is narrated by Luca—a dark-skinned, five-year-old boy—who gets hints of something going on in the street outside. Luca cannot tell, but an adult reader may presume that someone has been killed. The boy says that he first heard "angustiadas" [fearful] voices coming from the street talking about " un disparo… y de que había una mujer de color tirada en el suelo. ¿De qué color sería? No se porqué me la imagine verde" [a gunshot… and that a woman of color was lying on the ground. Of which color was she? I do not know why I pictured her green]. Luca's narration is deeply informed by that narrative of the innocent and color-blind child who does not know that 'of color' refers to people with dark skin, even though he is racially marked himself. The story continues protecting this child from the adult (racist) world; on the next page, Luca's grandmother pleads: "Bajad la voz que vais a asustar al niño!" [Lower your voices, you're going to frighten the child!]. As the shouting outside continues, the scared boy hides under a chair; his fear is dispelled later when the grandmother enters the room and starts tickling him. Luca laughs "y la risa espanta al miedo" [and the laughter shoos the fear away]. The boy does not get to know what happened and no further explanation is given to him or to the reader. Instead, the book goes about how the boy—born to a 'mixed' couple—is a child of two colors "que se aman" [which love each other]. This book, therefore, reproduces ideas of existing racial tensions that will only be solved by the new generations, an idea also framed in that broader cultural narrative of the redemptive child (Hillel) who is able to cure the illnesses of the adult society.

Sidelining the racism in these plots may end up justifying it even if the aim of the book is precisely the contrary. In *Susana Ojos Negros*, a boy of Turkish background is beaten in the street. The story is set in a German city and narrated by a local girl, who only gets confirmation of this aggression by overhearing a conversation in which the neighbors talk about the Turkish boy: "Qué más da de dónde vengan ni por qué? Están aquí y punto. ¡Podían dejarlos en paz!" [And why should we care where they come from and why? They are here and that's it. They could leave them alone!]. In this brief passage, the causes of immigration are quickly dismissed, as if digging into them would help the cause of the ones who feel compelled to attack foreigners. This uncritical report of the racist episode may reinforce the idea that it would be preferable not to have any immigrants. The complexities of human mobility and of globalized job markets are reduced to the terse statement 'they are here and that's it.' As a book that aims to educate on immigration and diversity, it misses the opportunity to reflect on how the host society and economy benefit from immigration or to explore the conditions imposed upon those labeled as 'guest workers,' of which Turkish immigration into Germany is an emblematic example. The sole anti-racist message that this story appears to convey is that native populations should accept immigrants and refrain from (physically) molesting them.

The circumvention of racism in these books may also derive from an effort to portray a society that welcomes foreigners. In all but one case— *Wie ich Papa die Angst vor Fremden nahm*, translated as *Cómo curé a Papá de su miedo a los extraños* and reviewed in more detail later in this chapter—the racist characters fade quickly out of the story. All those characters who discriminate on the basis of color get away without receiving censure from the others and are not given the narrative possibility of becoming transformed. They are not to be blamed; being racist is apparently a pre-modern feature of Western societies that will, nevertheless, become outmoded. Tomás Calvo Buezas, an anthropologist and sociologist who first studied racism in Spain, claims that one of the barriers to anti-racist education in the country is the widespread belief that Spaniards are not as racist as citizens from other Western countries (Calvo Buezas 238).

Oddly enough, the S.O.L. list of recommendations about racism includes one example of discrimination against Spaniards when immigrating to other European countries. *Antonio en el país del silencio* [Antonio in the Country of Silence] describes the discrimination experienced by a Spanish family in Germany. Very interestingly, the discrimination is here explicitly portrayed; racist characters take a significant place in the story, and they even get contested. There is no direct confrontation, but the Spanish family mocks the German neighbor downstairs, who despises them by calling her "la señora Tag" (since when responding to a greeting, the woman would just blurt out the 'Tag,' forgetting the 'guten') (22). Surprisingly, this book was labeled as about 'racism' when others in which racism is more directly thematized—such as *Luna de Senegal*, where the protagonist is, among others, called 'negra de mierda'—do not have this tag. Moreover, *Antonio en el país del Silencio* is presented as "una buena forma de conocer en la propia piel la situación por la que pasan personas de otros países que llegan al nuestro buscando trabajo" [a good way to get to know in our own skin what people go through when coming from abroad to our country looking for a job]. With this reference to 'our country' and 'our skin' the book is recommended to local children, the target group for the S.O.L. reader promotion as explained in Chapter 1. But this recommendation also reveals a need to find stories about immigration that do depict racism in Spain with some distance. Research done on Spanish textbooks shows a similar tendency. In them, racism is explained with examples of historic racial discrimination in the United States, South-African apartheid, or the Holocaust

(Calvo Buezas quoted in van Dijk *Racism and Discourse in Spain and Latin America* 60).

Racism is much more frequently addressed in stories that use anthropomorphized animals. When using human characters, books usually refer to examples set far from the contemporary social context of the European reader and refer to historical racism and slavery and segregation in the United States. A message that appears to be reinforced by doing so is that 'race' and racism are globally and historically grounded yet only occurring in the geographical distance or the distant past.

As briefly sketched in Chapter 4, discrimination is sidelined in the plots of most of the stories, and perpetrators quickly fade out of the story. Moreover, the victims never understand these acts as racist and fail to contest them as such. This circumvention of race may be related to that problematic arena in which intercultural education is being forced to prove that the idea of a hierarchical order of races has been replaced by one of a welcomed encounter between different cultures (Campani 165–68). Yet, 'culture' often takes the form of a destiny similarly to that of 'race' in biological racism; 'race' becomes invisible while remaining a prevalent marker.

Celebrating Diversity (and Colors!)

The most explicit approaches to the idea of the existence of different 'races' are found in very simple narrations that aim to show a scope of diverse physical features and colors among people. *¿Cómo es el color carne?* [What is skin-color?],[1] *Todos los colores del arco iris* [All the Rainbow Colors], *Teo aprende a convivir* [Teo learns to live together], and *The Colors of Us* are four books recommended to educate children younger than age eight on "human races" and "social diversity" (as labeled by the S.O.L. reviewers).

These four books focus on a character who discovers diversity in the close environment of a group of school friends or neighbors. These books also use similar visual narrations in which every new character is presented with an image that marks his or her difference not only regarding skin and eye color but also hair type, facial features, and clothing. These books balance the depiction of female and male characters ending up in what could be compared to the spirit of a United Colors of Benetton ad, assertively described by Stuart Hall as a "liberal mish-mash of 'difference'" (Hall *Representation: Cultural Representations and Signifying Practices* 273).

I may note some general differences between the three first books, which were originally published in Spain, and the latter, an American book. In *¿Cómo es el color carne? Todos los colores del arco iris*, and *Teo aprende a convivir*, the focalization is achieved through a character who defines himself or herself as White and is depicted as blonde or red-haired. In *The Colors of Us*, the American book, the narrator describes herself as having "cinnamon" (1) skin, and the entire story centers on how everyone she meets has a different tone; the concept of 'us' is formed by a diversity of shades that is very difficult to classify. In this way, *The Colors of Us* attempts to deconstruct the divide between 'us' (locals) versus 'them' (foreigners, racially marked characters) addressing the non-sense of categories like Black (African-American), Brown (Latino, Native Americans), Yellow (Asian), and White (American). Also, in this book, in opposition to the three Spanish examples, we find scarce references to how geographic origin may explain physical differences. Being a book about 'color,' it succeeds in de-essentializing physical appearance and in portraying diversity as constitutive of society.[2] In the Spanish books—most probably because immigration is a recent phenomenon—the physical differences are always coupled with a foreign origin. Very significant for our analysis is that in two of these books—*Teo aprende a convivir* and *Todos los colores del arco iris*—international adoptees and children with migrant backgrounds interact, making a parallel of two ways one might be racially/ethnically marked.[3]

Stereotypes and the Multimodal Construction of Meaning

I have sketched two recognizable subsets of books dealing with 'races:' those in which racism is—even if very tangentially—addressed and those that attempt to explain and celebrate the diversity of 'racial' features. In the next pages, I focus the analysis on an example of each of these textual strategies: *Wie ich Papa die Angst vor Fremden nahm* (*Cómo curé a papá de su miedo a los extraños*) by Rafik Schami illustrated by Ole Könnecke and *Madlenka*, by Peter Sís. Both books have received the White Ravens special mention—the most renowned prize for picturebooks in Europe—and appear recurrently in bibliographies on 'multiculturalism' and 'interculturalism' prepared in different countries.[4] Multimodal narrations—in this case, the interplay of the visual and the verbal—pose specific methodological challenges to the representational critique, and even if children's literature criticism has paid a lot of attention to picturebooks in the last years, very little research has focused on the ideological analysis of words and images (as argued by Robyn McCallum and John Stephens in their article "Ideology and Children's Books").

If we could agree on a picturebook canon, *Madlenka* would definitely have a place in it. It was written and illustrated by the Caldecott Medal winner Peter Sís and depicts a morning in the life of Madlenka, a girl who has a loose tooth and feels compelled to tell the world about it. To do so, she walks her Manhattan block and finds her neighbors to be representative of different world countries and regions: a French baker, an Italian ice-cream man, an Indian news vendor, a German old lady who tells fairytales, an Asian shopkeeper, her African schoolmate, and a Latino grocer. The world is contained in her block—the imaginary Manhattan as a multicultural mosaic—and she is able to familiarize herself with different cultural traits by having a curious stroll around.

This summary reduces the book, of course. If *Madlenka* can be placed among the best expressions of the picturebook genre, it is due to the complex and rich interaction between the words, the pictures, and the layout. The polysemic visuality opens the story by allowing a multiplicity of readings and decodings; Sís employs different fonts, cut-outs, and varied illustration techniques to highlight how ordinary events can be extraordinary and to suggest how these foreign neighbors may open windows to other worlds. Jack Zipes counts *Madlenka* among those books that use fantasy to foster alternative thinking (Zipes 85), but it may be the case that it cannot escape from a rather ethnocentric and yet not so alternative perspective. Despite its efforts, *Madlenka* represents foreign cultures in highly distorted and stereotypical ways. Walter Mignolo's postcolonial critique insists on how the establishment of the narratives of Modernity and Western civilization implied that knowledge was inscribed "to a geopolitical space (Western Europe) and erased the possibility of even thinking about a conceptualization and distribution of knowledge 'emanating' from other local histories" (Mignolo 59). A close reading of *Madlenka*'s textual strategies reveals the extent of how this Western logocentrism appears to shape postmodern appraisals of foreign cultures.

The idea of visual focalization—a category of narratological analysis previously introduced in this work (see Chapter 4)—sheds light on this projection of (Western) fantasies. In Madlenka's first pages, the story is zoomed in from an external point of view—a view of the planet

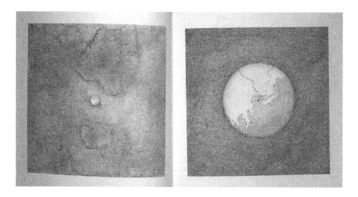

Figure 5.1 In *Madlenka*, the story zooms in to focus on the character who will act as the focalizer. Illustration by Peter Sís.

Earth—to Manhattan and, furthermore, to the window where a little blond girl awaits (Figure 5.1). The localization takes place in a visual narration, but a phrase displayed on the fifth page reinforces what the images were telling: "in the universe, on a planet, on a continent, in a country, in a city, on a block, in a house, in a window, in the rain, a little girl named Madlenka." And Madlenka stands in front of the reader.

The next pages underline that we, the readers, are invited to see the world as Madlenka does. She shouts that her tooth is loose and a new font emphasizes that the text has taken the first-person voice: "hey, everyone... my tooth is loose!" (Figure 5.2) The visual perspective is that that from below, the sight of a girl looking high up; on the opposed page, the visual focalization takes things a step further, presenting an altered vision of this world, and a new textual layout indicates that when we see the world as Madlenka, it may not correspond to what it actually is.

Madlenka is a postmodern picturebook that plays with conventions and perspective. I may read Madlenka as a story about 'getting the picture.' I mean this in the way illuminated by William J. Thomas Mitchell when he notes that a picture is, in its extended sense, "getting the picture" (Mitchell xiv), a whole that is more than just the snapshot. Mitchell quotes Martin Heidegger's reflection about how what distinguishes the modern age is that the world has become a picture. Mitchell claims that the reality is and has always been its representation. Madlenka may be read as the story of how a girl pictures others and how only some may have the possibility to project their images in this way. It may also be argued that if we look closely at the interplay of the visual and the verbal, Madlenka appears to be more engaged with the reproduction of stereotypes and the naturalization of ethnocentrism than with the recognition of diversities.

The story follows what Nodelman and Reimer define as the "home/away/home" (198–202) pattern, a recurrent plot structure in stories for children, in which a child goes away for adventure and returns to a safe home in the end. Madlenka has a loose tooth. She goes for a

Figure 5.2 Madlenka invites us to see the world as she does. The use of a new font underlines a change to the first-person voice, a point of view that is emphasized in the visual narration as well. Illustration by Peter Sís.

walk around the block meeting her neighbors and having access to their cultural backgrounds, which, we may suppose, changes her vision of the world. From the name of the girl, the reader or at least the reader of the English original, would expect the character to also have a foreign, probably Eastern European, background. Nevertheless, in the story the girl is the only character that is not 'ethnically' marked while she can project stereotypes on the rest. Very interestingly, these stereotypical neighbors include also her classmate Cleopatra who appears wearing a long "African" gown. Madlenka's parents, on the contrary, are white silhouettes; this deserves further analysis: are they just silhouettes emptied of meanings and representation precisely because they hold a position of authority? When the girl comes back home the two of them come close to the front door and ask worried: "Madlenka! Where have you been?" The girl, looks to the floor: "Well.... I went around the world" (twentieth double spread).

In the last two decades, scholars have dealt with the role of images in children's literature emphasizing how the visual and the verbal make a whole in "synergy" (Sipe 11), "interanimation" (Meek quoted in D. Lewis 39) or creating an "ecosystem"(D. Lewis 47). Perry Nodelman argues that words limit the pictures by indicating what to focus on, yet the pictures also limit the words by representing what otherwise would be vague (Nodelman *Words About Pictures: The Narrative Art of Children's Picture Books* 220). Maria Nikolajeva and Carole Scott have attempted to categorize different possible relationships between image and word and speak of a symmetrical relationship when both basically repeat the same information, complementary when words and pictures fill in each other's' gaps, expanding or enhancing picturebook when the visual narrative supports the verbal narrative and the other way around, and sylleptic when we find two or more narratives independent of each other. They also speak of the emergence in postmodern children's books of counterpointing relationships, in which we find two mutually dependent narratives that may even be contradictory. They argue that counterpointing picturebooks are "especially stimulating because they elicit many possible interpretations and involve the reader's imagination" (Nikolajeva and Scott 24). A book, may, of course, use different forms of these relationships.

Among Nikolajeva and Scott's categories, *Madlenka*'s would first have an enhancing or expanding narrative where both the verbal and the visual expand the meaning, yet how does this work? Nodelman's idea that images ground the meaning may help us to understand the role played by the visual representation of stereotypes. In *Madlenka*, images work as a dictionary defining meanings that the words alone would have left open. The visual appearance of Madlenka's neighbors, for instance, is not left to the readers' imagination but located and grounded, while their roles as sorts of ambassadors of ('exotic') cultures are stressed. The neighbors

Figure 5.3 Each character is presented as an ambassador from a different culture. Illustration by Peter Sís.

are dressed in traditional outfits and have shops decorated with all sorts of iconic elements from their lands of origin. The French baker has a "pâtisserie" with a French flag behind the window and the illustration insinuates that entering the bakery is like visiting Paris.

The layout of the book suggests certain distinctions between a more realistic portrayal and that of fantasy. Each character is presented on a full page facing another in which it is explained what sorts of things the character does/sells and what is to be found in the places where they come from. For example, in Picture 6 the different types of French breads a French baker would bake are described and illustrated.

Mr. Gaston's portrayal on the opposite page is certainly stereotypical, but it may not set one on alert for an ethnocentric and hierarchical construction of alterity. Some pages later though, Madlenka meets Mr. Eduardo, the Latino greengrocer (Picture 7). In the written text we only find a detail that may reveal some hierarchy among the neighbors. Mr. Gaston greets Madlenka saying "Bonjour, Madeleine," whereas Mr. Eduardo is more formal: "Hola Magdalena. Señorita Magdalena" (thirteenth double spread, the emphasis is mine). This may just be a detail, but a close looking to the visual depiction of Mr. Eduardo shows that certain ideas of hierarchies have been reproduced. Despite the rainy day (Madlenka holds her yellow umbrella), he wears ojotas. The poncho and an Indigenous-looking hat end up rounding the meaning: he appears to be from the Andean region with no traces of adaptation to the new landscape or weather conditions. In *Madlenka*, characters coming from Western countries—France, Italy, and Germany—wear Western outfits, whereas those coming from the rest of the world have all sorts of supposedly traditional outfits that mark their Otherness. This division recalls the claims of postcolonial studies and Edward Said's elaboration on how the Orient—and in this case all non-Western regions—are fantasies projected by the West in an opposition to a self-image. The West would embody culture, civilization, and democracy, while the rest of the world would embody a connection to nature and wildness.

To better assess the production of stereotypes we might ask to what extent these images wish to convey truth. We may first draw upon the concept of "visual modality" by Gunter Kress and Theo van Leeuwen (158–63) in *Reading Images The Grammar of Visual Design*. Kress and van Leeuwen claim that the division between 'abstract' and 'realistic' is not of much help to understand how an image does or does not present truth. The authors propose to look into what they call the modality markers that would distinguish images with high modality (truthful) from those with low modality (less truthful). The features they propose to view are color saturation, color differentiation (from monochrome to varied colors), modulation (if colors have different shades or are plain), contextualization (the use of background), representation (degree of abstraction), depth (perspective), illumination, and brightness. This may be brought down to a simple formula: the more an image looks like the photograph a camera would take—in its automatic mode, of course— the more truth it seeks to convey. This idea of modality helps us to understand the different depictions of the foreign characters in the book.

Mr. Eduardo provides us with a good example. He greets Madlenka on the page on the right, whereas the image on the left side is dedicated to a list of what can be found in his shop and in his continent: butterflies, jaguars, parrots, snakes, forests, rain, and also mountains, rivers, people, and pyramids. He represents quite an extensive territory. Among different expressions of nature, we are told that in his origin region we also find people. It is notable that the word 'people' is part of a list like this, as if there were world regions were no people were to be

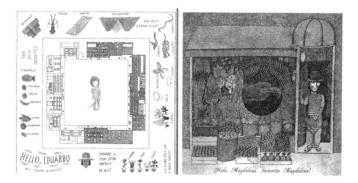

Figure 5.4 Mr. Eduardo is the ambassador for Latin America, represented as an Andean native yet nevertheless connected to the Amazonian tropical forest, Mayan and Aztecan iconographies. Illustration by Peter Sís.

found, but the way in which this word is visually defined is even more remarkable.

The visual narration tells us that 'people' in this region are indigenous people and, moreover, that indigenous people are those who go hunting with a bow and an arrow, do not wear clothes, and have a bunch of feathers on their heads. The image reproduces an imaginary view of non-Western regions—or specifically Latin America—as populated by tribes that would still go half-naked and survive by hunting. One could argue that it is just a simplified and stereotypical image not to be taken literally but instead as an ironic depiction. The way in which it is displayed—in simple lines as a list without a background—places it as a picture with low modality, not to be taken as a truthful depiction.

Every foreign country or region is referred to in three different illustrations: the visual dictionary, the presentation of the neighbor greeting Madlenka, and a collage that mixes different iconographic elements of the foreign culture meant to evoke Madlenka's journey to those different worlds. Each of these pictures responds to a different layer of narrative truth. Perhaps the most noticeable landmark of these layers is the use of cut-out windows that invite Madlenka, and the reader, to enter those foreign worlds. These cut-out windows bring us to double spreads where no rule of perspective is followed, a postmodern mishmash in which the truth only depends on perception. Mr. Eduardo's world (Figure 5.4), for example, combines a wild tropical forest with elements of Mesoamerican mythology. The modality markers—lack of perspective, monochromatic, abstract, dark—indicate the image's low modality, and the window that leaves Madlenka on another page—on another layer—reinforces the message: this is not the real world.

In contrast to these two levels of visual truth, the portrayals of the neighbors are to be taken as truthful or, at least, as the closest to a referential reality. The neighbors are depicted with perspective, using an ampler color palette and different shades suggesting that this is the level of reality, or at least in the storyworld of the book.

One could read the portrayals of the neighbors as ironic depictions of the multicultural imaginary associated with New York. The translation into Spanish may also facilitate this reading as a story that can only take place in Manhattan, the melting pot par excellence. Yet even if we read it like this, we may agree upon how the ethnocentric model is reproduced in these pages. In Madlenka, the West is organized on the base of national identities. The rest of the world is portrayed as existing in a previous stage of development and presents large cultural regions rather than determined nation-states. The book was published one year before the September 11, yet we may relate its circulation to the New York pride that followed the attacks and was transferred throughout the country and to other Western cities as well.

The three levels of narrative truth in Madlenka may be paralleled with the three modes of symbolic meaning construction described by German philosopher Ernst Cassirer: the expressive, the representative, and the significative functions. The expressive function (Ausdrucksfunktion) refers to mythical consciousness and its total disregard for the distinction between appearance and reality. This would be the symbolic function that structures meaning in the double spreads in which Madlenka is confronted with the mythical/fantastic orders of the different world regions. The significative function (Bedeutungsfunktion) is related to structuring knowledge and organizing explanations: it is a category of relations and abstraction that prevails in the sketch of the 'visual dictionary.' In between these two poles of symbolic meaning creation, we find the representative function (Darstellungsfunktion) related to the ordinary sense perception of what Cassirer calls intuitive space and intuitive time (Friedman), which would correspond to Madlenka's perceptions of her neighbors.

I am surprised by the book's lack of gestures indicating possible ironic readings. It could, for instance, have included details in the dictionary-like pages to displace and problematize its resemblance with a colonial catalogue. The depiction of the foreign characters appears not to be only deeply informed by stereotypes, but it also naturalizes the ethnocentrism from which these stereotypes emanate. It may be less evident than in the case of books such as *Tintin au Congo* from the early twentieth century, but *Madlenka* is informed by colonial narratives that appear to be overlooked when the book is promoted as educating about interculturalism and ethnic difference.

Wie ich Papa die Angst vor Fremden nahm by Rafik Schami and illustrated by Ole Könnecke uses an apparently opposite narrative strategy to address the question of racial and ethnic differences. The story describes a girl whose father is 'frightened by strangers.' The illustrations quickly show that by 'strangers' he refers to Black people and when the girl asks why, he tries to explain himself in a sequence in which a verbal and a visual point of view contradict each other.

Sie sind schmutzig...   und laut...   Sie sprechen Sprachen, die man nicht versteht...   und sehen anders aus, so grob.

Figure 5.5 Cómo curé a papá de su miedo a los extraños uses visual narration to contradict the verbal statements of the racist character. Illustration by Ole Könnecke.

— and they are dirty...
— and noisy
— they speak languages one cannot understand
— and they look different, so rude... (fourth double-spread)

The visual narration opposes each of the father's statements, evidencing his inability to see 'reality.' The pictures are focalized on the girl—who stops to watch Kofi Annan on TV—alerting the reader that there is another viewpoint to be taken into account. It is an auspicious beginning for an anti-racist book, even if its title is so euphemistic. The counter-pointing and even contradictory relations between the visual and the verbal stimulate to take distance from taken-for-granted assumptions. As many scholars point out, irony is a recurrent strategy in picturebooks that appeal to a deviation of the verbal and the visual (Sipe 9). This ironic sequence activates the reader's awareness and asks him or her not to believe everything just because an authoritarian voice says so. Yet, for some reason, this subversive relationship between the image and the word is not maintained throughout the book.

The story begins when the daughter—who is the first-person narrator—reveals she does not dare to invite her friend Banja home because she is dark skinned. Next, she plots a strategy to cure her racist father: she asks him to perform as a magician at Banja's birthday party. There, we expect, he will meet the family from Tanzania and will realize that they are not people to be afraid of. But what do we see when he gets to the friend's house? The visual narration is not anymore a counterpoint showing how African people—or people from African background—are

Figure 5.6 Despite a start in which stereotypes were deconstructed in the visual narration, the novel ends up reproducing a whole set of them. Illustration by Ole Könnecke.

similar to the imagined community of 'us.' Instead, the visual depiction (Figure 5.6) reproduces an extreme African 'ethnotype' that includes colorful masks, musical instruments, costumes, a naked chest, and feathers on the head.

These could have been ironic images or could have been representing the point of view of the father, but no hint is given to consider them as such. When I asked one of the S.O.L. mediators whether this image of the Africans was too stereotypical, she argued that it was not and that African people get dressed like that when they have important events to celebrate (S.O.L. reviewer).

How is the father 'cured' from his fear to strangers? As in *Madlenka*, the intercultural encounter is informed by a colonial imaginary in which the identity of the ethnic Other is constructed in opposition to a positive (Western) self-representation. The Other, as in *Madlenka* and as in the large majority of books of the sample, is constructed as pre-modern, backward (often emphasized through the presentation of fixed gender roles), and solicitous. Here, intercultural communication resembles the hierarchies and subordination of colonial encounters, now disguised as a relation in which difference is valued. In *Madlenka*, the subordination of the ('multicultural') neighbors to the (blonde) girl is not explicit but structural to a story in which a girl can tour the world just by walking her Manhattan block. In *Wie ich Papa die Angst vor Fremden nahm* the subordination becomes even more explicit when the only White man is the only one who gets a drink and the group of funny dressed Black people stares at him with admiration while he performs as a magician. In this visual narration, the racist father is honored while the African birthday girl is left aside.

Instead of conveying an anti-racist message, *Cómo cure a Papá...* suggests that Black people may not be dirty and rude as the father originally tells to his daughter, but that they are nevertheless different from that imagined community of 'us.' In the end, 'race' and ethnicity are coupled and a set of stereotypes is reproduced to maintain the hierarchical position of the Western White man. The very ending of the story is quite revealing of a hidden and unwittingly racist rhetoric in the book; the White father's anxiety about Black people is finally dispelled only when he performs as a magician in front of them and realizes that they can be fooled by his tricks.

In the Place of Conclusions: The Diverse Majority in *Toño se queda solo*

As reviewed throughout this chapter, 'race' and racism are avoided subjects in the list of the recommendations and may only become visible as occasional marks of ethnicity. I listed two recurrent strategies to deal with and explain 'races' to children and how both coincide in marking this category as mainly irrelevant by putting forward a color-blind ideology. On one hand, we find some books that include episodes of discrimination and tension, yet they almost always become supplementary events within the plots; moreover, racist characters fade out from the stories, and their victims are portrayed as passive characters who do not react against aggressions. These books may be read as efforts to acknowledge discrimination while naturalizing it as the death rattle of a soon-to-be-forgotten racism in society. The second very common strategy is that of depicting a welcoming and celebratory multiracial society, a colorful neighborhood. Interestingly, these books often include adopted characters in which their different features are acknowledged while marking how they are similar to the group of 'us.' At the same time, children from migrant parents are implied as being somehow different.

The close reading and looking at of two praised picturebooks used in different countries to educate in cultural and ethnical diversity showed how the visual text might jeopardize the verbal text and its sensitivity toward power relationships. In both picturebooks, we noted how the authors were aware of the possibilities opened by the composition of multimodal messages but failed in using these possibilities to deconstruct the dynamics of the production of otherness.

Viva la France (*Toño se queda solo*) a picturebook by Thierry Lenain illustrated by Delphine Durand, is much lesser known than the previous two examples: it has not been included on the White Ravens lists, it has only been translated into Spanish (from French), and was one of those books the S.O.L. mediators could hardly remember having read. None of the reviewers recalled this book when talking about examples of books about cultural diversity and it was not included in the different annotated bibliographies as were *Madlenka* and *Cómo curé a Papá...* . I raise these contextual matters here to underscore how the two books discussed previously may be taken as more representative of the type of books used to educate on diversity in Spain and in other European countries.

As one might note, none of these three examples was originally written in Spanish. The fact that they are translations from different languages may also speak to the different social contexts in which they were written. We could trace certain particular traits of the discourses on 'race,' 'ethnicity,' and 'national identity' according to the countries in which they were originally published (the United States, Germany, and France). It could be argued, for instance, that the Peter Sís' book—located in Manhattan—reveals certain features of a progressive American East Coast discourse on immigration as colorful and tasteful multiculturalism, while the German book may be read as fleshing out the difficulties to name racism after the Holocaust as in it the racist character is solely described as being afraid of strangers and not even xenophobic. A similar analytical approach would understand *Viva la France* as indicative of the French discourse on assimilation and the emphasis on the school as the place in which the French citizens become equals. Yet, rather than delving into these differences, I instead note how the circulation of these books, their translations, and their inclusion in lists of recommended readings on multiculturalism in different countries may be indicative of a shared Western discourse in relation to belonging and exclusion.

Viva la France—the French book that has only been translated into Spanish—tells about the day when Lucien, the leader of a group at school, decides to exclude Khélifa, a girl, because "she is Arab and not French" (third double spread). When forced to give explanations by Lao, a child of Asian features, Lucien ends up expelling him also, because Lao is also different: his father is Chinese. But then, other children in the group stand against Lucien. Manuel argues that as his grandfather only speaks Portuguese so he will also leave the group. One by one, the girls and boys of the group decide to join with Khélifa. The visual narration is apparently "symmetrical" (Nikolajeva and Scott 17) illustrating what the verbal text tells. What is revealing here is a small detail at the end that challenges this supposedly symmetrical relationship between words and images, while at the same time it deconstructs the coupling of 'race' and ethnicity. Tarik, a dark-skinned child, also decides to fight Lucien. The verbal text does not mention his ethnic affiliations or ancestors apart from what may be deduced from his name; it only says that there is a boy named Tarik who is angry with Lucien and decides to join the others. In that verbal account, Tarik may be as French as Lucien; the pictures, however, show that he is Black. It may have been the case that despite the Arabic root of the name, the reader would have imagined Tarik as White, if we follow Richard Dyer's claim that White is the "unmarked, unspecific, universal" (45) color that we put on the faces of those characters we do not know what they look like (Dyer). The visual depiction, therefore, anchors the words. Does Tarik's skin color make any difference? It does and does not, and probably in this ambivalence is located a potentially productive relation between words and pictures in an anti-racist book. Tarik's racial origin does not make any difference in the story, but it challenges the deeply ingrained assumption of the White Western nation. This detail adds to the meaning conveyed: a diverse majority forms the nation. If there is a minority in this play-yard it is that of Lucien, who persists in excluding and categorizing.

These three books also indicate a path to follow in this analysis. In them 'race' and ethnicity are coupled and intersected by other social categories such as gender, class, religion, and kinship. In the next chapter, I approach the question of how 'race' and 'ethnicity' are marked focusing on how the cultural signifier of race is negotiated among different 'axes of social power' (Yuval-Davis "Intersectionality and Feminist Politics" 198) in the construction of origin narratives.

Notes

1 'Color carne' refers, in Spain, to the light pinkish/orange skin tone that White people supposedly have.

2 Nevertheless, this book may also be criticized for reproducing stereotypes such as that of the man portrayed as a stereotypical Indian-Pakistani who sells spices, the dark-skinned (Southern-) Italian who prepares Pizzas, and the babysitter of the protagonist, who is the only Afro-American character. One could make a point, nevertheless, for the use of these stereotypes as a form of tactical essentialism for narrative purposes.

3 It may be also revealing of how international adoption influences the publishing of books about 'race' that the American author of *The Colors of Us* is an adoptive mother, even if no explicit reference to this is made in the book itself.

4 Such as lists made by IBBY (International Board for Books for Young People) or those provided by the Bibliothèque nationale de France (http://www.udaf60.fr/IMG/pdf/Bibliographie_contre_le_racisme.pdf).

6　Intersected Identities

Nationality, Class, Gender, and Ableism in the Making of 'Race'

In this chapter, I explore the construction of 'race' by examining its relationships with other social signifiers such as origin, social class, gender, nationality, and ableism. Using an intersectional approach, I inquire into how 'racially marked' characters are often placed in subordinated positions among different axes of difference exploring at the same time how these books may be regarded as narrative strategies to recode and resist these categorizations.

Transnationally adopted characters add tension to social categories unearthing how 'race' is coupled with belonging and ethnicity and how it intersects with class and nationality quite strongly, especially in European countries in which 'race' is quickly connected to foreignness and immigration. Claudia Castañeda proposes the view that international adoption is a "technology of race" that not only 'reflects' existing forms of racial categorization and attribution, but that makes 'race' in particular ways (Castañeda 1). Indeed, during the last decades psychologists and social workers on adoption have been beginning to pay attention to the ways racism and forms of racial subjectivation affect non-White adopted children raised in predominantly White contexts. In the United States it is often recommended that families get engaged in what is called the "ethnic-racial socialization" (Bebiroglu and Pinderhughes 133; Hughes et al. 747). The term refers to a scope of different types of involvement with the (imagined) 'birth culture' of the adopted children ranging from language lessons, books, special meals, participation in certain cultural festivities, and trips to countries of origin. The goal is to turn the racially marked origin into an asset developing pride for a specific cultural heritage. Researchers in the cultural construction of international adoption in Europe have called attention to how this approach very often pathologizes adoptees and psychologizes the "deep social and ideological contradictions adoptive families encounter" (De Graeve 369). In this chapter, I keep the question for these contradictions in the foreground while I explore the makings and unmakings of 'race' not only within adoption discourses but also in relation to migration (and especially exploring the tensions when comparing these two discourses). By the end of this chapter, I relate 'race' to ableism—that is, to discourses on disability—arguing that 'race' is constructed as a gap to be overcome.

Recoding the Origin

Most of the books about adoption avoid any explicit references to possible experiences of discrimination or racism. Instead, they opt for presenting the adoptee's difference from the start as attractive and valued by a group of friends. In these books, the adoptee's 'race' is either overlooked or highlighted as a mark of desired exoticism, and the adopted child happily accepts the fate that turned him or her into a national of a foreign country. Only two books of our sample—which are coincidently those dealing with preadolescent adopted characters—question even if very superficially the parents' account about the adoption is what may open a reflection about the complex politics of transnational adoption which is, nevertheless, successfully avoided in the stories. Moreover, if we look into the broader picture of the books about adoption that have been published to young readers in Spain, we only find two texts that depict problematic adoptions: *Piel Color Miel*, a graphic novel originally published in French by a Korean adoptee and Belgian author, Jung, and *El precio de la verdad* by German book author Carolin Phillips (Jung; Philipps). The first is an autobiographical account in which Jung tells about his failed integration into a Belgian family and the complexities of dealing with 'race' in a (supposedly) color-blind environment. *El precio de la verdad*, on the other hand, deals with the boom of Chinese adoptions and the implications of the one-child-only policy. It features a Chinese adoptee who searches for her origin and criticizes her parents' approach to her adoption; even if the publisher labels this book for children from nine years old, the experts of the S.O.L. have recommend it for readers over fifteen and, therefore, it does not appear as an example of children's literature on adoption as the ones studied throughout this book. Interestingly, the posts by adoptive parents in the blog La Adopteca—devoted to recommend stories about adoption—also reveal that fear that children may get access to these books at what is believed to be inappropriate ages: the first is praised by a reader who warns that *Piel Color Miel* is "absolutely recommendable, but not for children," while El precio de la verdad is reviewed with a warning in red letters: "even if the book is labeled as for children between 9 and 12 years old, it may be necessary to be read first by an adult, especially on those cases of children adopted in that country."[1]

Adopted children appear to be carefully protected from stories that would unsettle the narrative order created for them from infancy. This may be partly explained by the studies that show that adolescent adoptees are expected to have higher incidence of psychological mental disturbance (a fact that, nevertheless, needs to take into consideration that precisely because this is expected, adopted children are taken more frequently to the psychologist, cf. Brodzinsky 154–55). The S.O.L. recommends three books about adoption that would be safe reads for pre-adolescents younger than eleven years, the age category that usually is referred to as children's literature. Two of them share a story about an adopted girl who begins to question the parental story about her adoption and through the course of that questioning, 'race' emerges and intersects with gendered ideals of beauty. *Isha, nacida del corazón* [Isha, Born from the Heart] and *¿Por qué no tengo los ojos azules?* [Why Do I not Have Blue Eyes?] coincide in featuring young adopted girls who experience what we may call racial anxiety. These issues are very often related to developing feelings of self-hatred or inadequacy within the adoptive family and its larger social context due to their physical features.

Isha, nacida del corazón opens with a dialog that may recall a conversation 'transracial' adoptive parents fear:

> —Mamá, yo quiero ser blanca como tú.
> —Pero, Isha, ¿qué me dices?
> —Que quiero tener la piel como tú, quiero ser blanca.
> —¡Anda ya! Si ahora te descoloras, me muero.
> —No te rías, mamá; eso se puede hacer... Michael Jackson...
> —No digas tonterías, tesoro. ¡Pero si eres preciosa! Tienes bonita la piel y el alma.
>
> Isha vuelve a ser un pájaro azul perdido en el aire, y Sara intenta convencerla del privilegio que supone tener esa deliciosa piel canela propia de las gentes que nacen en los mágicos territorios hindúes.
> —¿No te das cuenta, corazón mío, de que en la playa todo el mundo se tumba al sol, sufriendo y sudando, para que se le oscurezca la piel? (9–10)

[Mom, I want to be white as you./But, Isha, what are you saying?/ That I want to have the skin like you, that I want to be white/Come on! If you lose your color, I'll die./Don't laugh, mom; it can be done... Michael Jackson.../Don't be silly, sweetheart. You are beautiful! You have a beautiful skin and soul./Isha is again a blue bird lost in the sky, and Sara tries to convince her of the privilege of having that delicious cinnamon skin typical of the people born in the magical hinduist territories./Don't you notice, my sweetheart, that at the beach everyone lies under the sun, suffering and sweating to get their skins darkened?]

The reader soon knows that Isha's desire to whiten her skin was triggered by a comment by a classmate who said that her mother could not be her real mother because she is Black. Isha comes home with an unbearable sense of unease which is not dispelled with her mother's well-intentioned compliments, but only later when the father intervenes to tell Isha, again, that origin story about how they wanted so much to have her that she was born in a country far away from them. As suggested in Chapter 3, adoption books appear to be more tailored to the needs of the adoptive parents than to those of the children, providing adopters with stories in which they find explanations, justifications, and possible scripts to refer to in their own domestic storytelling.

The quoted dialogue presents a possible script for adoptive parents in need of dealing with the rather uncomfortable matter of 'race.' In the mother's response, Isha is placed outside the Black/White binarism: the girl is not Black as her classmate has said but has "piel canela" [cinnamon skin] and is told that the others envy her color and that they actually suffer under the sun to try to achieve the same tone. Anthropological research conducted by Beatriz San Roman and Diana Marre in Barcelona shows how adoptive parents often resort to this script of other children being 'jealous' of their colors and that they do indeed use this idea of everyone going to the beach to be like them (San Román and Marre 10). This approach toward dark skin may only be possible in a society that does not include significant Black communities—or that they are only related to recent migration. In the United States, the National Association of Black Social Workers (NABSW) took a vehement stand against the placement of Black children in White homes where the parents would be unable to understand the 'racial' issues their children face (Howell and Melhuus 64).

Isha's parents fail to acknowledge racism in society. The girl is told that if she feels treated differently it is because she does not understand her unique privileged condition. The mother assures Isha that her color is a privilege of those born in the 'magical Hinduist territories.' Magic, as already sketched in Chapter 3, appears to be necessary for the successful "transubstantiation" (Howell 68–73) of the adopted child into an as-if-biological child and recodes 'race.' The mother may be aware that foreigners are not automatically discriminated but also likely to be admired and that this admiration takes usually the form of a fascination for a perceived exoticism. The adopted child, therefore, embodies Homi Bhabha's ambivalent colonial subject, who motivates feelings of repression and repulsion, sympathy, and attraction (cf. Bhabha 85–92). Without acknowledging the possible discrimination, Isha's mother highlights the girl's exoticism as her key to get through.

Isha, nacida del corazón may be symptomatic of the deep interrelation between class and 'race,' identifiers that are mediated through kinship. The adopted girl is recurrently reaffirmed with the message that her privileged origin—being adopted from that magic land—places her beyond the Black/White binarism. In the embedded origin story in the book, Isha is depicted as a sort of Indian princess while the illustrations show her in a Persian castle that recalls the Taj Mahal. The origin story recodes 'race' as cultural origin, making Isha a unique child not to be mistaken with other Indian children or with other children to be adopted. She has always been a chosen one; her place among the privileged is granted by origin.

¿Por qué no tengo los ojos azules?, originally published in French under the title *Pourquoi j'ai pas les yeux bleus?*, also places this idea of a white canon of beauty at the center of the argument. Maya, a dark-skinned adoptee from Colombia, cannot bear to hear more comments about how attractive her blonde and blue-eyed mother is and develops a deep self-hatred feeling: she not only wants to be White but also to have blue eyes. Among the books about immigrant children we find a character with a similar problem. In *No soy rubia ¿y qué?* [I'm not blonde. So what?], Amira, who came from Tunisia, wants to be blonde (and blue-eyed) like Hollywood actresses and like Amaia, an attractive classmate at school. Isha, Maya, and Amira are all dissatisfied with their physical appearances and wonder why they were not given the chance to have features that canons of beauty would praise: white skin, blonde hair, and blue eyes. The way each of these three stories is resolved is highly revealing of how the cultural discourse on 'race' and ethnicity intersects with categories of class that appear to structure the divide between migrants and adoptees.

Isha's racial anxiety is not resolved when her skin color is rephrased as 'cinnamon' and as a feature others envy but only after she hears again the retelling of her origin story. As the title announces, Isha is told that she has been gestated in her mother's heart instead of in her womb and that her belonging to that Spanish family had been orchestrated by magical forces. Instead of dealing with the racism in society and with socio-cultural constructions of beauty, this story displaces 'race,' focusing instead on an exploration of a fictionalized origin. By the telling of the 'right' story about this origin, the narrative of the orphaned and abandoned helpless child is overwritten. The American scholar Margaret Homans argues that adoption needs to be understood as a "fiction-generating machine," in which the past is constructed for the needs of the present (5). These books aim to cater to this need of inventing a past that would allow self-confidence in the adoptees of the present. Very interestingly, the parents of Maya, the Colombian adoptee in *¿Por qué no tengo los ojos azules?*, react in a similar way to Isha's parents; they approach the racial anxiety of the child by providing her with a story in which the apparent subordination of 'race' would be resisted.

Maya, adopted in Colombia as a baby, has been so ashamed of her eye color that she wears dark sunglasses at school to keep them hidden (which appears to imply that everyone at that school has blue or green eyes). The schoolteacher tells Maya's mother about it, and the mother approaches the girl for a talk:

> "Mamá hizo café para ellos y a mí me dio un vaso de leche caliente. Me dijo que era muy guapa tal y como era, con mi pelo rizado y oscuro y mis ojos negros. Y creo que lo piensa de verdad" (55)

[Mom made coffee for them and gave me a glass of warm milk. She told me that I was very pretty as I am, with my curly dark hair and my black eyes. It seems like she really believes it].

As in *Isha, nacida del corazón*, the mother's compliments regarding the girl's beauty are followed by an origin story that is assertively told by the father. Maya's father brings an Atlas to explain to her than in Colombia, the country where she was born, "casi todos están mezclados ('mestizos', dijo Papá). Papá dijo incluso que seguramente yo tenía sangre india y africana. Eso sí que me gustó porque mis compañeros se morirán de envidia." (55) [Almost all have mixed backgrounds ('mestizos', said Dad). Dad even said that most probably I had Indigenous and African blood. I really liked that: my classmates would die of envy]. Notably, here 'race' is disdained at the same time that it is naturalized. The father misses the opportunity to point out how human 'races' are social constructs that have been instrumental to the subordination of determined groups, how 'races' do not exist. Instead of explaining that intra-group differences are bigger than those between people of presumably different races, he reproduces the idea of distinguishable Indigenous and African blood. Maya's parents coincide with Isha's in putting forward the idea that the girls' physical features generate envy from their (very white) classmates. Both sets of parents, therefore, fail to acknowledge the possible microaggressions and everyday racism their daughters face and reproduce the hegemonic whiteness while positioning their adopted daughters as different/other to what would be a homogenous group of nationals.

The three books mentioned—*Isha, nacida del corazón*, *¿Por qué no tengo los ojos azules?*, and *No soy rubia. ¿Y qué?* aim to convey the idea that we live in a post-racial world in which 'race' is in fact a sign of ethnicity of which should be proud. The three protagonists—Isha, Maya, and Amira—pose the question of how should they deal with the fact that they have darker skin colors than the ones they wish they had. The question is not answered directly, but through stories; in the case of the two books with adopted characters, it is addressed in the embedded stories told by the fathers who provide them with a sort of 'narrative explanation' of their differences. By narrative explanation, I relate to the idea that stories are more persuasive than logical-scientific thinking and that by narrating and listening to stories we make relationships between causes and effects and use these to structure the world (cf. Bruner *The Culture of Education* 39). In these books, we may trace a narrative explanation to the question of why Isha and Maya have darker skin colors than their classmates and why they should not envy their classmates who would fit better into an apparently predominant canon of beauty. Contrastingly, no origin story is offered for the migrant character, Amira, with which she can come to terms with her desired blondeness.

We now return to look at some other details of the cultural work performed for the Colombia adoptee, Maya. After the father brings the Atlas and tells her about her mixed Latin-American origin, Maya is more comforted and believes that her classmates would envy her, but the narration does not conclude there. Going back to Nöel Carroll's ideas, we could argue that the story up to that point has not achieved that desired 'narrative closure,' that "phenomenological feeling of finality that is generated when all the questions saliently posed by the narrative are answered" (1). The final happy ending comes, therefore, only some days later, on Maya's tenth birthday, when the girl receives a very special present from her blonde and blue-eyed mother. The mother works as a goldsmith and has made two earrings with the form of blue eyes, reproducing, as she explains, a design from ancient Egyptian jewelry. The woman says that in Egypt, where women were dark-skinned as Maya, it was fashionable to wear earrings with the shape and color of blue-eyes. Maya is thrilled.

> "Me he tocado la oreja para comprobar que mis ojitos azules están en su sitio. Mamá ha tenido una idea genial.
>
> Es que no es fácil tener una madre con los ojos azules. Pero esta noche tengo ya diez años y unos pendientes más bonitos todavía que los suyos. Dentro de poco me pareceré a ella, seré tan guapa como ella y sabré hacer montones de cosas, como ella.
>
> Al final... ¡es estupendo tener una madre así! ¿no es verdad?" (75)

> [I've touched one of my ears to make sure my little blue eyes are in place. Mom has had a terrific idea. It's not easy to have a mother with blue eyes. But tonight I'm ten years old, and I have earrings that are even nicer than hers. Soon I will look like her, I'll be as pretty as she is and I'll know how to do lots of things, like she does. In the end, it's great to have a mother like her! Right?]

The happy ending, therefore, does not counter the original premise of the White beauty as the desired and rather only form of being attractive but also frames this canon as if it was historically funded, that is, to be found through history and, moreover, in different cultures. The tale of the Egyptian 'blue-eyes' appears to reproduce the idea that a rather fixed hierarchy of 'races' can only be modified through assertive cultural work and class belonging. In the end, Maya concludes, what matters is that her mother has those physical features that can be transferred to her by her privileged place in society.

In *Isha, nacida del corazón*, the racial anxiety of the adopted child is also positioned as deriving from that comparison between the daughter and the mother. This dismisses that racial subjectivation the characters (may) experience in their quotidian lives and recodes it as anxiety more related with the artificial bond of the adoptive family. Anthropological research conducted in Spain and Norway has shown how adoptive mothers anxiously state that their children look like them regardless of their different (and racially marked) features (Howell and Marre 301). Interestingly, Maya's happy ending suggests that having a blonde and blue-eyed mother makes the girl—at least artificially—White. The earrings—manufactured by this blonde woman—symbolize those efforts by the adoptive parents on delivering the most assertive story, the most assertive cultural work to boost the self-confidence of the adopted child. The reader can note that they also have the economic and social means to do it. The belonging to a certain social group that has access to privileges is not explicitly acknowledged in these narrations. Yet, as it is predominant in the portrayal of families in realistic modern fiction for children published in Spain, the families depicted could easily be assumed to be middle- or upper-class families. Parents appear to have qualified jobs that allow them to go on rather expensive trips and are able to take their children out for dinner, for example.

The life standard of Amira's family, the Tunisian family that immigrated to Spain, is different. They do go on a family outing—to the cinema—but the narrator tells us how special this event is: it is the very first time that

(Picture by Mikel Valverde)

Figure 6.1 Amira is now integrated: she leads the action and the local children follow her. Illustration by Mikel Valverde.

they all go to watch a movie together. Perhaps coincidently, the racial anxiety of Amira is not solved as Maya's and Isha's. The last lines of the book sketch the limits of a happy ending for the immigrant girl:

> "Yo quiero ser rubia, es verdad. Pero miro a la calle y me doy cuenta de que en Vitoria hay muy poca gente rubia. La mayoría tiene el pelo castaño y la piel más bien morena, como yo. Quiero ser rubia, pero ya tendré tiempo de teñirme el pelo. Cuando crezca, tal vez" (30)

> [I want to be blonde, that's true. But I look to the street and realize that in Vitoria there are few blonde people. Most of them have brown hair and the skin is rather dark, as mine. I want to be blonde, but I will have time to dye my hair. When I grow up, maybe].

This is one of the very few stories that acknowledge how the local society is already diverse and not as White as it is symbolically constructed. Amira tells us that 'tal vez' [maybe] she will later decide whether to pursue her blonde dream by dying her hair with an artificial product. We may read the illustration (Picture 10) on the last page as suggesting that she will not. If we analyze its visual grammar following Gunter Kress and Theo van Leeuwen's categories, we may notice how Amira is the "Actor" (Kress and Van Leeuwen 63–67) leading the agency by jumping with her arms opened, as if a bird, followed by her playmates. Even Amaia, the (blonde) girl who proffered some offensive comment when the Tunisian child first came to school, follows her. The picture, therefore, plays a role in confirming Amira's successful integration as if witnessed by an external, impartial viewer. This image tells us that Amira is accepted as she is and may even predict that the girl will come to terms with her own insecurities, flying away from that blonde ideal.

Monolithic Authenticity

As explained in Chapter 4, Amira became popular in school after writing the names of her classmates in Arabic, that is, after presenting her original culture and language in an attractive way to the group. Dying her hair would be an opposed strategy, opting for an inauthentic, artificial assimilation. Amira's story reproduces that narrative of the exotic immigrant in which a desired authenticity is performed. Anthony K. Appiah claims that the efforts to preserve the cultural identities of minorities go against the right to individual identities—that is, that the claim for authenticity limits and constricts the movements of those who are requested to perform "too tightly scripted" identities (Appiah "Identity, Authenticity, Survival: Multicultural Societies and Social Reproduction" 165). In the same line, Vincent J. Cheng highlights how contemporary society is taken by an "anxiety over authentic cultural identity" that paradoxically ends up constructing artificially what is meant to be authentic (Cheng 1–8).

Identities seem to be more flexible for adoptees, even if they are still asked to fulfill expectations of a rather stereotypical authenticity. A book that illustrates clearly this difference is *Todos los colores del arco iris*. Aimed at readers between six and eight years old, it starts with the celebratory premise that the classmates of the narrator-protagonist form a 'rainbow of colors.' The characters are an Ecuadorian girl, a Moroccan boy, and four internationally adopted children: two siblings from Ethiopia, a girl from China, and another girl from Russia. The narrator explains that the Ecuadorian and the Moroccan boy not only share a skin tone but also the fact of having foreign parents. As in other examples, the narrator presents these children as if newcomers without making any reference to how the places where they were born and socialized may have a say in their identity formation. Locals, on the contrary, are presented as (very) White despite the centuries of emigration and immigration that have shaped a rather heterogeneous composition of the Spanish people.

This highlighted whiteness, as well as the rather sharp divide between adopted and immigrant characters, is clearly exposed in the passage in which the Ecuadorian character is introduced:

> "Y también está Celina 'piel roja'. Así la llamaban algunos niños que querían molestarla solo porque ella tiene la piel del color del cobre. Pero Celina es muy atrevida y nunca se calla. De color rojo se les ponía a ellos la cara en cuanto se le soltaba la lengua: 'rostro pálido' era el primero de una cascada de insultos que tengo prohibido reproducir aquí. Así que 'piel roja' se le quedó de mote, pero ella dice que no le importa, que a ella eso no le duele como nos pasa a nosotros cuando nos ha dado el sol y parecemos auténticos 'piel roja'" (seventh double spread).

> [We also have 'redskin' Celina. Some kids who wanted to bother her called her that, just because her skin has the color of copper. But Celina is very cheeky and never holds back. Their faces turned red too when her tongue ran away with her: 'pale face' was the first of a lot of insults, which I am not allowed to repeat here. The 'redskin' nickname stayed, but now she says she doesn't care; she says it doesn't hurt her like it hurts us when we stay too long in the sun and we turn into real 'redskins'].

It is implied that Spanish people have such a white skin that they get totally red and burned when exposed to the sun. The characters with foreign backgrounds are to be opposed to this (racially) homogeneous group of 'us.' More importantly, contesting (White) racism—as 'cheeky' Celina did—does not help. The Ecuadorian girl has failed in taking advantage of her difference by self-fashioning herself as an exotic girl, and this resistance wins her the nickname of redskin. Completely unaware of how this perpetuates the racist attack, the narrator introduces her with that nickname. This narrator is aware that there are correct and incorrect ways of calling things and people, but that seems to apply only to Celina's insults, which he does not feel allowed to reproduce in the text.

We may wonder if an adopted character would have been equally harassed. Interestingly, in the very first page of this book, the narrator introduces his adopted sister with an effort to resist racial essentialisms:

> "Dicen que es amarilla porque nació en China... Tiene los ojos rasgados y el pelo liso y muy negro, pero yo lo que se dice la piel, cuando la miro, la veo completamente blanca, sin mucha diferencia con mi propia piel" (second double spread).

> [They say she is yellow because she was born in China...She has slanted eyes and very straight and black hair, but when it comes to her skin, when I look at it, it looks completely white, not much different from my own skin]

In this brief introduction, the trope of the Asian yellow skin is contested while the narrator problematizes his own whiteness as a cultural construct. Pages later, though, when referring to the immigrant girl, this narrator is so White that he is among those who would get totally burned if exposed to the sun.

Nevertheless, the ending attempts to depict a society that welcomes diversity:

> "Aunque por fuera somos todos distintos, por dentro somos todos iguales. Y yo lo creo, aunque es muy divertido vernos a todos juntos cuando salimos de clase y nos unimos para formar todos los colores del arco iris" (fifteenth double spread)

> [Although we are all different on the outside, on the inside we are all the same. And I believe this, even if it is really funny when we get out of school and we get together forming all the colors of the rainbow].

This paragraph contradicts again that first statement of how the Chinese sister does not look different from the narrator, a contradiction that appears to be at the core of this celebration of difference anchored in a superficial utopian multiculturalism. As pointed out in Chapter 5, the trope of the rainbow of diversity is informed by a very superficial and naïve approach to 'race,' if only because the colors of a rainbow do not resemble at all the different shades of human skin.

Gendered Destinies

Celina's depiction is gendered. In these books, paths for integration are different for male and female characters. In *No soy Rubia*, for instance, we get to know that Amira's brother, Najib, is "un fenómeno en el fútbol y tiene un montón de amigos. Regatea a todos y mete más goles que nadie" [a football genius and has lots of friends. He swerves past all and scores more than anyone]. Sports are not only a ticket to becoming popular and feeling integrated, but also to naturalization. Foreign football players in Europe go through fast-track processes and are often taken as examples of how the nation welcomes difference—a matter that has been researched in different European countries (cf. DuBois; Tomlinson and Young; Carrington and Mcdonald). Would Amira's brother be as well integrated if he had different talents? Stuart Hall's ideas on the "racialized regime of representation" (249) suggest that he will not. Hall stresses how Black people are often presented with attention to physical rather than mental attributes and frequently portrayed as excellent athletes (Hall *Representation: Cultural Representations and Signifying Practices* 249). Western society appears to be prepared to admire Black athletes but not Black philosophers, to give an example. The stereotype of Black physical power illuminates how we find different 'integration-plots' for female and male characters. This racialized regime of representation is gendered and focuses on the female characters and the problematic interplay of 'race' and beauty.

Forty-six of the sixty books in our sample of recommended books feature girls as protagonists. In *Gender and Nation*, Nira Yuval-Davis reformulates that binary of women/nature versus men/culture by claiming that women are "symbolic border guards" of the nation bearing the responsibility for the reproduction of the culture and of carrying the "tradition" to next generations (61). The predominance of female protagonists may reflect this emphasis in the role of women in reproducing the nation. In some cases, as in *El diario de La* or in *Susana Ojos Negros*, a local girl 'mothers' the foreign Other, facilitating his difficult adaptation. Other stories are focused on the experiences of an immigrant girl to whom discourses about how to behave properly are projected. Celina's 'misbehavior,' for example, explains the verbal violence of her classmates. Celina is, nevertheless, an exception to the portrayal of immigrant girls who are in most cases smart, attractive, and submissive: their very appropriate behavior usually grants them recognition within the group.

In this group we find a number of books in which a girl is troubled with her physical appearance but learns to appreciate her features—a transformation that implies accepting and embodying the desired exoticism. Along with Amira, Isha, and Maya, we have the case of Khoedi, who immigrates with her family from Senegal to Vigo. The story of Khoedi describes her own preparations to deal with discrimination and racism, and it is recommended by the S.O.L. as a story "de integración y de esperanzas" [of integration and hope]. The narration alternates an internal focalization 'into' the girl—a first-person narrator—with an external focalization 'on' her—a third-person narrator who has access to her feelings and thoughts, which is commonly called 'free indirect speech' (cf. Bal *Narratology: Introduction to the Theory of Narrative* 97–103). The story is told alternating the two voices, quite an effective device, as changes of narrator are uncommon in children's literature and, in this case, appear to be unnecessary, since both narrators seem to have the same access to Khoedi's feelings and thoughts; both narrators also have the same information about the events and appear to share points of view about the storyworld. Both of them, for instance, assure that the girl is not ashamed of her racial physical features but proud of them and describe her color as the Black of Senegalese people, the most beautiful of all ("el más hermoso de todos" 87). Both narrators recount too how Khoedi was initially frightened by the accounts of fellow Senegalese girls in Spain who had suffered bullying by their local classmates.

Khoedi arrives in Spain some months before the beginning of the school year, which gives her some time to adapt and to strengthen her self-esteem before confronting an environment that she expects to be hostile. Why use two different narrators to narrate this? It may not have been orchestrated as such by the author, but this duality of voices appears to give more credibility to Khoedi's first-person account. It is believed that an immigrant narrator would present an alien perspective to the reader (Nikolajeva "Exit Children's Literature?" 20), and, as I have reviewed before, these books are recommended, in the first place, to Spanish readers (that is, those born to Spanish parents). The dual point of view facilitates the identification of the reader with the Senegalese immigrant establishing and reinforcing some facts from an external point of view. The first and most important fact is that Khoedi, we are recurrently told, is beautiful because of her skin color. This is assured by the external narrator and later rephrased in Khoedi's first-person narration: we are to take this as a true fact and not as the girl's perception of herself. 'Racially marked' women are, in positive representations, beautiful because of their exotic, exuberant features. In its effort to dismantle stereotypes, the narrator needs to first establish Khoedi's beauty in order to then sketch a character who is confident, smart, and assertive.

The duality of narrative voices in *Luna de Senegal* facilitates addressing racism with distance. We have, for instance, the passage in which Beidu, a fellow Senegalese girl, tells Khoedi how she has been harassed at school. Beidu's classmates have called her 'mona chita' (the Spanish name for Cheetah, Tarzan's chimpanzee), and 'Conguito' (literally, a diminutive for the Congo, but also the name of some sweets with the figure of a tribal African boy, which, despite protests by anti-racism activists, are still sold in Spanish shops). They even told to go back "con los monos a África y cosas peores" [with the monkeys to Africa and even worse things] (93). Beidu does not give any hint of what those "cosas peores" [worse things] were and looks down to the floor after saying this. This is recounted by the third-person narrator who has superficial access to Khoedi's feelings while listening to Beidu. In this way, the harshest racism is mediated, and the reader is, presumably, protected. Moreover, a first-person narration of this passage is more unlikely, as the narrator then would have had to enunciate further what those 'even worse things' were. This external narrator works, therefore, as a bridge between the harsh (and apparently untellable) experiences of immigrant children and the reader. It might also be that the story of hope that this book intends to portray needed an external narrator as a witness to confirm that the successful adaptation is possible and not only that it depends on the perception and feelings of the foreigner. The external narrator's role is, therefore, to assure us that even if a girl faces a rather constant discrimination, she may not grow in resentment, or develop an internalized racism, but may skillfully use her origin culture to self-fashion herself to the locals and gain a place within a group.

The focalization in *Luna de Senegal* may be described as a superficial internal focalization, as the narrator has access to Khoedi's feelings and points of view but still refrains from delving into them. The girl, for instance, does not reflect on the discrimination she suffers. This dual access, therefore, appears to be only productive in minding the gap between that perceived distance between the implied reader of the book (a local child) and the immigrant child who tells her story but does not delve further into the feelings and fears of the migrant girl.

How Kin Whitens

In *Luna de Senegal*, Khoedi manages to overcome the initial hostility of her classmates, amusing the class with a tale from the Senegalese oral tradition, which she used to hear from her grandmother. *Mi abuela es africana*—originally published in German as *Meine Oma lebt in Afrika*—provides an opposite integration narrative for a child who is also physically different from his fellow classmates; yet, he is not depicted as an immigrant but as a local child with a migration background. This book gives an excellent example with which we may understand how racial identitarian construction depends on its interaction with other axes of diversity.

Mi abuela es africana is one of few books that deal with the perceived ethnic-racial difference of children born to transnational ("mixed") couples. Eric—born to a German mother and a Ghanaian father—is in the first chapter verbally attacked by Mr. Frank, the neighbor of his friend Flo. Interestingly, as soon as Mr. Frank finds out that the Black child is Flo's friend, he excuses himself. The episode occurs when the two friends play in the neighbor's cornfield imagining that they are in the jungle, singing, and hitting some barrels as if they were drums. When the farmer comes, he only sees Eric to whom he shouts: "¡Esto es increíble! ¿Es que estamos en el medio de África?" [¡This is incredible! Are we in the middle of Africa?]. And adds: "Cuántos negros más andan correteando por mi maizal? ¿no podíais quedaros en vuestra tierra, en vuestra selva, y dejarnos a nosotros en paz?" (19) [How many more ne-gros are running around my cornfield? Couldn't you stay in your land, in your jungle, and leave us in peace?]. The man threatens to call the police, but just after that he notices that the Black boy is playing with his young German neighbor, Flo. Mr. Frank instantly calms down and after saying "¡no me rompáis ninguna planta!" [don't ruin any of my plants!] (20), walks away. In this short passage, Eric is mistaken for a threatening—or at least disturbing—foreigner to be then safely passed to the category of 'welcomed' citizen because of his friendship with the German boy. The words of the farmer keep resounding in Eric's head:

> ¿Por qué tenía que volver a la selva y dejarle en paz? ¿Qué había querido decir con eso? Por supuesto que desaba ir a África, pero no por lo que dijese aquel hombre, sino porque quería ir a visitar a mi abuela. Después regresaría a Alemania, el país donde nací." (20)

> [Why should I go back to the jungle and leave him in peace? What was he trying to say with that? Of course I wanted to go to Africa, but not for what that man said, but because I wanted to go visit my grandmother. Afterwards I would come back to Germany, the coun-try where I was born]

As in other books, racism here is not confronted and not even iden-tified as such. The characters remain passive and unaware. Instead of reflecting on why a person apparently of African descent should be sent home, Eric sets his own 'route' (born in Germany) to explain why for him Africa is a continent only attractive for a short visit. Eric has been mistaken for an immigrant, but he is not one. Notably, his friend Flo does not comment on the event. This episode, at the very beginning of the story, serves to introduce these two main characters who later travel to Africa together with Eric's Ghanaian father. An underlying narrative insists in how African ways of doing things are very different and how the Black boy is as German as his friend when compared to them. Both Eric and Flo will be surprised by life in a Ghanaian village: the kitchen without appliances, the houses without electric light, the time it takes to prepare a meal, the funny traditions, the mosquitos. Eric may be dark-skinned, but culturally he is (fully) German.

Meine Oma lebt in Africa attempts to show how there is no direct relationship between physical appearance and cultural belonging. Sig-nificantly, the German author writes upon a similar experience with her grandson born to an African father. The book may be taken as an or-igin narrative for this child and for the children born in Europe from 'transracial' couples. The textual strategy resembles that of the adop-tion books in the way this connection between 'race' and ethnicity is problematized and decoupled. This critical approach to the relationship between physical attributes and cultural belongings, this decoupling of 'race' and ethnicity is rare among books about migration. We may here note just one example, *Cuál es mi color*, originally published in French by Antoine Guilloppé, which recounts the problematic affiliation and subjetivization of a child considered to be Arab by the Spaniards and Spanish by the Arabs. In Meine Oma lebt in Afrika, the figure of the author, inspired by her grandson's story, recalls how adoptive parents became children's book writers to provide their adopted children with stories that would position them outside structures of racial subordination. These stories may be considered artifacts that make visible how kin (and class) whitens. We may relate the circulation of these stories to the pair of blue eyes that Maya receives from her blond mother. Kin (and class) need cultural artifacts to 'repair' the stratifications of race.

The racial anxiety of the adoptee is most often presented as deriving from the lack of resemblance to the parents. This effectively sidelines the impact that social racism may have for the adoptee's identity construction. 'Race' and racism are, as I have described in the previous chapter, circumvented in these stories, and the racial features of the adopted characters appear to be addressed as indicating the singular form that

Figure 6.2 Physical similarity between the (adoptive) mother and the child is suggested with the use of the (Chinese) silk robe and the slanted eyes of both. Illustration by Jane Dyer.

Figure 6.3 When they finally meet, the adoptive parents embrace the child, and they all look alike with slanted eyes. Illustration by Emilio Amade.

this non-normative family takes rather as a social issue to deal with. In the picturebooks with adopted characters, we may trace ambivalences in the way 'race' is gapped. In some cases, it is 'bridged' by making the adoptee and the parents look alike in the illustrations, and, in some others, it goes on in an apparently opposite direction, highlighting it as the visible mark of that unique story that founds the bond of the adoptive family.

I Love You Like Crazy Cakes (*Te quiero, niña bonita*) shows how 'race' is bridged. Even if differences between mother and baby are acknowledged—red-haired adopter versus dark-haired adoptee—similarity is nevertheless suggested with the use of a (Chinese) silk robe by the mother and her somehow slanted eyes combined with a lack of recognizable Asian features in the baby (Picture 11). Something similar happens when the parents in *En algún lugar de China* finally meet the baby: the three of them look alike with slanted eyes embracing each other (Picture 12). Anthropologist Heather Jacobson's research on adoption culture in the United States shows that families adopting in China often define themselves as Chinese-American families (Jacobson 6) and this effort to become the Other can be also traced in picturebooks about transnational adoption published on both sides of the Atlantic.

Research conducted in Spain by Beatriz San Román and Diana Marre shows that 'race' is most often silenced and phrased as ethnicity; stakeholders speak of the 'ethnic features' and the 'cultural origin' of adopted babies even if they came to Spain as infants, that is, before being socialized in the country where they were born (Marre; San Román and Marre). In this discourse, the transnational adoption of a child would lead to a cultural transformation of the adopters, who would become strongly attached to the chosen origin land. This 'ethnic origin' emerges as a euphemism to call out the complexities of transracial adoption, an emphasis that appears to be common to adoptions from Asia, Latin

America, and Africa. In Spain, these are called 'transracial adoptions' in contrast to families adopting in Eastern Europe and Russia, which are uncritically labeled as 'same race' adoptions by adoption professionals (Reinoso et al.). The ethnic origin euphemism is all but non-existent in stories about this category.

It goes beyond the scope of this study to identify and analyze the differences and nuances of the race narratives offered to adoptees from different origins, but we may do some schematic commentaries. In the books here considered, the idea of 'race' does not appear to be very relevant in the depiction of (Central) Asian and European (mainly Russian and Ukrainian) adoptions as for adoptions from Africa, South America, or South Asia. In the latter, the differences are acknowledged in either the visual depiction or in the textual account. When portraying children coming from the Global South, the racial features are contrasted to those of the adoptive parents and siblings, who are always very white and, in most cases, blonde and blue- or green-eyed, at least in the visual depictions. The representation of the Other disguises a self-representation, and, in this case, it works in both directions: the highlighted blondness and whiteness of the adopters marks racial difference without insisting in the blackness of the offspring. This self-representation may also be understood as deriving from Spaniards' identitarian construction as Europeans stressing a whiteness that would position them closer to Northern Europe than haunting images of Northern Africa. It also responds to a larger cultural tradition of representation in which White is the unmarked, universal color. As Richard Dyer argues "whites are not of a certain race, they're just the human race" (Dyer 3). Finally, this highlighted whiteness of Spanish adopters may be related to ideas on transnational adoption as a humanitarian practice: as a country with high rates of adoptions from the Global South, Spain moves higher up in that world system that places Western/Northern Europe up in a position of responsibility over the Southern hemisphere.

Sara K. Dorow argues that (Central) Asian adoption into the United States must be understood in relation to a 'race' imaginary in which Asian-Americans occupy a 'liminal space' outside of the binary opposition of White and Black (Dorow "Racialized Choices: Chinese Adoption and the `White Noise' of Blackness" 358). In the United States, Asian-Americans are considered a model minority, and this image is transferred to a preference for Asian adoptees. China holds a special position within Asian adoptions too, as its current geopolitical power enables new ways of negotiating 'race.' In these books, we may trace how the Western humanitarian narrative—what some researchers have analyzed as a rescue discourse in transnational adoptions (cf Dorow *Transnational Adoption: A Cultural Economy of Race, Gender, and Kinship* 50; Ortiz and Briggs 41)—is more clearly related to the adoption of dark-skinned adoptees from South Asia and Africa.

These books may be regarded as attempts to offer what we could label as 'preventive racial identities.' The stories suggest that these cute
adopted children could be discriminated in the future; without acknowledging racism, they aim to train adoptees to replace inquiries about their
racial features with questions about where they came from. Adoptive
families insist in the 'cultural heritage' of their children as a way of in-
verting the hierarchies of 'race' by conveying a proud affiliation. The
front covers of the collection *Llegué de...* illustrate this point soundly
(Picture 13). In them, each of the adoptees is dressed with a folkloric
costume suggesting that these children have assimilated cultural traits
of the regions where they come from.

This book series may be related to a number of other examples of
collections in which each book presents a character coming from a
different region dressed up with some exotic outfit. Adopted children
are, as children from migrant backgrounds, also subjected as ethnotypes. In Spain the idea of the 'race' of the adoptee appears to be such
a taboo that official documents about international adoption speak of
the importance of acknowledging the ethnic origin of adoptees (San
Román and Marre 124). In the spirit of a liberal, celebratory multiculturalism, difference is erased and at the same time superficially
marked. The basket with fruits on top of the head of the Colombian
adoptee is meant to denote a tropical, tasteful, and close-to-nature
provenance that would probably not be implied if his skin would have
had a lighter color.

Anthropologist Claudia Castañeda categorizes different processes
of 're-racialization' in contemporary adoption: those of total "assimilation"—the adoptee who identifies him/herself with the race of the
adoptive parents, explicitly claiming this affiliation: 'I look Asian but
I'm white'—to "immersion"—when the adoptees claim that their birth
countries are 'home' (Castañeda 2–3). Contemporary adoption narratives would be closer to the second alternative as adopters are becoming
increasingly aware that 'race' cannot be written off. Yet, these books do
attempt to write it off while acknowledging a difference. Children's literature on the subject of transnational adoption may be assisting a process

Figure 6.4 The front covers of the collection *Llegué de...* present international adoptees
as if exotic ambassadors of ethnic groups. Illustrations by Luci Gutiérrez.

in which both cultural scripts—'assimilation' and 'immersion'—are combined disregarding the contradictions. In these books, the adopted children overcome the perceived differences and have the privilege of a dual belonging: they preserve a connection with their origins while being citizens of the destination country.

Adoption scholar and Korean adoptee in Sweden Tobias Hübinnette claims that the 'subjectivization' of Asian adoptees as White has alienated them from their bodies ("Disembedded and Free-Floating Bodies Out-of-Place and Out-of-Control: Examining the Borderline Existence of Adopted Koreans"). Hübinnette uses Homi Bhabha's concept of hybridity and third space to claim that transnational adoptees provide the perfect example of a third-space identity because in them all the classical categories associated with ethnicities and diasporas, "like kinship and territory, culture, religion, and language, and memory and myth" (155) are estranged. We may consider that the children's books reviewed here—meant to help a new generation of transnational adoptees, which would be brought up without repeating the mistake of neglecting race—are attempts to bring together those estranged categories and, therefore, to achieve the liberating promise of hybrid, non-essentialist identities. Yet, and despite the alleged awareness of these new adoptive families, these new narratives about transnational adoption and belonging appear to fail to acknowledge racism and microaggressions that appear naturalized in these stories.

Tobias Hübinette argues that "the dilemma of the Korean adoptee also sends out signals to other non-Western immigrants in Western countries who struggle deeply and painfully to fit in, 'assimilate,' and 'integrate': this struggle is meaningless, as they will never be fully acknowledged as Westerners" (Hübinette "Disembedded and Free-Floating Bodies Out-of-Place and Out-of-Control: Examining the Borderline Existence of Adopted Koreans" 144). This claim is based on his own experience as well as on his research with Korean adoptees in Northern Europe. As explained in Chapter 3, the cultural construction of Korean adoption differs from that of a later wave of contemporary adoptions in that today adoptees are not forced to develop a White subjectivity—or, at least, not in the same way in which previous generations of international adopted children were (T.A. Volkman 5). Moreover, Korean adoption differs from contemporary transnational adoption in that it was mainly constructed as a humanitarian enterprise, an idea that from the mid-1990s onward has been put in suspense (Selman "Intercountry Adoption in the New Millennium; the 'Quiet Migration' Revisited" 223). Arguing in Spain that the motive to adopt is saving or helping out third-world children is reason enough in failing to obtain the determination of suitability to adopt in Spain (Casalilla Galán et al. 137–39). Nevertheless, as these stories show, the humanitarian discourse still informs circulating cultural narratives.

Embodiments of Western Humanitarism

Mi hermana Aixa illustrates the Western well-intentioned yet patronizing humanitarian aim quite transparently. This book tells the story of an African girl who lost a leg stepping into a landmine and was adopted by a Spanish family. In it multiple markers of diversity coincide, most visibly, those of being racially marked and disabled. As may be clear by now, we do not find many examples in which different (explicit) discourses of diversity coincide: in the books studied here, we do not find, for example, characters deviating from heteronormativity, nor do we see examples of gender non-conformity. Likewise, marks of religious affiliation are rare. *Mi hermana Aixa* has been mentioned by the British newspaper *The Guardian* in a blog post about children's books about disability that could—or rather should—be translated into English: "A whole manner of diversities are included in this book - narrated by a young boy about his adopted, disabled sister from Africa: perfect for the #WeNeedDiverseBooks campaign!" The We Need Diverse Books campaign was initiated in the United States after a Twitter exchange in which Ellen Oh and Malinda Lo, two American authors, expressed their frustration with the lack of diversity in children's and young adult literature. They were then writing in response to an all-white and all-male panel of authors assembled for the BookCon reader event. Several other authors, bloggers, publishers, and mediators praised using the hashtag #WeNeedDiverseBooks and soon this crystalized in an initiative that promotes books about diversity through awards, events, lists of resources, and a blog. This campaign has helped to raise awareness of the very limited representation of minorities in children's literature, while it has also pointed out the need to understand how different discourses of diversity may converge. Drawing upon intersectional theory, Malinda Lo speaks of characters having "intersectional identities" when they could be described as facing oppression in more than one front such as LGBT characters who also belong to an ethnic minority (Lo "2014 LGBT YA by the Numbers").

In our sample we find few books in which the convergence of markers of diversity is highlighted. *Mi hermana Aixa* is one of them and this makes this book a very interesting object to analyze the recognition of differences. Fiona Kumari Campbell calls attention to the similitudes of discourses on 'race' and disability claiming that 'internalized racism' (self-hatred) resembles 'internalized ableism' (Campbell 151–52). Ableism refers to the set of practices and beliefs that assign inferior value (worth) to people who have developmental, emotional, physical, and/or psychiatric disabilities, while 'internalized ableism' refers to how disabled people may uncritically share these beliefs.

In *Mi hermana Aixa* discourses about 'race,' national origin, family, and disability overlap. Coming from a war-torn country, Aixa gets the

love and care she could not have in her origin country, and, symbolically enough, she also receives a prosthesis that will enable her to walk
without crutches. Significantly, this story is not focalized on the girl, but
narrated by her White, blonde-haired brother, Arnau, who happens to
be a biological son of their parents. Throughout the entire book, we do
not get to listen to Aixa's voice but are driven to believe that she is very
grateful to the Spanish family that has adopted (and saved her). The narration is imbued by those symbolic binarisms between the West and the
rest of the world: nature (Africa) is opposed to science (Europe), body
to intellect, underdevelopment, and war to civilization and humanitarism. Moreover, and perhaps because of the liminal place of Spain in the
symbolic Western world, Aixa's new leg is not requested from a Spanish
but from an English doctor, who travels to assist the girl in this. Aixa's
brother tells us that the African girl calls him: "Hombre-de-algodón
porque tiene la piel y el pelo completamente blancos. Con la bata blanca,
Aixa dijo que parecía una bombilla encendida" [the Cotton Man, because he has both completely white skin and hair. Aixa said that he
looked like a lightened bulb in his white coat] (32). Aixa gets the ultimate advanced medicine to repair her traumatic past. Her image of him
as a 'lightened bulb' may be related to the iconography of being illuminated by knowledge: he will do something as crucial to Aixa's body
as electricity for development. Aixa, on the other end, is Black, a girl,
a child, disabled, and adopted. I draw these oppositions to reveal how
they all intersect and stress the girl's subordinated position. Moreover,
the story told is rendered by her brother who is a biological child of her
parents. At the end of the book, Arnau tells that a TV team will come
home to make a story about Aixa. He is very excited about this and tells
the readers that his adopted sister has asked the people from the TV to
interview him. As you may already infer, this story appears to be more
about a boy that has a Black adopted sister than about this girl.

In *Mi hermana Aixa*, we only get to listen to the boy's telling about
his sister's experience. We are also told that the girl is pleased with this
situation, as she has asked the journalists to interview his brother to
know about her story. This focalization is praised in the recommending
review, which states: "the anecdotes and the humor notes by Arnau give
the reader complicity and invite a reflection." The idea of complicity here
implies—as in the references to 'our country' highlighted in Chapter 4
when reviewing stories about migrants—that the reader may only access
Aixa's intimacy by first relating to characters that belong to their White
and able-bodied Spanish world. The idea of an imagined reader who
cannot connect to the experience of being different appears to be trans-
versal to the practice of reviewing. Malinda Lo, one of the instigators
of the WeNeedDiverseBooks campaign and blogger of the Diversity in
YA (Young Adult Literature), analyzes how in the book reviews, the
recommendations are catered to White readers who would need to make

an effort to decode other cultural markers and experience in one or another way diversity. Lo identifies biases and points out how novels with characters marked by difference—as LGBTQ characters—are often catalogued as "problem novels" (Lo "Perceptions of Diversity in Book Reviews").

Mi hermana Aixa was one of the first books about international adoption published in Spain, in 1999. By then, adopting children transnationally was still a very new phenomenon regarded as a humanitarian practice, which may explain that a rescue discourse is in this book much more transparent than in subsequent examples. The passivity of the adoptee depends in this story from her position among other power binarisms: male/female, chosen/abandoned, developed/underdeveloped, biological/adopted, and White/'ethnic,' among others. Aixa's story also raises the question of whether 'race' is, altogether with 'abandonment,' a lack to be repaired by the adoptive family. It may be the case that the humanitarian plot that shaped intercountry adoption in previous decades takes today the form of a celebratory utopian 'post racial' encounter in which 'race' is phrased as ethnicity and becomes a symbol of Western progressiveness. Color is recoded as 'rainbow colors' and stripped from any historical subordination, cultural heritages, or familial and intra-ethnic bonds. Therefore, these stories appear engaged not only in bridging the 'race' gap, but also in 'repairing' race as if it was a deficit to be overcome.

I review two cases in which this reparation of 'race' is explicitly embodied: in Aixa's leg and in Maya's 'blue eyes.' Yet, it may be the case that this reparation is to be traced in the aims behind these books: to provide adoptees with origin stories that would counter that predominant Western narrative that (nuclear) families are those formed by blood that sticks together. These adoption stories would narrate and, moreover, perform a new familial bond to resist the discourse about the importance of blood bonds, thus providing the adoptees with stories to build their own. Notably, we do not find similar aims in the books with characters from migrant backgrounds; in books about immigration, 'ethnicity' and 'race' are coupled and the origins not only explain where the characters came from, but also the directions their lives will follow.

In the Place of Conclusions: Kin and Bond Beyond Blood in *Korazón de Pararrayos*

Following on the previous chapter's ideas about how 'race' is circumvented, I explore here how it intersects with other social categories. The discourses surrounding international adoption shed light on how class, nationality, and gender may be narrated to make 'race' in particular ways. I analyze too how the 'racial' difference between the child and the adoptive parents is either gapped in the illustrations or highlighted as an exoticism to be proud of and how these strategies obscure the social and economic contradictions that surround international adoption. The comparison between the stories about adoption and about migration unearths how the first are meant to assist the production of 'preventive racial identities,' an emphasis that is not paralleled in the books about immigrants.

Throughout this chapter, I pay consistent attention to the intersection of gender and 'race' with other social categories. I explore integration narratives offered to children with migrant backgrounds and how girls are presented as desiring to be White and blonde to fit into a supposedly widespread ideal of beauty. I also look briefly into the local mothers as figures that may 'whiten' their racially marked children, a script into which I delve deeper in the next chapter devoted to the analysis of family narratives in these books. Yet before moving on, I may here focus on the third book that the S.O.L. recommends about adoption to preadolescent readers (nine to eleven years old). This book, *Korazón de pararrayos*, is quite a rare book in our sample. It is narrated by an eleven-year-old Chinese adoptee, yet it focuses on the story of her twenty-four-year-old brother who lives as a squatter and has an affair with an older woman before he decides to join a nongovernmental organization (NGO) in Africa. It may be actually regarded as having an inverted focalizing relationship as that of *Mi Hermana Aixa*: in this case the story is seen through the eyes of the adopted sister even if it recounts that of the White brother. Luna—the protagonist—tells us about the very special relationship they have, a relationship marked by a platonic crush she has on him. Luna also recounts his brother's tense relationship with the father who opposes his volunteering in Africa—"¡no te hemos pagado la carrera de medicina para que te vayas a clavar inyeciones (sic) a los negros!" (36) [We haven't paid for your degree in medicine so that you go to give the Blacks some injection shots!]. The conflict of the story occurs after this brother has a car accident while in the African mission and is brought back to Spain. Her adoption, therefore, is not important to the plot at all and only poses some questions about the possible relationships between non-biological siblings. This story also deals in indirect ways with issues about 'race,' as the quoted statement of the father shows. This book, therefore, problematizes at the same time that it simplifies the consequences of international adoption. Luna, who likes to be called Yung, her Chinese name, does not feel that her adoption is pivotal in her life, even if it is such an important identity marker.

This book is quite exceptional in how it stresses that the adoptive mother is not a biological mother. They do have a strong bond but it is not to be plainly equated to that given by biological reproduction but rather to be related to other traditions of kinship, like that of stepmothers. This is highlighted in the story by the fact that Luna's brother is only the biological son of the father, who after his wife died remarried. Luna considers then that both are adoptive children of this mother.

The way this story ends also opens other possible narratives about adoption, immigration, and (national) belonging. The brother finally joins a mission of Doctors Without Borders in Africa with a new girl-friend. Soon after, Luna meets Sekou, a child of her age born to African parents in Spain. In the end, Luna overcomes her platonic crush on her brother and is ready to begin a sentimental relationship. Significantly, Luna's friend is also subjected as an immigrant while also a local: as in Luna's case belongings are not easy to explain.

Note

1 Adopteca.blogspot.com (retrieved on Aug. 8, 2015) is a blog intended to review and recommend media for adopted children.

7 Nation-as-Family
Tropes of Kin and Orphanhood

The family has been recurrently described as the basic social unit upon which society is built. The cognitive linguist George Lakoff argues that Nation-as-Family is a 'conceptual metaphor' from which others emerge, such as that of the government as a parent and the citizens as children (Lakoff 155). We may also trace the Nation-as-Family in those phrasings of a motherland, of founding fathers of a nation or in the diplomacy of a family of nations and brother countries. In Lakoff's argument, the idea of the nation being a family is shared across the political spectrum and structures the moral of politics in the United States for both liberals and conservatives. The ideological differences, therefore, would be organized around preferred modes of parenting: conservatives would claim a need for a 'Strict Father' setting clear rules for everyone, whereas liberals would appeal to the idea of a 'Nurturant Parent' focused on providing for each in their own need (81).

George Lakoff's idea on the power of the Nation-as-Family metaphor builds upon his previous work with Mark Johnson on metaphors. In *Metaphors We Live By*, they claim that metaphors structure how we perceive the world and become invisible forces shaping our understanding and actions (Lakoff and Johnson 4). They illustrate their theory with examples such as "argument is war," showing how from this root metaphor others emerge: "your claims are indefensible," "he attacked every weak point in my argument," "his criticisms were right on target," "I demolished his argument," "I've never won an argument with him," "You disagree? Okay, shoot!" "If you use that strategy, he'll wipe you out," "He shot down all of my arguments" (4). The authors argue that these metaphors reside in thought and not only reflect our ways of thinking but also make us think in certain ways.

Interestingly, the public and political rhetoric on Nation-as-Family does not match with metaphors used in social theory, where the society is usually understood as a living organism, a body of which different parts are dependent on others (cf. Maclay). Thus, what differences may we identify between these two models? If the nation is a family, do we have to obey those holding parental positions in society? Does the Nation-as-Family metaphor also imply that kin organizes structures of inclusion and care? Remarkably, traditional anthropology argued that bloodline kinship was the base of the community and, therefore, of the society, a view later contended by David M. Schneider in his groundbreaking *A Critique of the Study of Kinship*. Schneider argues that Anglo-American anthropologists constructed the idea of 'blood is thicker than water,' which appears to be an organizing principle only in European Western contexts. Schneider blamed anthropologists for being unable to understand how social relatedness was more important than biological kin in numerous societies. In other words, blood bonds do not necessarily lead to an organization of care.

In this chapter, I inquire into cultural constructions of ideal families and how they may be related to dynamics of belonging to the nation. I review some recurrent tropes in the representation of migrant parents focusing then on the figure of the mothers as marginalized from society and on the grandparents who establish close affective relationships with their children and present the value of preserving ancestral knowledge. Next, I delve into how the metaphors of kin and orphanhood overlap with metaphors of nation and care shedding light on how exclusion is culturally reproduced.

The Divide between Migrant and Local Parents

The representation of local and foreign families is deeply informed by stereotypes. Families with migration backgrounds are mostly large families in which the mother stays at home and the father is the breadwinner who works hard in a blue-collar job. Contrastingly, most of local, European parents are presented as professionals and are much more equally involved in the childrearing. Research done on American books about Latino minorities by Opal Moore and Donnarae MacCann showed that children's literature authors tended to represent migrant parents rather in "negative or insubstantial" ways lacking the agency in stories (Moore and MacCann 99). Moore and MacCann argued that most of the stories about Hispanic youth involved an Anglo character that played the role of a rescuer, exemplar, or surrogate parent figure. The depiction of immigrants in the books here studied follows similar lines. Even if we trace numerous efforts to put forward the idea that, regardless of our external differences, we are all the same, migrant parents are strongly subjected as ethnic others. A case in point might be that depiction of Banja's family in *Wie ich Papa die Angst vor Fremden nahm* reviewed in Chapter 4. The illustrations in the book highlight strongly the exoticism of the African adults while the little girl, Banja, is kept dressed in modern outfit. I deal at length with the trope of the immigrant as an ethnotype in Chapter 4, so here I focus on other features often shared by immigrant families, exploring how these characteristics can be contrasted to those of local family units.

In almost all of these books, immigrants have many children. With only one exception—*Mehdi y las lunas del zoo*—immigrant mothers do not work, or, at least, we find no references of them doing any kind of paid job outside the house. Rather the opposite, they are often portrayed in typical housewives roles—cooking, cleaning, taking care of the children—and are very often quite marginalized from social exchanges out of the household. Their husbands work hard in non-qualified jobs that leave them with scarce time to engage in domestic activities. Asha's Moroccan father in *Un ordenador muy especial* is so exhausted after work that he falls asleep in front of the TV, and the only way the girl is able to gain his attention is by intervening this TV with a message in which she asks him to spend time with her (she manages to get her broadcast on the TV). Amira's father in *No soy rubia. ¿Y qué?* is also burned out and falls asleep on the only day the family is able to go to the movies. An exception to this absent immigrant father may the one in *Mi abuela es africana*, where the Ghanaian father takes his son and his best friend on a journey to Africa, while the German mother stays at home to work: Interestingly, as mentioned before, this book takes distance from recurrent immigration narratives. *Mi abuela es africana* was written by a German author whose grandson has an African father and recalls the aim of the books about adoption in which the origin is not presented as a destiny.

Perhaps coincidently, most of the local children who are either the narrators or focalizers of the stories are single children. The lack of siblings is actually a force that moves the narration: many stories go about how this single child meets an ethnic Other who pushes him or her out of the comfort zone, thus opening their eyes to realities they were not aware of. Most of the stories are focalized on a local child who is transformed after meeting a foreigner to whom they offer help. In some few cases, this immigrant works illegally, yet in most cases it is a classmate or neighbor in need of feeling understood and welcomed into the group. Very often, the local protagonists meet the foreign families at their immigrant homes. In many of these stories—such as in *Susana Ojos Negros*, *El diario de La*, *La bicicleta de Selva*, and *Teo aprende a convivir*—the focalizer remarks upon the cultural differences between that family and the local protagonist's family. Nevertheless, those differences appear to be welcome; moreover, the appraisal of those ways of doing things leads them often to question their own culture. Tania, the local protagonist, in *Susana Ojos Negros* is invited to a party at her Turkish neighbors' house and afterward tells her father: "ha sido divertido. Lo divertido no puede explicarse. Tendrías que haber estado allí. Tú también te habrías reído" [it was fun. Fun cannot be explained. You should have been there. You would have laughed too]. Tania feels isolated as an only child and can reflect about her lack openly: "Pero si no llegara a tener una hermana me ilusionaría mucho tener una amiga" [if I do not get to have a sister,

I would love to have a friend]. Her neighbor—the girl she calls Susana, but whose real name we never get to know—might be that friend she has been longing for as a replacement for a sibling. Or perhaps what Tania longs for is a family like the neighbors. She joins them at a party and enjoys how they celebrate loudly and without making a fuss if someone breaks a dish while playing a joke.

The Italian La has a similar experience when she visits her classmate Ahmed. La is an only child and is impressed by how lively Ahmed's house is. He has three siblings and his mother is expecting a fourth child, plus their grandfather lives with them. La recounts the visit in her diary and does it by deconstructing some stereotypes on immigrants; even if she does not include as critical perception of her own culture as Tania does. La writes:

> "Por cierto, que estuve ayer y me pareció muy pequeña. Estaba limpísima y tenía un olor dulce y fresco a la vez. Es como vivir en el campo, aunque está en el número 154 de Via Spalato, en medio de unas naves grises. Olía incluso a hierba, y a especias, como en casa de la abuela cuando íbamos a verla antes de que se pusiera enferma. Creo que hasta olía mejor" (55)

> [By the way, I was there yesterday and it seemed too small. It was very neat and had a sweet and fresh smell. It's like living in the countryside, but it is in between some grey industrial units in Via Spalato 154. It smelled like Grandma's when we visited her before she became ill. It even smelled better].

El diario de La takes the form of a diary narration, which may explain why she gives certain details—as the address of the house—that are useless for a reader who is not familiar with Turin. Nevertheless, the reference to a house between industrial units added to that the observation of the place being 'too small' gives us a hint: Ahmed's family endures hardship. This image of the poor immigrant family is immediately contrasted with a positive representation: the place is 'very neat.' Compared to what? To La's own house or to her expectations of how immigrants live? The 'sweet and fresh smell' recalls her grandmother's place. Immigrants are often presented as more connected to nature— it smelled like the countryside—and to tradition—like grandmother's place. Later La eats a pastry made by Ahmed's mother. Most likely, the mother is responsible for that welcoming and cozy environment, the one who cleans and cooks, but La dedicates only a brief passage to her: "La madre de Am no ha dicho casi nada: eso sí, estaba allí sentada con las manos apoyadas en la barriga y dejaba siempre que hablase el padre" [Am's mother didn't say anything: she was there sitting with her hands on her belly and always let the father speak]. The mother appears to be portrayed as a stereotypically submissive (Arab) wife. In this passage we may trace how the so-called positive stereotypes are closely bound to what may be negative stereotypes. The portrayal of Ahmed's mother recalls Ali Rattansi's claim about the 'ambivalence' in the representation of British Asian women, who are usually portrayed positively as pillars of the "tightly knit" Asian family, much admired because of its family values, but also depicted as symbols of backwardness (Rattansi "Racism, "Postmodernism" and Reflexive Multiculturalism" 97). The depiction of Ahmed's family and mother is intended to be a positive representation, but it can only be built among those positive features 'available' for immigrants such as neatness and friendliness, a positive depiction then contrasted with the suggestion of backwardness.

The portrayal of migrant mothers as unable to speak the local language is rather common. In many cases, the children act as language brokers, translating for them, as Amira for her Tunesian mother and Antonio for her Spanish mother in Germany. It might be the case that Ahmed's mother does not know Italian and, therefore, is unable to speak, yet the reader cannot tell because La does not seem to be interested enough in her to let us know whether she does not speak because she cannot or because she is culturally trained to step aside.

So apparently evident is the assumption that immigrant mothers bear more children than locals that Tania, in *Susana Ojos Negros*, asks her (highly educated) mother: "¿las personas de ojos negros tienen más hijos que las de ojos azules?" [People with dark eyes have more children than those with blue eyes?]. I would like to remark here again how the stereotypical construction of the racial Other involves that contrasting self-representation of the locals as being predominantly blonde and having blue eyes. Strikingly, Tania does not ask whether immigrants are more prone to have more children, but makes a reference to what would be an innocent remark upon her own experience perceiving 'races.' As the books studied here convey, the portrayal of White and blue-eyed locals is very prominent, remarkably too in those books originally published in Spanish, even if they are far from the physical features of the majority of Spanish people.

Susana Ojos Negros was originally published in German and refers quite explicitly to the Turkish immigration. The question made by Tania may be reflecting on how children organize locals and foreigners along color divides at the same time that shows how parents attempt to pass on a color-blind ideology. The mother's answer misses an opportunity to inquire into how and why people are seemingly organized under such categories. The mother does not counter to ask Tania why she thinks that blue-eyed women may have fewer children and does not inquire into which cultural constructs are underpinning Tania's conclusions or whether she truly sees so many blue-eyed women around her; instead, this mother (just) laughs and says: "¡Eso no tiene nada que ver con el color de los ojos!" [That has nothing to do with eye color!]. Yet after reading all these books one may come up with a similar question: why are the White and blonde local mothers so contrasted to the characters of foreign mothers (with dark eyes)?

Tania's question about the 'ethnicity' of mothers directs us again to how gender intersects with ethnic categories. Nira Yuval-Davis claims that women's task is to reproduce the nation even if they are also the group put aside from most decisions regarding the collectivity (*Gender & Nation* 26). Yuval-Davis distinguishes between Staatnation (administrative nation state), Kulturnation (the cultural or religious nation), and Volknation (the authentic people forming the nation) and claims that women have an under-recognized role in maintaining the latter two types (21). This role is, of course, exercised differently in different cultural contexts yet appears very clearly among Jews and their belief that the ethnic belonging can only be passed on by a Jewish mother. Yuval-Davis claims that women are entitled to reproduce the nation and are turned into symbolic "border guards" (46) who protect at the same time that they are being protected by the nation. In Chapter 6, I explore the recurrent trope of the White and blonde mother to analyze how kin whitens; I inquire into the role played by the mothers in establishing the cultural and, moreover, 'racial' belongings of their children even if they are not their biological children. Migrant mothers may be marginalized in these stories precisely because of this key role in reproducing culture: the migrant mothers cannot transmit a (strong) ethnic belonging if their children are to be integrated/assimilated into the ways of doing things in the new society,

Surveying the agency of the characters in these stories, we note how immigrant children do not—or cannot—rely on their parents as local children do. In *Luna de Senegal*, the troubled Khoedi acknowledges that her parents are already too burdened with their own issues to share with them her own fears. On the contrary, many of the local children playing protagonist roles do get their parents involved in their adventures and seek their advice and help. In *Viruta* and *El balonazo*, the local parents are not only able to assist their children but also take responsibility over the irregular immigrants they have befriended. Moreover, the sets of parents in these stories are key in supporting their children in their rescue narratives and have the power to confront abusive mafia organizations. If we apply J. A. Greimas' typology of roles in narration, we note how immigrant parents never play the role of the 'helper,' while local parents often do (cf. "Actantial Model" in Herman 27). Regardless of whether the 'subject' (or 'hero' as named in other typologies) is an immigrant or a local child, the adult immigrants do not play a part in the child's quest to obtain his or her object of desire.

Forty-nine of the sixty books analyzed here portray at least one mother that in all but one case includes the mother of the protagonist. As already sketched, local mothers are White (in many cases portrayed as very white and blonde). This whiteness is stressed for most adoptive mothers, perhaps to remark upon the 'race' gap without insisting on the adoptees' colors. Foreign, immigrant mothers may also be strongly marked as a way to avoid showing greater differences among the group of children. Foreign mothers do not only have different skin, hair, and eye colors, but they are also ethnically marked by the ways they dress. For instance, none of the girl characters wear headscarves, but many mothers do. We find three boys called Ahmed in these books (in *La Mirada de Ahmed*, *El diario de La*, and in *Teo aprende a convivir*), and all of their mothers are depicted wearing scarves. The mothers of the girls in *Caja de Cartón*, *Susana Ojos Negros*, *Sola y Sincola*, *No soy Rubia*, and *Mi miel, mi dulzura* also do. The existence of different religions is only rarely acknowledged in these books, but it may be traced in these forms of depicting cultural belonging. Differences are also marked in the representations of family structures: while local families have one or two children—very often just one isolated child who seeks friends that open new worlds to them—foreign mothers have large families and appear to devote their lives to them even if by doing so they close to other social influences and end up unable to reproduce culture. They are unable to transfer their own cultural marks—at least that is not highlighted in any of these texts—and appear to be unaware of the codes of the place where their children are growing up. Even if migrant fathers are most often kept out of the picture, they appear to have a little more agency.

Contrastingly, local mothers do work, and their professional lives are often explicit in the narration. Foreign mothers are with very few exceptions kept in the background of the story and are portrayed undertaking the household tasks and, as remarked above, appear to be unable to understand the challenges that their children are confronting.

The Wise Ethnic Grandparents

Grandparents have more active roles than parents in migration narratives. A number of books use their figure to incarnate that origin culture and, quite often, to reflect on how identities may come into conflict. In the grandparents' portrayals, we may trace some conceptual metaphors such as 'origin as land,' 'people as plants,' and 'families as trees' (cf. Lakoff and Johnson). Grandparents are rooting devices. When we speak of the origin of someone or something, we most often refer to a geographic land or region; migration is seen as causing uprooted individuals who will find it difficult to flourish and whose growing will be hindered. Moreover, families are trees—think of genealogical trees and of family branches—which makes migration not only unnatural but unfruitful: the individual cannot get rooted somewhere else because the individual without a family is a small branch without a trunk. Interestingly enough, genealogical trees did not always have the aspect for which they are known today. In the Middle Ages, when genealogical trees began to be drawn, they placed greater emphasis on contemporary figures of kin—cousins, uncles, and aunts—than on ancestors. They were thus used to determine whether a kin-connection fell under incest prohibitions rather than to trace lineage (Teuscher 83–84).

In the books in this study, grandparents suffer from the consequences of this unnatural migration. They either long for their homelands when they have immigrated with their children and grandchildren (*in El diario de La, La bicicleta de Selva, El árbol de los abuelos*), or are left behind longing for their grandchildren (*Vamos a ver a Papá, Mi miel, mi dulzura, Mi abuela es africana, Luna de Senegal*). In the first cases, they share the household with the child protagonist and are the best examples of 'uprooted' individuals who know that they are not part of the productive capitalist order and have no reason to stay in the country to which they immigrated. The grandfathers in *El diario de La* and in *La bicicleta de Selva* are desolated, and their grandchildren are the only ones who understand their suffering and are able to help them. These old men long for certain objects that might bring them comfort, and their grandchildren are assisted by their local friends in providing them with this comfort. In *La bicicleta de Selva*, the Spanish protagonist helps 'foreign' Selva to bring her grandfather bottles with sand from the desert, and in *El diario de La* La helps Ahmed to find a guembri, the beloved musical instrument that his grandfather had lost in the immigration journey. In these two books the trope of the White savior is not mobilized to help the immigrant child integrate—an integration that is taken for granted—but to come to terms with his or her own background symbolized in this figure of the uprooted grandparent, who suffers now that he is not part of the productive force in the destination land.

The grandfather in *El árbol de los abuelos* also came from Africa and is likewise nostalgic about his life in a little village in the Saharan desert, yet he is not powerless and sad as the previous two characters are. Karamoko, the grandfather, is very proud of his origin. Rather than taking the place of the receiver, he acts as a 'magical helper' in the plot. Karamoko means 'lion hunter,' and he loves to tell stories about his childhood, but his granddaughter feels uncomfortable with his name and origin. When the girl is asked by the teacher to draw a genealogical tree and to explain her ancestors' lives, she wants to lie, saying that her grandfather is a butcher called Mauricio. She regrets that the desert he came from would not be as attractive for her classmates as one of the parents who has been to the Paris-Dakar race. The girl is ashamed and refuses to complete her genealogical tree, but the teacher insists:

> "La historia de vuestra familia empezó muchísimo antes de que vosotros naciérais y vosotros la continuaréis. Si la olvidáis, se perderá. Saber de dónde se proviene es como tener raíces. Y los niños, como los árboles, necesitan tener raíces para crecer" (29)

[Your family history began long before you were born, and you will continue it. If you forget it, it will be lost. To know from where you come from is like having roots. And children, like trees, need to have roots to grow]

This passage fleshes out that shared ideology, which asserts that one must be connected and continue the ancestors' culture. If we go deeper into the conceptual metaphor of origin as roots, we may come to the conclusion that immigration hinders migrants and their children, who will never be fully adapted to the 'new soil.' Significantly, children who are adopted are not portrayed as uprooted, and the stories mobilized to explain their origins do mark their journeys—the routes instead of the roots.

Let us return to *El árbol de los abuelos*. After the teacher insists in how important it is to acknowledge our origins, she announces a surprise for the class and Karamoko enters dressed in a long gown with his tamtam (drum). He performs as a storyteller, attempting in this way to persuade his granddaughter with the gleam of their cultural heritage. Karamoko proudly assumes the ethnotype that we have described in Chapter 4. As argued there, these stories recommend migrants and children with migrant backgrounds to mark their differences in order to become attractive for the locals.

Grandparents play roles that immigrant parents seem to be unable to perform. While parents are apparently too busy to even consider the importance of emotional well-being, grandparents connect to their grandchildren and are the means for the reproduction of cultural belonging—through folk music, stories, and crafts. This connection also implies that the children are the only ones who understand their grandparents' distress. An illustrative example is that of Ahmed's grandfather who is depressed after immigrating to Italy, a situation that only Ahmed understands. Assisted by the Italian La, who plays the role of the 'magic helper' and who has a much more extended and influential social network, Ahmed can bring his grandfather a guembri, his beloved musical instrument.

Perhaps the most extreme example of the negative portrayal of migrant parents is that in *Sola y Sincola*. A gas station attendant, who every summer sees how people from African origin travel south carrying loads of baggage and animals, narrates the story. He recounts how a family with seven children, a goat, and three hens got off at the station, how the father extended a rug on the floor to pray, and how they all got back into the van and took off without realizing that they left behind one of the daughters. The attendant—the 'subject-hero' in the story—tracks the family of the girl by calling the next gas stations down the road and asking them to stop a van carrying a rug to pray. Strikingly enough, the girl's family had not noticed her absence until they are adverted in one of these gas stations. When they come back for the girl they express their gratitude to the attendant:

> "Me han dicho que les avisaron en una gasolinera, que la idea de la llamada había sido muy buena.
> —Sukran— se han despedido al final, como hacen los africanos a los que lleno el depósito". (37)

> [They told me that they were notified at a gas station and that calling them was a very good idea. Sukran—they said as they left, as the African people say after I fill in their tanks].

Interestingly, the narrator insists that this African family shares the recognizable cultural traits of immigrant African families. They all carry the same kinds of goods, they all travel at the same time of the year, and they all say 'sukran' instead of 'gracias.' Are all African parents as careless as these? The gas attendant does not appear to be surprised that this family has forgotten a child, and strikingly, the family only notices her absence when adverted by the attendants of another gas station. It not a plausible story, yet one cannot help wondering if it would have been even less plausible if a family of locals had left behind a child.

Sola y Sincola depicts a very negligent family. As reviewed before, in most of the other books, immigrant children are either helped out by their local classmates (*Me llamo Yoon, El diario de La, La bicicleta de Selva, No soy rubia..., Toño se queda solo, La Mirada de Ahmed*), neighbors (*Antonio en el país del silencio*), or schoolteachers (*Mila..., Mehdi..., Yoon y el brazalete...*). The foreign parents rarely notice the difficulties and adventures their children go through. With very few exceptions, foreign families are not depicted as part of social networks: they do not have friends or participate in broader communities. On the contrary, immigrating is predominantly portrayed as a process that involves cutting off with social belongings and family relationships. As in *El árbol de los abuelos*, identity is better thought of as a continuation of the ancestors' history. These books avoid reflections on the fluidity of identities and the multiplicity of belongings to reproduce concepts of fixed cultures and origins as a land where people grow as plants that have enough soil and water.

Symbolic Orphans

Sola y Sincola also provides an interesting case for our study in its depiction of abandonment. The stories about adoption avoid referring to these episodes and often explain abandonment as deriving from a rather thoughtful decision of the biological mother seeking to provide the child a better future—as it is explained for example in the case of *Usoa, llegaste por el aire*. Explanations about the reasons behind the relinquishing of children or about the processes that they follow are always very brief. In *Motherbridge of Love*—the only book of the sample in which a biological mother is visually portrayed—the mother has found "a home for you that she could not provide" (eighth double spread). The depiction of this biological mother working in a rice field under the sun is contrasted with the Western (and blonde) mother running with the adopted daughter, reinforcing that message that it was done with best interests of the child in mind. In *Korazón de Pararrayos*, a short novel addressed to readers between ages nine and eleven years old, Luna, the adopted protagonist, explains:

> "Resulta que, al nacer yo, se ve que mi madre biológica me llevó a un asilo del gobierno, porque en mi país los chinos eran muy pobres, y muchos padres no podían mantener a sus hijos. En mi país, muchas niñas chinas como yo tuvimos que ser dejadas en el asilo por nuestras madres// Un asilo es algo así como una guardería en la que esperas cada día que te vengan a buscar los padres de otro país" (14–15)

> [When I was born, my biological mother took me to a government shelter because in my country the Chinese people were very poor, and many parents could not provide for their children. In my country, many Chinese girls like me had to be taken to this shelter by our mothers// A shelter is something like a daycare center where you wait every day for parents from another country to pick you up].

Books about adoption avoid using the word 'orphanage' and try out new terms such as 'asilo' (shelter) or 'casa de los niños' (children's house). As explained in Chapter 3, international adoption is presented as an adventure for the adopted parents and the child who travels 'back home' on a plane. These books may be, therefore, regarded as devices meant to overwrite the story of abandonment with one in which the child is a precious child. Overwriting abandonment is crucial if we read these books acknowledging the impact of John Bowlby's attachment theory in childrearing. The idea that children with maternal deprivation in the early years face later nearly irreversible psychological damage has had a huge impact on upbringing culture since the 1960s (Fulcher and Scott 131). In these books, adoptees are presented as redemptive figures who at once represent the unfortunate conditions in some world regions, but at the same their own potential to overcome those conditions and, in the end, to triumph over global inequity.

Adopted children appear to be represented against the cultural narrative of the orphan. Orphan characters come in all shapes and sizes and have been prevalent figures in different traditions of children's literature. Here I refer to the trope emanating from the recurrent figure of the Victorian orphan. Melanie Kimball describes the recurrence of the orphan figure, arguing:

"They do not belong to even the most basic of groups, the family unit, and in some cultures this is enough to cut them off from society at large. In other cultures, orphans are regarded as special people who must be protected and cared for at all costs. In either case, orphans are clearly marked as being different from the rest of society. They are the eternal Other" (Kimball 559).

Isha in *Isha, nacida del corazón* wonders about her own origin after watching a news report about a baby who has been found in a trash can, presumably left there by her Colombian mother. The baby is encountered by a man who believes he has heard a cat whining; when he finds out it is a baby thrown inside the container, he takes her to the nearest hospital. After watching the news, Isha approaches her parents with anxiety: was she also found abandoned in the trash? No, she was not: she has always been loved, her mother assures.

> —¿La mujer que me tenía en la barriga también?
> —¡Por supuesto! Esa mujer también te quería.
> —¿Dónde está ahora? No quiero que venga a buscarme (…)
> Aquella señora te amaba muchísimo. Era una buena mujer, por eso renunció a ti y te dejó en Hyderabad. Así nosotros pudimos ir allí a buscarte (…) Ella tuvo que marcharse con Yama (…) Un poderosísimo guía indio, hijo del Sol, que conoce los caminos que llevan a otras vidas diferentes… Vive en un palacio en el cielo" (20)

[The woman who had me in her tummy also loved me?/Of course, that woman also loved you./Where is she now? I don't want her to come looking for me (…)/That lady loved you a lot. She was a good woman, that's why she gave you up and left you in Hyderabad. So that we could go there and find you (…) She had to go away with Yama. (…) A very powerful Indian guide, the Sun's son, who knows the paths to different lives… Now she lives in a palace in Heaven].

As often remarked, adoptees are not orphans as in most of the cases their parents are alive (Kim 262). Nevertheless, the international legislation on adoption requires the children to be legally labeled as such before being adopted, a formality that erases the rights of the biological parents and grants an exclusive belonging to the adoptive family. Yet, can such a thing truly be granted? This question appears to haunt both adoptees and adoptive parents and underpins this dialogue between Isha and her mother. Isha asks about her past, and the mother answers by telling her a story that avoids dealing with the details of the adoption process. This brings us back to the 'impossible contradictions' of international adoption (cf. Dorow, chapter 3). In the story told by the mother, these contradictions are apparently resolved. Isha is turned into a child of a very special kind who has been gestated by a woman who is not referred as a (biological) mother but only as a woman who had her in her tummy. Isha's trajectory, therefore, does not recall that of Oliver Twist, Cinderella, or Huckleberry Finn, to name some literary orphans; she has not experienced the misfortunes and lack of care that follow abandonment and/or the death of the parents. Interestingly, Isha's (biological) mother died without even dying: she went to Heaven following some exotic, god-like figure. To make that awkward way of dying possible, the author resorts to an image that stems from Indian mythology. The inclusion of pieces of supposedly local cultural traditions is recurrent in contemporary adoption narratives and appears to respond to a need for culturally justifying the increasingly controversial practice of Western adoption of non-Western children as culturally grounded in that foreign culture (García González and Wesseling 259). Before dying, this mother is able to provide the girl with care: Isha, therefore, was not abandoned, but placed.

Isha was never an orphan: her story is much more privileged than that of orphans. She was not an orphan, in the first place, because in the strategic phrasing of the novel, the biological mother was just someone who had her in her tummy. The novel also tells us about the moment in which Isha as a baby starts calling her (adoptive) parents "Mamá" and "Papá." Moreover, that moment signals the end of the embedded origin story told by César, the adoptive father. Once he has completed this piece of storytelling, Isha is prepared to go to bed and have a peaceful night's sleep. Yet, the girl is still uneasy and cannot fall asleep. The mother comes to her room to check on her, and Isha confesses that she is still troubled with this story on the news about that baby abandoned in the trash. What happened to that baby? The mother needs to come up with a happy ending to that other story introduced by the media. She then finds a solution: the baby has been adopted by a nurse at the hospital. Isha is now comforted. The novel can end there, as this second adoption marks a happy ending for that sub-plot in *Isha, nacida del corazón*.

We may wonder why is this ending the 'tell-able' ending (Andrews 9). Would it have been possible to reunite this baby with her biological mother had she been suffering from a terrible post-partum depression? Or perhaps, might the baby have been given to some other relatives who might have been looking desperately for the child? Or perhaps the baby had not been abandoned like that but instead was taken away from a desperate mother? We may also wonder why this episode was included in the novel; the girl's problem with her adoption is already set at the very beginning of the story when a classmate tells her that her mother cannot possibly be her real mother. Isha had already been suffering a crisis about her adoption that is very connected to the racial difference with her mother: what role does this other story play? And, moreover, why is the mother of that abandoned baby in the trash identified? The news report speaks of a Colombian mother. How is it possible to identify this mother if the baby was just rescued when a man thought it was a kitten?

The way a story comes to a happy ending is usually indicative of its ideological stances as it fleshes out which are the issues that have to be resolved to re-establish equilibrium and peace. This is more the case in stories that achieve what Nöel Carroll calls a "narrative closure," in which the issues that have troubled the characters are solved with an implicit promise that they will not bother our protagonists again. The adoption of this baby is, therefore, key for the message in *Isha, nacida del corazón*, and I read it as achieving two goals: on one hand, this episode reframes Isha's anxiety as mostly concerned with her condition of being adopted (the traumatic past of being abandoned at the same time that the possibility that she might be abandoned—again—in the future) rather than with being racially marked in a predominantly White context; on the other hand, it assists the naturalization and justification of transnational adoptions. The identification of the biological mother as Colombian may reinforce the message that these adoptions are done on the 'best interests' of the child as it suggests that the Spanish nurse would make a better mother than a presumably marginalized Colombian. This happy ending draws upon a deeply ingrained assumption—found also on other stories—that Western cultures of parenting are better than those from non-Western countries.

In 2009, the city of Madrid launched an adoption campaign targeted to migrants. The campaign first took the form of posters placed at metro stations stating, "Before you leave me in the street, make a call to 012. Many families want to adopt me" (86). Anthropologist Jessaca Leinaweaver tracked down how the campaign involved a second phase in which flyers were left in places where different migrant communities would meet (immigrant aid centers, restaurants and locutorios, small businesses that provide Internet access and foreign calls). Leinaweaver also found that only every two or three years a baby was found in the garbage and that, therefore, the campaign could be better described as aiming to impede undesired pregnancies that end with an abortion (87). The idea that marginalized, third-world mothers would be more prompt to abandon their babies informed the campaign even if it had no correlation with real practices.

The figure of this marginalized, third-world mother is to be connected to a broader figure in which third-world countries and societies are unable to provide a space for proper families. This idea is also reproduced in *¿Por qué no tengo los ojos azules?*. Maya, who is coincidentally born in Colombia, tells:

> "Mi madre, la verdadera, la que no conozco, no tenía nada para mí y no quería que me muriera. Una mañana me abandonó en una iglesia de Medellín. Quería que creciera lejos, muy lejos, en Europa o en Norteamérica, en una verdadera familia que no me dejara morir de hambre" (44).

[My mother, the real one, the one I did not meet, did not have anything for me and did not want me to die. One morning she abandoned me in front of a church in Medellín. She wanted for me to
grow up far away, very far away, in Europe or in North America,
within a real family that would not let me starve to death]

Two ideas of what is 'real' kin are confronted here: on one side, the
'real' mother who gave birth to her, yet a 'real family' is the one that
can provide for its members. The family is coupled with material means,
a link that recalls the historical importance of kin as a way to regulate
investments and multiply capital. Interestingly, the 'real families' are to
be found in Europe or North America. The family is not only coupled
with material means but also inscribed in that long-standing tradition
of the Western advances and civilized values against a fairly 'wild' order
in the rest of the world. Interestingly, in this order, the child becomes a
redemptive child able to escape the fate of 'ethnicity' through education
or, in this case, through 'kinning' (Howell).

In contrast to the books about adoption in which the portrayal of the
adoptees distances them from the imagery of the orphan, certain books
about immigration tend to present migrants as if they were orphans. In
the next pages, I explore tropes of orphanhood in three books depicting irregular immigration to complete the argument on how nation and
family overlap to organize dynamics of belonging and exclusion. I read
these books as arguing that irregular immigrants are orphaned from
states that cannot provide for them; in order to belong to a new state
they need to be 'kinned,' taken under the wing of a local and proper
family.

The S.O.L. recommends three books that depict irregular immigration in explicit ways portraying characters that arrived on pateras or
were 'smuggled' by mafias. Two books—already reviewed in Chapter
4—have strikingly similar plots, *Viruta* and *El balonazo*. These two
books reveal not only some paradoxes of the discourses about (illegal)
immigration, but also a rather imperceptible normative discourse on
kinship and family as a rule that explains exclusion. In both stories,
a Spanish boy befriends an irregular immigrant who is controlled and
extorted by the mafias that trafficked him into Spain. Both immigrants,
Jalal and Maxama, are forced to work in the informal economy in order to pay abusive debts that the mafias claim, and are helped out by
their Spanish friends, who manage to involve their parents and other
adults in the complex adventure of rescuing them. In *Viruta*, Jalal is
finally released from the persecutions of the mafia organization when
it is dismantled, and in *El balonazo* Maxama is set free after a trial at
a Spanish court that had threatened to deport him. In the two books,
therefore, the immigrants are liberated by their Spanish friends, yet in
both cases, this happy ending is followed by another happier ending in

which narrative closure is achieved. In other words, a first happy ending in which the migrants are liberated from the mafias is not enough to solve the problem, and the stories carry on to achieve a final solution to all problems. If these stories had ended when the migrants were set free, these books would have conveyed the idea that irregular immigration is an acceptable way to become a part of 'our' society. And what these books say is that it is not.

Strikingly enough, in both books that final, happier ending has the same twist: the immigrants are sent off to another European country—Jalal to Germany, and Maxama to France. In both cases, the reason put forward is that there they are supposed to meet their relatives. No reflection is given to whether in those other countries they will become legal workers or residents, whether they can speak the foreign language, or what kind of care they might expect from those relatives. The message passed on soundly is that life is only possible within a family structure and, implicitly, that individuals without a family are threatening to the social order. If there is hope in these stories, it is the hope that familial relationships can provide what the state cannot give.

Perry Nodelman and Mavis Reimer argue that a plot of parental control underpins orphan narratives in children's literature (197). In them, the adventurous homeless child finally finds security and care, a home, either through adoption or through re-encountering relatives. Interestingly, the books reviewed here re-affirm that need of parental control that recalls and overlaps with a government's control over citizens. Notably, the irregular immigrants are only 'rescued' after the (Spanish) parents take a part in the story. These sets of parents could be assimilated to Lakoff's idea of a "Nurturant parent" (Lakoff 15) who provides to each in relation to what each needs to accomplish its potential. This nurturant approach is to be opposed to that of the "Strict Father" (65–68), in which clear rules for everyone are set from the beginning. Nevertheless, they also end up accepting strict rules that organize a broader system.

Interestingly, the immigrant characters in these stories are presented as if they were children. We do not get any clear reference to their age, but they befriend the children and are protected by the adults. We may even argue that irregular immigrants appear to be symbolic orphans from those nations that could not provide for them, and an implicit question that underlies the narration is whether the European countries should 'adopt' them. These novels do not dare to answer this question; instead, a happy ending is fabricated in which the irregular migrant is happy to immigrate once more. A reason put forward is that of the relatives who exist in some other part of the desirable Global North. These happy endings appear to reproduce the European immigration policy on family reunification. As the Home Affairs division of the European Commission assures, family reunification "helps to create socio-cultural stability, facilitating the integration of non-EU nationals within EU States, thus promoting economic and social cohesion – a fundamental EU objective" (Home Affairs Division of the European Commission).

Laura Peters argues that recurrent orphan characters in Victorian Fiction responded to the emergent ideal of the family: "in order to reaffirm itself, the family needed a scapegoat. It found one in the orphan figure" (Peters 1). Might it be the case that today's representations of immigrants play the roles of scapegoats for an elusive national cohesion? Nation-states are allegedly under menace by globalizing forces but also by internal nationalism, such as the Catalan and Basque separatist movements in Spain. Immigrants, as if orphans, reinforce the need of the family as the first, basic unit upon which the nation is built.

Books with adopted characters are in almost all cases recommended as books for adoptees, their families, and friends. Books depicting (irregular) immigrants are, on the contrary, meant to 'bring closer' a phenomenon that is distanced from the experiences of the reader. This for/about divide—for adoptees, about migrants—sketches the limits of the Nation-as-Family. Adoptees are, despite the differences, one of 'us' with whom we are meant to bond; the book itself becomes a cultural artifact to provide what biology did not. Books about (undocumented) immigrants do the opposite: they are descriptive and end up explaining and normalizing the unfortunate exclusion.

A third book dealing with irregular immigration, *Blanca y Viernes*, refers to the pateras (open boats) that cross Gibraltar Strait and end too often in tragedies. In this case, the focal character is Blanca, an only child, who is bored in her holidays at the Southern coast and reads *Robinson Crusoe*. The action of the plot starts the day she encounters a young Black child hidden in her garden's dollhouse. She calls him Viernes (the Spanish for Friday) and tries to instruct him in the way Robinson did with his Friday. That evening, she realizes that this boy must be one of the survivors of a patera that has arrived to the village's beach. She watches a news report on TV showing how the fellow travelers were detained, and, as her parents appear unable to explain what future they can expect, she decides to guard her Viernes and keep his existence a secret. Some days later, though, the holidays are over, and she is forced to go back to the city with her parents. She leaves Viernes provided with food, but it is only enough for a few days, after which the boy manages to call Blanca saying the only Spanish word he apparently knows: "hambre" [hunger]. Blanca realizes that she has failed to provide him with means for his own survival and rushes to the seaside with a bag full of groceries without noticing that her parents are following her and that, out of worry, they have called the police. Once everyone is there, the boy is detained. Blanca, who narrates the entire story, tells us that she felt so miserable after that that she refused to speak for days. The story, up to here, only has a very sad ending.

Irregular immigration is a rare topic in European children's literature.[1] In the United States, the Latino community has managed to write and publish some stories reflecting the difficult experiences and journeys of Latin American immigrants (Campbell; Naidoo). In Spain, we do not find such examples, and irregular immigration appears to be depicted along the lines of criminality and marginalization: the only possible story is that in which the 'illegal' is sent off. Interestingly enough, in *Blanca y Viernes*, the undocumented boy is not sent off but adopted by a local family.

Blanca does not wonder who Viernes' parents were or are probably because in that third world she imagines him coming from there are no "real" families, to paraphrase Maya. Viernes is a state-orphan, and, as such, he is adoptable.

The ending of *Blanca y Viernes* is a case in point. After days spent dealing with the girl's obstinate silence, Blanca's parents decide to look out for Viernes. They find him in a center for young refugees, where the director explains he came from a place where:

> "de la noche a la mañana, pueblos enteros… **desaparecen**. Y no por causas naturales. Y es muy posible que él haya presenciado eso…, es muy posible que viese **desaparecer** ante sus ojos a la gente que le había rodeado desde que nació." (139, in bold what was in italic in the original)

> [from day to night entire towns… disappear. And not from natural causes. And it is very likely that he witnessed that…, it is very likely that he has witnessed with his own eyes how the people who had surrounded him since birth just disappeared.]

Both the suspension points and the italics—here in bold letters—mark this text as one to be de-coded by a reader with social literacy. It may not be suitable to speak of genocide in a children's book; moreover, the death of the progenitors and/or details of violence that the child or his family may have suffered have been a long-held taboo in children's literature (MacLeod 179–80). After meeting the center's director, the parents decide to adopt Viernes to give Blanca a brother. Adoption is much easier in this story than in real life and Viernes can be easily adopted. As in previous stories, the happy ending is only possible after a family provides the care other institutions are unable to give. Adoption will be the refugee's ticket not only to a family, but also to a state that looks after its people and where we shall find no examples of genocide like the one suggested by the center's director.

Significantly, *Blanca y Viernes* is not recommended as a book about adoption. It has little to nothing in common with the books that have adoptees as protagonists. Here the bond with that new member of the family has not been magically arranged and written by destiny, but responds to a fortuitous event. Moreover, this adoptee has not always been privileged but deals with a traumatic past of which, nevertheless, no one speaks. Viernes is that type of orphan that other adopted children are not. Very interestingly, in Spain adoptive parents may fail to receive the 'certificado de idoneidad'—the certificate of suitability to adopt—if they give as a reason to adopt the desire to give their first biological child a sibling. One of the criteria is that the adoption does not respond to anything other than the desire to parent, as if such desire would always be explained as independent from other factors. *Blanca y Viernes* ends with an illustration of the two children playing while Blanca narrates about how happily they spend their days together. Significantly, Viernes does not receive another name: he will always be Friday, as if he is a projection of Blanca's desire to become a *Robinson Crusoe*–style savior.

In the Place of Conclusions: Finding and Creating Home in *Tea with Milk*

"At home she had rice and miso soup and plain green tea for breakfast. At her friends' houses she ate pancakes and muffins and drank tea with milk and sugar" (4). Her parents, a couple of Japanese immigrants, called her Masako whereas Americans called her May. "When she graduated from high school, she wanted to go to college and then live in San Francisco. But her parents were homesick and decided to return to Japan, which was their homeland" (6). Masako has to go back with them and to leave "the only home she had ever known" (7). In Japan, she is required to wear a Kimono and to learn the language; when a matchmaker offers her as a bride, she decides to run away from her parents' home.

In *Tea with Milk*, the Japanese-American author Allen Say tells the story of his mother and how she came to meet his father. Masako manages to get to Osaka, the biggest city in the region, where she becomes a department store's guide for foreign businessmen. One of these men is also, even if in a different way, struggling with the identities projected onto him. Joseph is Japanese but grew up in China: "'I went to an English school in Shanghai,'" (24) he says to explain why his English is so much better than his Japanese: "They called me Joseph. Won't you have tea with me?" (24). In her answer, the narrator remarks, Masako brings together the seemingly conflicting identities: "'I would enjoy that very much' she said in her very best English, and bowed as a proper Japanese lady should" (24). The narrator continues telling us that when they meet for tea—she had it with milk—she asked him to call her by her American name, May. Joseph works in Japan for a Chinese bank.

> "Are you planning to stay in Japan?" May asked.
> "That depends," he said. "If you have certain things, I think one place is as good as any other."

"What sort of things?"

"Oh, a home, work you enjoy, food you like, good conversation. How about you? Would you like to go back to America?"

"I think so, someday," she said. "I wouldn't have to be such a proper lady there. I could get a job or drive a car and nobody would think anything of it." (28)

That was—Allen writes—"the beginning of their friendship" (28). They meet frequently, yet, after some months he is told that he will be re-located to Yokohama. Surprisingly, it is only then, on the next-to-last page, that he tells her that he was adopted by British parents: "There were six of us, all adopted and all scattered now and looking for a home. May, home isn't a place or a building that's ready and waiting for you, in America or anywhere else" (30). For Joseph, kin is not linked to home and home is not attached to geography. As in *Blanca y Viernes*, adoption is narrated differently in those books that are not addressed to adopted children. In this case, being adopted by British parents does not make him more British than the fact that he attended a British school.

By the time this conversation happens, the visual narration shows the characters holding hands.

"What about us?" Joseph said. "We can do it together."

"Yes," May said, nodding.

"We can start here. We can adopt this country," he said.

"One country is as good as another?" May smiled. "Yes, Joseph, let's make a home."

So they were married in Yokohama and made a home there. I was their first child. My father called my mother May, but to everyone else she was Masako. At home they spoke English to each other and Japanese to me. Sometimes my mother wore a kimono, but she never got used to sitting on the floor for very long.

All this happened a long time ago, but even today I always drink my tea with milk and sugar. (30–32)

Tea With Milk is one of very few books in which cultural differences are sites of negotiation. Home is not a place you come from, but the place you want to be and that may evolve with time. Moreover, geography is not conflated with nation and becomes a much more complex category. For example, once Masako/May is in Osaka after leaving her parents' home, she feels as if she is back in the United States because of the energy of a big city. There is an acknowledgment of the locality of cultural traditions alongside an understanding of them as layers that depend on multiple other factors and contexts. It is also remarkable that in this book we may trace a critical approach to how identities are projected differently onto women than onto men. Joseph appears to be free while moving countries, while Masako/May must fulfill what she considers to be constrictive gender codes.

We may also read this story in light of the home/away/home pattern described by Nodelman and Reimer, even with the twist that returning home is finding and founding a new one. The characters are not defined by their parents' cultural identities but by their own decisions, routes, and affiliations. The tea with milk functions as a metaphor for that proud cultural hybridity.

Interestingly, despite this presentation of the complexity of social identities, the book also coincides with others in depicting the couple of foreign parents as unable to adapt to new discourses and ways of doing. Joseph's parents appear to have failed in making a home for their family in China, and Masako's parents decide to move back to Japan, where they expect their American-raised daughter to marry according to a traditional and outmoded Japanese custom of arranged marriages. Masako's parents seem to be quite attached to the Japanese traditions, yet, paradoxically, they failed in transmitting them to their daughter. They were not even able to teach her the language, which she had to learn from scratch once 'back home' in Japan. They—as other foreign parents depicted in these books—are also unable to understand May's emotional distress and her difficulties in adapting to a new context.

It is remarkable, that in the recommending review by the S.O.L. *Tea with Milk* is not described as a story that presents a case of intersecting forms of identification revealing the problematic category of ethnic identity. On the contrary, the idea of an insurmountable difference between people of different cultural backgrounds is put forward:

> "Los obstáculos en la convivencia entre diferentes culturas se reflejan en las contradicciones que Masako encuentra en su vida. Esta obra muestra un recorrido por las etapas principales de su vida. Masako nació en Estados Unidos en el seno de una familia emigrante japonesa y vivió su infancia entre dos mundos diferentes. De adolescente regresa a Japón donde el choque cultural le hará sentirse extranjera en el país de sus padres. El distinto papel de la mujer en una y otra sociedad desencadenará el conflicto que le lleva a buscar su sitio y a encontrar un equilibrio entre ambas formas de vida."

> [The obstacles in the coexistence between different cultures are reflected in the contradictions Masako finds in her life. This text goes through the main life stages of her life. Masako was born in the United States in the bosom of a Japanese migrant family and lived her childhood between two different worlds. As a teenager, she goes back to Japan where the cultural clash makes her feel a foreigner

in her parents' country. The different roles for women in one and another society trigger a conflict that leads her to find her place and a balance between both ways of living.]

This review reproduces the narrative of cultural clashes and of different cultures as different 'worlds.' May's problems do not derive from the conflict with her parents or from having to accommodate to very particular gender roles in Japan but rather to her condition as an immigrant child trapped between these different worlds. An underlying narrative in this review identifies immigration as unnatural; the reviewer identifies her as 'Masako'—the Japanese name, which the character rejects—and phrases her move to Japan as a 'return.' In this recommendation, we may be led to believe that Masako has been burdened by her parents' immigration opening up for her a world to which she does not belong. Her place is, therefore, to marry a Japanese man, even if this Japanese man also feels displaced and foreign and struggles with a broken biography.

Note

1 The very few examples dealing with it are targeted to young adults (Eccleshare).

Conclusions

"Un día vinieron unos franceses. Todos los niños vimos acercarse un potente Land Rover y corrimos asustados para averiguar qué ocurría. Mi padre decía que sí, que nosotros mismos podíamos verlo, que aquellas personas tenían la piel de color blanco. En el poblado había un gran alboroto. Yo ya había oído hablar muchas veces de los hombres blancos, pero nunca había visto uno. Estuvimos mucho rato mirándolos y diciéndoles cosas, practicando el francés que habíamos aprendido en la escuela. Eran dos, los enviaba una cooperativa de agricultores de algodón y querían ver nuestras cosechas. "Eran un hombre y una mujer" dijo uno de mis compañeros, convencido, cuando se fueron. Nos quedamos boquiabiertos. Todos los demás habíamos visto solo a dos blancos. ¿Cuál de los dos era la mujer?, nos preguntábamos. Oímos que decían "hasta mañana. de manera que nos organizamos para volverlos a ver. Queríamos comprobar lo que decía nuestro amigo. En mi pueblo las mujeres visten largas y alegres faldas, ropas con los colores de las flores y la fruta madura, nunca llevan pantalones ni gorra, se cubren la cabeza con un pañuelo".

"Volvieron con el mismo Land Rover. Después supe que siempre venían con Land Rover. Mirábamos de arriba abajo para descubrir quién era la mujer, pero nada de nada. "Fijaos bien", dijo mi compañero, mientras nosotros los rodeábamos intrigados, "fijaos en los pechos, la diferencia está en los pechos" ¡He ahí la diferencia!; aún éramos muy pequeños" (10–11).

[One day some French people came. We saw a powerful Land Rover coming, and we ran, afraid to find out what was going on. My father said that yes, that we could see it, that those people had white skin. The town was stirred up. I had heard many times about the white men, but haven't yet seen any. We stayed there for a while looking at them and saying things to them, practicing the French we had learnt at school. There were two of them who were sent by a cotton farmer's cooperative, and they wanted to see our harvests. 'They were a man and a woman,' said one of the children, convinced, when they left. We were open-mouthed. We had just seen two White men. Which one was the woman? we wondered. We heard that they said "until tomorrow," so we organized ourselves to see them again. We wanted to prove what our friend had said. In my town, women wear long and happy skirts, clothes with the colors of flowers and ripe fruits, they never wear jeans or a cap, they cover they heads with a headscarves.

They came back with the same Land Rover. Later I knew that they always came with a Land Rover. We looked carefully at them to find out who was the woman, but we couldn't find out. "Pay attention," said my friend, as we gathered around them curious, "pay attention to the breasts, the difference is in the breasts." That was it! We were still very young].

This fragment is taken from one of the first books about immigration published in Spain, *Bully. Yo vengo de Doubirou*. In it, a Gambian immigrant, Bully Jangana, recounts his childhood in African cotton fields, his reasons for emigrating, a complicated first journey to Paris where he could not find a job, and how he finally settled in Santa Coloma de Farners, in Catalonia. It was published as part of a collection initiated by the Teachers' Association Rosa Sensat in Barcelona with La Galera, a publishing house strongly committed to diversity. The aim of the collection was to feature migrants from different countries recounting their life stories before and after settling in Spain.

As may already be evident here, *Bully. Yo vengo de…* is considerably distinct from the other books discussed throughout this book. First, because it may be the only one in which the reader identifies the author as an immigrant able to bring in another perspective.[1] In *Bully. Yo vengo de…*, the written testimony is accompanied by numerous photographs depicting life in Gambia as well as illustrating the author's European journeys. The front cover includes a picture of him with his family—Jangana with his wife and two children—and the back cover confirms that we should understand this text as autobiographical:

> "La vida, las inquietudes y las dificultades de una persona extranjera que se ha integrado en el entorno socio-cultural de nuestro país. Una perspectiva que ayuda a comprender las diferencias y las similitudes entre culturas fomentando el respeto mutuo".

> [The life, concerns, and difficulties of a foreign person who has integrated into the socio-cultural environment of our country (sic). A perspective that helps us understand the differences and similarities between cultures promoting the mutual respect] (back cover).

This paragraph confirms that the book is to be considered an autobiography that gives us a new perspective. It would be unfair not to recognize how 'race' and ethnicity are narrated here in a way that differs greatly from what is prevalent in the other books of our sample. In *Bully. Yo vengo de…*, the reader is invited, for instance, to imagine how Other is a White man—or, moreover, a White woman—to a Black boy born in an

African village; moreover, as in the anecdote of misrecognizing the gender of the French woman visiting the village, this perspective may also unveil how gender and other social categories may become naturalized in discourses while remaining cultural conventions and how different social categories intersect in the creation of differences.

Yet the publishers' note in the paragraph quoted above does follow a common narrative in the promotion of these books. In it, the idea of fixed cultures is reproduced, and the phrasing 'our country' emphasizes that binary structure of us/them, in which immigrants do not belong and the addressed reader is, unmistakably, a local.

Bully. Yo vengo de Doubirou provides us with an interesting example of the tensions between the discourse on integration and that practical philosophy on assimilation that Ricard Zapata sketches as characteristic of the Spanish approach to immigration (Zapata-Barrero "Managing Diversity in Spanish Society: A Practical Approach"). We may trace in this book numerous efforts to counter stereotypes and common narratives about immigration. The sole fact to publish the autobiographical text of an immigrant stands out from common approaches to immigration in children's literature, where migrant characters are most often superficially and stereotypically depicted and not very often the focalizers of the stories. The importance of the focalizer has been discussed throughout this book and corresponds also to one of the most salient debates about the possibilities and shortcomings of so-called multicultural children's literature. As John Stephens argues, the focalization on a character who is a member of a minority community is a very powerful method of expressing subjectivity; Stephens, as other scholars, has raised a claim for more children's books written by members of the represented minorities (*Advocating Multiculturalism* 181). *Bully...* renders that migrant view and is written as a nonfictional text by a migrant author, but we may still be skeptical regarding the extent to which this 'other' voice is as other as it is claimed.

There are some other details that mark this book as exceptional in this context. For instance, the title introduces the character as coming from Doubirou, a little village, most probably unknown to the reader. This phrasing stands apart from a very common use of the nation as the overarching marker of identity. We may recall here how in the renowned and awarded picturebook *Madlenka*—analyzed in the final section of Chapter 5—foreign characters could only represent countries when they were Western (the Italian, French, and the German neighbor), whereas African, Asian, and Latin American characters were to be taken as ambassadors of large and diverse regions (while Madlenka herself was representative of New York City as a melting pot of world influences). Interestingly, Bully is not meant to represent all African migrant experiences but his own as a young man coming from a small village in times in which Gambians could travel to Europe without the current regulations for visas. This is Bully's story and it may coincide with that of other fellow African migrants, but it is not to be generalized. Another small yet meaningful detail in the publishers' paragraph on the back cover is that Bully is not just a foreigner but a foreign person, denoting how among many other qualifiers he may also have in addition to being foreign.

Despite these details, the publisher's voice on the back cover still suggests that Bully's voice is not to be listened to in his own right, but because he embodies the desirable 'good immigrant,' who is well-integrated into the "socio-cultural environment of our country." This sentence can be illuminated by Gayatri Spivak's resonant question: "Can the subaltern speak?" (Spivak). Spivak wondered about the difficulty—or impossibility—of subaltern women to produce narrative, to be able to speak as political subjects in a patriarchal India. The essay—and the question in its title—has been recurrently evoked in postcolonial studies to question whether Western scholars studying the colonized reproduce the conditions of marginality of the studied subjects and whether subaltern subjects in general (colonized, working class, women, among others) are able to get their voices and perspectives through. Spivak's claim resounds when we wonder how other is Bully's account to the stories told about immigration. How is his narration modeled to be "tell-able"?

As explored in the previous chapters, the reviews elaborated by the S.O.L. experts speak of a mediation in which a divide between 'us' (the Spaniards) and 'them' (the foreigners and people with foreign backgrounds) is set clear. This divide appears to be reproduced again in this book when its peritextual material refers to 'our country.' In this work, I have traced how the construction of alterity opposes the positive self-presentation of the group of 'us' (the Europeans) welcoming the Other, the migrant. Foreign people are rarely depicted in (explicitly) negative ways, yet this positive self-presentation, as Teun van Dijk claims conveys (White) supremacy in an indirect way (van Dijk *Racism and Discourse in Spain and Latin America* 6). Immigrants are invited to integrate but are, nevertheless, subject to essentialized identities suggesting (and explaining) their exclusion. In this world order, the migrant characters lack agency and are in need of the interventions of the locals. Immigrants are presumably grateful for the help provided; we cannot find, for example, any example or episode in which a migrant refuses to be helped by the locals apart from that of the African Amadou that manages to get through helping rather than being helped by his Spanish 'rescuer,' Rita. As Mireille Rosello argues, migrants in Europe inherit a "perpetual identity as guests" (Rosello 127) without the possibility of exercising a right to feel at home.

In Chapter 4, I identified recurrent tropes in the depiction of foreigners as exotic, connected to ancestral traditions, and to nature, while local characters welcome this difference. Many stories evolve around what happens when a migrant child comes into a new class feeling isolated, a problem usually solved after the teacher or a local classmate intervenes making the child realize that she or he is welcomed. Spanish society is recurrently depicted as homogenous and White but open to diversity and embodying that European ideal of commitment to equality. Nevertheless, foreign origins end up explaining exclusions. The books that refer to irregular immigration—such as those analyzed in more detail in Chapter 7—end up reproducing the idea of a need to control the borders. Even if stories such as *Viruta* and *El balonazo* attempt to serve as instruments to deal with the migration phenomenon from an inclusive and self-critical perspective, the way these stories are resolved speak of a need to naturalize exclusion rather than the other way around. European humanitarism is, nevertheless, entrusted with the responsibility of protecting its territory.

In Chapter 5, I explore the rather inexplicit approaches to 'race' and racism showing how in most cases the foreign characters feel isolated but are not portrayed—at least not recurrently—as experiencing (racist) discrimination. In the few explicit depictions of racism, the perpetrator quickly fades out from the story and is never blamed. These narrations suggest that the best possible reaction to racism is to ignore it and carry on. Mediators might, of course, foster a critical reading of these texts encouraging the questioning of the perpetrators attitudes, yet at least the S.O.L. reviews do not encourage these readings.

The plot structure and perspective put forward in *Bully. Yo vengo de...* is quite different. Bully overstays a tourist visa and works on the black market until he succeeds in obtaining a residence permit, a very common process for migrants coming from outside Europe (cf. González-Enríquez). The book recounts the unfairness and difficulties he faced, and depicts the treatments irregular immigrants receive: he tells about the extremely low wages, about a local government that harassed migrants even when they already had residence permits, and about violent racist attacks against his fellow African neighbors. Yet, as in the other books, Bully does not take civic or political action against the discrimination but understands the incidents as trials to be endured. Bully is a model immigrant, perhaps because he is able to understand that if he decided to come, he should not complain. Bully can just hope for things to get better and works hard for them. With this resilient approach he manages to get a better job, proper housing, buy a car, get married, and have children. In *Bully. Yo vengo de Doubirou*, assimilation, integration, and exclusion are deeply intertwined.

We are told that Bully is an integrated immigrant, and we may wonder what integration means here. Bully understands and praises many different features of Catalonia and is able to speak both Spanish and Catalan, while he is proud to tell that his children will probably speak these languages better than him. He is a Muslim, but he says in Spain he came to realize that all religions are equally valid. Moreover, he also openly questions some doctrines of the religious culture in which he was raised:

> "La planificación familiar es un tema polémico para algunas religiones. En mi pueblo hay la convicción de que tener muchos hijos es sinónimo de riqueza y prueba de gratitud divina. Yo prefiero tener pocos niños y poder cubrir sus necesidades." (34)

> [Birth control is a controversial topic in some religions. In my village, the conviction is that having many children reveals wealth and divine gratitude. I prefer to have few children and to be able to cover their needs].

Notably, Bully questions Islam precisely in its attention to family planning, which is often related to ideas of immigrants taking advantage of European welfare system, since with their numerous family members, they would get housing benefits (Doughty). In this paragraph, integration appears to be close to assimilation, yet, in another fragment Bully tells us how he is part of a close-knit diaspora community with whom he celebrates festivities and provides assistance to newly arrived migrants. This assistance, nevertheless, follows the rules imposed by the host land. For example, Bully warns us that immigrating today is not as easy as it was when he came, and that even if there are companies willing to employ people without permits, it is illegal to do so. Bully reproduces that pro-diversity discourse in which migrants are welcomed yet the most common form of migration (irregular migration) is condemned. He also reproduces that paradox in which irregular immigration is widely tolerated, but still illegal.

We are told that Bully has successfully integrated, but he shares a plan to move back with his family to set up a business in his homeland. Bully embodies that figure of the Gastarbeiter, a term originally designated to refer to the workers who came primarily from Turkey to Germany in the 1960s and 1970s in the frame of agreements with different countries to provide the booming industry with much needed labor. The Gastarbeiter were expected to move back after some years, even if most of them stayed. The German term for 'guest worker' speaks to that paradigm in which immigrants are guests, whereas the locals take the powerful position of hosts, and—moreover—it suggests that they are welcome as long as they are productive. Throughout this book, we have analyzed how the good immigrant is the productive immigrant who contributes to the local work force as an employee. Bully, as a model immigrant, is happy to be a guest and is grateful to his hosts.

A question that has surfaced at several points in this work is that revolving around how these stories seek for affective investments of the readers and how they may be related to the reproduction of national belonging. A study of reader engagement would probably unveil how readers make sense of these books in different ways to those planned or imagined by the writer/publisher/mediator. The question here, neverthe-less, is not about possible readings but about the type of readers these books appear to be looking for. What do these books and the ways they are recommended tell us about belonging and exclusion?

I compare books that depict adopted and migrant characters based on the understanding that international adoption of children is a form of migration. International adoptees share with migrant children countries of origin and physical features. They are subjects of similar processes of racialization. Migrant and adopted children also share being taken from one to another land without being consulted about their wishes.

As explained in Chapter 3, many of the books about adoption are written by adoptive parents or their close friends based upon the stories they use to tell to their adopted children; these stories are meant to assist adoptees in their formation of (racialized) narrative identities. In past de-cades, adopted characters in children's literature were resilient orphans who, after numerous misfortunes, were lucky enough to be encountered and cared for by a loving family. In the books analyzed here, the stories start either with the adoption process or by presenting the adopted child: the past and misfortunes are quickly overcome. Instead of revolving around abandonment, these stories stress the unbreakable commitment of the adoptive parents: they narrate and, moreover, perform the family, overwriting the abandonment and dismissing that shared narrative of the family as a bond built by blood.

Notably, books about adoption are aimed at adopted children and their siblings, whereas those about immigration are not recommended to readers with migrant backgrounds. Following the S.O.L. reviews, the imagined reader of the books about immigration is one of 'us,' a group clearly distinguished from 'them' (the foreigners). In this division we may trace those different approaches to origin—flexible for adoptees and essentialized for migrants—as well as certain ideas on how read-ing and writing may have an effect upon identity construction. Books about adoption may be taken as examples of "bibliotherapy" (Crago 183) meant to heal the (traumatic) past of the adopted child through the performance of belonging to the adoptive family and, by extension, to the adoptive land. The telling of the right story transforms that past into a narrated origin presented under the light of privilege and exoti-cism. In this transformation, 'race' becomes an ethnicity to be proud of and, moreover, becomes the mark of a magical explanation. Adoptees are transformed into one-of-kin through magical transubstantiation: we cannot explain their existence by following only rational explanations. As I trace in Chapter 3, stories about adoption do recall biblical narra-tives that may respond to this need to invoke the magical and religious to explain that (new) form of family reproduction. The stories about adoption are to be opposed to the odds of global circulation of children and stratified reproduction.

Adopted children appear to form a group of reader-citizens requiring us to adapt cultural scripts that have limited the family to its biological norm. Books featuring immigration, contrastingly, do not aim to rewrite the scripts that organize our understanding of the world. Not only are simple stereotypes reproduced in them, but national borders are also produced and reproduced. Cultural diversity appears to be welcome only if the Other plays the role of a (grateful) guest and the locals can feel safe while being tolerant and open hosts.

This opposition appears to inform the initiatives of La Galera, a renowned publisher committed to pro-diversity approaches. As mentioned before, *Bully. Yo vengo de Doiborou* was one of the first books about immigration by La Galera. This ego-document is part of a series that includes biographical accounts by migrants of diverse origins: Reykjavik, Belgrade, Nador, Jehlum, Guajará-Mirim, Cochabamba, Benin, Marruecos, Noruega, Estados Unidos, El Salvador, Japan, and China. The last of these titles was published in 2001, a year usually marked as the turning point in the discourse about immigration and belonging following the 9/11 attacks. Nira Yuval-Davis argues in *The Politics of Belonging: Intersectional Contestations* that the question of who is 'a stranger' and who 'does not belong' was modified along with growing ethnic, cultural, and religious tensions in the aftermath of 9/11: "The politics of belonging have come to occupy the heart of the political agenda almost everywhere in the world, even when reified assumptions about 'the class of civilizations' (Huntington, 1993) are not necessarily applied" (Yuval-Davis *The Politics of Belonging: Intersectional Contestations* 2). In children's literature these tensions are downplayed, yet they certainly underpin the stories written, published, and recommended.

Some years after interrupting the collection of testimonial books about immigration, La Galera launched a series about international adoption. These books also shared a common title only modified according to the origin country: *Llegué de (…). Cuéntame mi historia* [I arrived from (…). Tell me my story]. A comparison of the title templates in these two collections is already quite revealing of the opposed discourses in relation to belonging. The ones about immigrants use either "yo soy de" (I am from) or "yo vengo de" (I came from); in both cases the present tense indicates that the geographical origin is not just a departure point but a place where they are (always) coming from. Instead, in the collection about adoption, origin is referred to in past tense—'I came from'— conveying how identity is constructed by that journey: the story told in each picturebook will explain this origin while de-essentializing it. The two title templates reflect the tension between 'roots' and 'routes:' migrants are uprooted when abroad and will go back to their origin (roots) at a certain point, while adoptees have trajectories (routes) to acknowledge and tell. Migrants are always coming, following their routes, whereas adoptees have arrived and allowed to grow roots that are forbidden to the "permanent guest" immigrants.

An approach to these books as examples of testimonial life writing illuminates what these stories are meant to do. Both series are inspired by real events, yet they differ in what is expected from this account. The 'tell me my story' in the title of the books about adoptions puts forward the idea that the adoptee has the right to a special narrative identity. In Bully's book, contrastingly, we do not find traces of an acknowledgment of how events are mediated and enacted through the telling of stories.

The visual narration in these books also fleshes out differing approaches to the testimonial. The collection about adoption has low modality and referentiality (cf. Kress and Van Leeuwen 158–63): the illustrations have no backgrounds, they use very simple lines and saturated colors. The front covers are indicative of this approach, presenting the adopted child dressed up in folkloric outfits and reduced to "clean" stereotypes. These books are not to be taken as documentary, but as mediated and simplified accounts of lived experiences. The series about immigration, on the other hand, has a very different cover design: in them, the characters are introduced with a picture of the protagonist with his or her family and a background picture with a detailed map of the origin country. The books about migrants present these texts as testimonials and, moreover, emphasize how, through this testimony, the reader will learn true facts about life in a foreign country.

Both book series may be understood as fulfilling what Philippe Lejeune calls the autobiographical pact. In this pact the author, narrator, and protagonist of a story coincide (Lejeune). The pact appears to be looser in the books about adoption not only because of what I have mentioned about the visual narration, but also because the peritextual material does not explicitly identify the author with the narrator. They are and are not testimonial accounts, and this ambivalence opens up the story as a text to be appropriated by any child coming from the same country of origin. This ambivalence may also indicate a more flexible approach toward self-narration understanding how what occurred may be remediated and adapted to make a good story. The flexibility toward the 'facts' of the adoption may be paralleled with the relationship established in these books toward 'race,' as a category that is to be highlighted at the same time that it is dismissed and relabeled as ethnicity.

In this work, I put special focus on analyzing the interplay between the verbal and the visual, a focus that responds to the large number of picturebooks analyzed as well as to the topic at stake—'race,' a fundamentally visual mark of difference. As noted, 'race' is circumvented and frequently overlaps with ethnicity. New publications on cultural diversity often reproduce what I call the 'rainbow trope' in which diversity is superficially celebrated and reduced to colors—black, brown, yellow, white—that would comprise a beautiful rainbow, an aesthetic informed by a utopian discourse of sameness in which differences are neglected even if they appear to be welcomed. Most of the books analyzed here do reproduce the fiction of clear-cut classifications that end up naturalizing the socio-construct of 'race' at the same time that they pass on a color-blind ideology. An exception to this approach may be noted in *Los colores de nuestra piel*, a book originally published in the United States in which a girl realizes that skin tones are enormously varied and nearly unclassifiable.[2]

As mentioned in Chapter 2, most of the translated books recommended by the S.O.L. were originally published in other European countries, which may reflect a pan-European approach to 'race,' cultural diversity, and migration discourses. We do find one praised and awarded American title among the list, *Madlenka*, by Peter Sís. Madlenka depicts a multicultural Manhattan in which foreigners are rigidly stereotyped yet the idea of a city encompassing different worlds is presented and celebrated. I read this book inquiring into the interplay of the verbal and the visual in Chapter 5 to argue how the visual conveys meanings that a power-sensitive verbal text suppresses. As argued there, *Madlenka*—as the much-praised German book *Wie ich Papa die Angst vor Fremden nahm*—presents foreign characters who are not only connected to exotic regions but are also subordinated to a colonial epistemology that founds ethnocentrism. The close reading of the multimodality in these awarded picturebooks suggests that the polysemic image inherits the world order of White supremacy. This is found not only in the visual narration of sophisticated picturebooks, but also in a number of books in which the locals are always White and opposed to racially marked characters.

Strikingly, in these books recommended to educate children about cultural diversity, identity appears to be fixed and unchangeable. We find only scarce references to the tension between projected social identities and everyday life practices in which individuals appropriate and modify social codes. *Bully. Yo vengo de…* may be one of the few cases in which an ethnocentric narrative is contended, yet it still reproduces categories of 'race' and ethnicity that are bound to the reproduction of belonging and exclusion. That the book is written by an author of the same minority group represented marks a difference from other approaches, yet meanings are still not subverted and that trope of the good and grateful guest immigrant is still reproduced.

¿Cuál es mi color? originally published in French as *Quelle est ma couleur?*, may be the only example in which the protagonist reflects critically on how different identities are projected onto him. The Spaniards consider him to be Arab, and Arabs to be a Spanish child, since he was born and raised there. The boy understands these categories as fictional projections always depending on a context, and he resists internalizing them. The protagonist mentions, for instance, how we may find Spanish people with different racial features. In *¿Cuál es mi color?*, people may

be associated with a multiplicity of social identities without it being problematic. The story avoids that integration narrative in which foreigners adapt to local practices and, moreover, it playfully avoids the binary opposition between local and foreign as one of many categorizations that we could eliminate. The book ends with a picture of the boy lying face up on his bed yawning half naked and upside down with his feet by the headboard. He looks relaxed while also ready to start the day. His dog awaits him with a red ball, and the boy exclaims: "Mi perro sí que lo ha comprendido. ¡Él es de muchos colores!" [my dog really got it. He has many colors!].

Notes

1 However, it is not the only one by an author who has immigrated: Peter Sís, the author of *Madlenka* immigrated from the Czech Republic to the United States; a German illustrator based in Barcelona, Stephanie Pfeil, authored *Pipocas*; and Rafik Schami, a German author born in Syria and one of the leading figures of *Migrantenliteratur*, depicts a family of African origin in *Wie ich Papa die Angst vor Fremden nahm*.
2 Originally published as *The Colors of Us* by Karen Katz.

Works Cited

Abril, Paco and María Luisa Torcida. *¿Sóis Vosotros Los Reyes Magos?* Barcelona: La Galera and Anne Decis, 2002. Print.

Abril, Paco. *Colores Que Se Aman.* León: Everest, 2008. Print.

Alamán, Olga and Clara Roca. *¿Cómo Es El Color Carne?* Barcelona: Destino, 2004. Print.

Anónimo. *Mi Madre.* Oxfam, 2009. Print.

Arnal, Txabi and Hassan Amekan. *Caja De Cartón.* Pontevedra: O'QO Editora, 2010. Print.

Benavides González, Antonio and Jesús Egido. *Buscando a Baltazar.* Madrid: Didáctico, 2003. Print.

Cannals, Anna and Luci Gutiérrez. *Llegué De Etiopía... Cuéntame Mi Historia.* Barcelona: La Galera, 2005. Print.

Capdevila, Bet. *Un Ordenador Muy Especial.* Barcelona: Cromosoma, 2009. Print.

Casalderrey, Fina. *Isha, Nacida Del Corazón.* Madrid: Edebé, 2006. Print.

Curtis, Jamie Lee. *Cuéntame Otra Vez De La Noche Que Nací.* Barcelona: Serres, 2008. Print.

Denou, Violeta. *Teo Aprende a Convivir.* Barcelona: CEAC, 2003. Print.

Duran, Teresa. *Mila Va Al Cole.* Barcelona: La Galera, 1998. Print.

Elfa, Albert and Luci Gutiérrez. *Llegué De ....Rusia: Cuéntame Mi Historia.* Barcelona: La Galera, 2005. Print.

Falip Esther, Joan Molet and Luci Gutiérrez. *Llegué De... Ucrania: Cuéntame Mi Historia.* Barcelona: La Galera, 2005. Print.

Farías, Marta and Aitana Carrasco. *El Viaje Del Bisabuelo.* Sevilla: Kalandraka, 2008. Print.

Fernández Paz, Agustín. *Luna De Senegal.* Madrid: Anaya, 2009. Print.

Folgueira, Ana and Emilio Amade. *En Algún Lugar De China.* Madrid: Syllabus, 2009. Print.

Fossette, Daniele. *El Árbol De Los Abuelos.* Zaragoza: Edelvives, 2002. Print.

García, J., M. Martín, and I. Furlanetto. *Todos Los Colores Del Arcoiris.* Bilbao: MPC Ediciones, 2005. Print.

Gibert, Miquel and Luci Gutiérrez. *Llegué De ....China: Cuéntame Mi Historia.* Barcelona: La Galera, 2005. Print.

Gopegui, Belén. *El balonazo.* Madrid: Ediciones Sm, 2008. Print.

Greder, Armin. *La Isla: Una Historia Cotidiana.* Salamanca: Lóguez, 2003. Print.

Guilloppé, Antoine. *¿Cuál Es Mi Color?* Madrid: Anaya, 2006. Print.

Guinea, J. and M. J. Cordero. *Una Fiesta Sin Igual.* Bilbao: A fortiori, 2011. Print.

Janer Manila, Gabriel. *Mehdi Y Las Lunas Del Zoo.* Barcelona: Edebé, 2005. Print.

Jangana, Bully. *Bully. Yo Vengo De Doubirou.* Barcelona: La Galera/Associación de Maestros Rosa Sensat, 1998. Print.

Katz, Karen. *Los Colores De Nuestra Piel.* Barcelona: Intermon Oxfam, 2005. Print.

Lembcke, Marjaleena. *Susana Ojos Negros.* Madrid: Barco de Vapor, 2003. Print.

Lenain, Thierry. *Toño Se Queda Solo.* Zaragoza: Edelvives, 2006. Print.

Lewis, Rose and Jane Dyer. *Te Quiero, Niña Bonita.* Barcelona: Serres, 2003. Print.

Limb, Sue. *Ruby Rogers, ¿Te Lo Puedes Creer?* Madrid: Anaya, 2009. Print.

Lofthouse, Liz. *Ziba Vino En Barco.* Salamanca: Loguez, 2008. Print.

Martínez Gimeno, Carmen. *Viruta.* Zaragoza: Edelvives, 2005. Print.

Montoriol, Mónica and Luci Gutiérrez. *Llegué De... Colombia: Cuéntame Mi Historia.* Barcelona: La Galera, 2005. Print.

Neuschafer-Carlon, Mercedes. *Antonio En El País Del Silencio.* León: Everest, 1999. Print.

Pellicer i Sòria, María Dolors and Eva Garcés. *La Mirada De Ahmed.* Valencia: Tándem Edicions, 2007. Print.

Pfeil, Stephanie. *¿Pipocas?, ¿Qué Es Eso?* Barcelona: Takatuka, 2009. Print.

Piquemal, Michel. *Mi Miel, Mi Dulzura.* Edelvives: Zaragoza, 2005. Print.

Piumini, Roberto. *El Diario De La.* Zaragoza: Edelvives, 2007. Print.

Ponç Pons and Francesc Rovira. *El Rey Negro.* Barcelona: La Galera, SAU, 2002. Print.

Prats Pijoan, Joan de Déu. *Noche De Reyes.* Barcelona: Edebé, 2002. Print.

Raventós, Joan, Queti Vinyals and Luci Gutiérrez. *Llegue De ....Nepal: Cuéntame Mi Historia.* Barcelona: La Galera, 2005. Print.

Recorvits, Helen and Gabi Swiatkowska. *Me Llamo Yoon.* Barcelona: Editorial Juventud, 2006. Print.

Recorvits, Helen and Gabi Swiatkowska. *Yoon Y La Pulsera De Jade.* Barcelona: Juventud, 2009. Print.

Rodríguez, Mónica. *La Bicicleta De Selva.* Madrid: Anaya, 2010. Print.

Sarti, Javier. *Blanca Y Viernes.* Madrid: Anaya, 2007. Print.

Say, Allen. *Té Con Leche.* León: Everest, 2001. Print.

Schami, Rafik and Ole Könnecke. *Cómo Curé a Papá De Su Miedo a Los Extraños.* Barcelona: RqueR Editorial, 2005. Print.

Schimel, Lawrence and Alba Marina Rivera. *¡Vamos a Ver a Papá!* Barcelona: Ekaré, 2010. Print.

Schwarz, Annelies. *Mi Abuela Es Africana.* Zaragoza: Edelvives, 2003. Print.

Sís, Peter. *Madlenka.* Barcelona: Blumen, 2001. Print.

Sotorra, Andreu. *Korazón De Pararrayos.* Madrid: Edebé, 2003. Print.

Torner, Carles. *Noaga Y Juana.* Barcelona: Octaedro, 1997. Print.

Torras, Meri and Mikel Valverde. *Mi Hermana Aixa.* Barcelona: La Galera, 2006. Print.

Uribe, Kirmen and Mikel Valverde. *No Soy Rubia.* Barcelona: Editores Asociados, 2004. Print.

Valverde, Mikel. *Rita Robinson.* Madrid: McMillan, 2008. Print.

Vantal, Anne. *¿Por Qué No Tengo Los Ojos Azules?* Zaragoza: Edelvives, 2005. Print.

Villanueva Sanz, David. *Wamba Y El Viaje De La Miel.* Madrid: Demipage, 2005. Print.

Wilsdorf, Anne. *Yuyuba.* Ed. Barcelona: Destino, 2000. Print.

Zubizarreta, Patxi and Noemí Villamuza. *Sola Y Sincola.* Zaragoza: Edelvives, 2005. Print.

Zubizarreta, Patxi and Elena Odriozola. *Usoa, Llegaste Por El Aire.* Barcelona: La Galera, 1999. Print.

References

Abbey, Ruth. "Liberalism, Pluralism, Multiculturalism: Contemporary Debates." *Modern Pluralism: Anglo-American Debates since 1880.* Ed. Bevir, M.: Cambridge University Press, 2012. 154–78. Print.

Abdallah-Pretceille, Martine. "Interculturalism as a Paradigm for Thinking About Diversity." *Intercultural Education* 17.5 (2006): 475–83. Print.

Andrews, Molly. *Shaping History: Narratives of Political Change.* Cambridge University Press, 2007. Print.

Andrews, Molly, Corinne Squire and Maria Tamboukou. *Doing Narrative Research.* SAGE Publications, 2013. Print.

Anónimo. Auto De Los Reyes Magos. 2012. Web <https://books.google.ch/books?id=KStZcApLsO8C>.

Anthias, Flora and Nira Yuval-Davis. *Racialized Boundaries: Race, Nation, Gender, Colour and Class and the Anti-Racist Struggle.* Taylor & Francis, 1993. Print.

Appadurai, Arjun. *Modernity at Large: Cultural Dimensions of Globalization.* U of Minnesota P, 1996. Print.

Appiah, Anthony K. "Identity, Authenticity, Survival: Multicultural Societies and Social Reproduction." *Multiculturalism* (Expanded Paperback Edition). Ed. Gutmann, A. Princeton, NJ: Princeton UP, 1994. 149–64. Print.

———. "Race, Culture, Identity: Misunderstood Connections." The Tanner Lectures on Human Values. 1994. Print.

Arizpe, Evelyn, Teresa Colomer and Carmen Martínez-Roldán. *Visual Journeys through Wordless Narratives: An International Inquiry with Immigrant Children and the Arrival.* Bloomsbury Publishing, 2014. Print.

Arizpe, Evelyn, Caroline Bagelman, Alison M. Devlin, Maureen Farrell and Julie E. McAdam. "Visualizing Intercultural Literacy: Engaging Critically with Diversity and Migration in the Classroom through an Image-Based Approach." *Language and Intercultural Communication* 14.3 (2014): 304–21. Print.

Baaz, M.E. *The Paternalism of Partnership: A Postcolonial Reading of Identity in Development Aid.* Zed Books, 2005. Print.

Baker, Martin. *The New Racism: Conservatives and the Ideology of the Tribe.* London: Junction Books (1981). Print.

Bal, Mieke. "Introduction: Another Kind of Image." *Nomadikon.* Web. 02–08–2012.

———. *Narratology: Introduction to the Theory of Narrative.* U of Toronto P, 1997. Print.

Balibar, Étienne. "Is There a 'Neo-Racism'?" *Race, Nation, Class: Ambiguous Identities.* Eds. Balibar, E. and I.M. Wallerstein: Verso, 1991. 17–28. Print.

Barker, Chris. *Cultural Studies: Theory and Practice.* SAGE Publications, 2007. Print.

Barrena, Pablo. "Phone Interview." 25.11.13.

Bassnett, Susanne. *Translation Studies.* Taylor & Francis, 2002. Print.

Bebiroglu, Neda and Ellen Pinderhughes. "Mothers Raising Daughters: New Complexities in Cultural Socialization for Children Adopted from China." *Adoption Quarterly* 15.2 (2012): 116–39. Print.

Beck, Ulrich and Elizabeth Beck-Gernsheim. *The Normal Chaos of Love.* Wiley, 1995. Print.

Beller, Manfred and Joep T. Leerssen. *Imagology: The Cultural Construction and Literary Representation of National Characters: A Critical Survey.* Rodopi, 2007. Print.

Bergquist, Kathleen Ja Sook. "Operation Babylift or Babyabduction? Implications of the Hague Convention on the Humanitarian Evacuation and 'Rescue' of Children." *International Social Work* 52.5 (2009): 621–33. Print.

Bernstein, Robin. *Racial Innocence: Performing American Childhood from Slavery to Civil Rights.* New York UP, 2011. Print.

Bhabha, Homi K. *The Location of Culture.* Taylor & Francis, 2004. Print.

Bonilla-Silva, Eduardo. *Racism without Racists: Color-Blind Racism and the Persistence of Racial Inequality in the United States.* Rowman & Littlefield Publishers, 2010. Print.

Booth, Wayne. *The Rhetoric of Fiction.* U of Chicago P, 1983. Print.

Botelho, M.J., and M.K. Rudman. *Critical Multicultural Analysis of Children's Literature: Mirrors, Windows, and Doors.* Taylor & Francis, 2009. Print.

Bourdieu, Pierre. "Intellectual Field and Creative Project." *Social Science Information* 8.2 (1969): 89–119. Print.

Bradford, Clare. *Unsettling Narratives: Postcolonial Readings of Children's Literature.* Wilfrid Laurier UP, 2007. Print.

Brodzinsky, Daniel. "Long-Term Outcomes in Adoption." *The Future of Children* 3 3.1 (1993): 153–66. Print.

Bruner, Jerome. *The Culture of Education.* Harvard UP, 1996. Print.

———. "Life as Narrative." *Social Research* 54.1 (1987). Print.

———. "Self-Making and World-Making." *Narrative and Identity: Studies in Autobiography, Self and Culture.* Eds. Brockmeier, Jens and D.A. Carbaugh: John Benjamins Publishing Company, 2001. 25–38. Print.

Burchianti, Flora and Ricard Zapata-Barrero. "Is Catalonia Immune to Racism? An Analysis of Intolerant Political Discourses of Mainstream Party Representatives (2010, 2011)." *Journal of Immigrant & Refugee Studies* 12.4 (2014): 401–17. Print.

Burton, Richard Francis. *Book of the Thousand Nights and a Night.* Kessinger Publishing, 2003. Print.

Cai, Mingshui. *Multicultural Literature for Children and Young Adults.* Information Age Publishing, 2006. Print.

Callahan, Cinthya. *Kin of Another Kind: Transracial Adoption in American Literature.* U of Michigan P, 2011. Print.

Calvo Buezas, Tomás. *Inmigración Y Racismo: Así Sienten Los Jóvenes Del Siglo Xxi.* Madrid: Cauce, 2000. Print.

Campani, Giovanna. "The Role and Forms of Education." *Europe's New Racism: Causes, Manifestations, and Solutions.* Ed. Foundation, Evens: Berghahn Books, 2002. 165–86. Print.

Campbell, Fiona A. Kumari. "Exploring Internalized Ableism Using Critical Race Theory." *Disability & Society* 23.2 (2008): 151–62. Print.

Canal Lector. "Te con Leche" Webpage. http://www.canallector.com/1161/ T%C3%A9_con_leche Retrieved 06.02.17.

Carp, E. Wayne. *Family Matters: Secrecy and Disclosure in the History of Adoption*. Cambridge, MA: Harvard UP, 1998. Print.

Carrington, B., and I. Mcdonald. *'Race', Sport and British Society*. Taylor & Francis, 2002. Print.

Carroll, Nöell. "Narrative Closure." *Philosophical Studies* 135.1 (2007): 1–15. Print.

Cartwright, Lisa. "Photographs of 'Waiting Children': The Transnational Adoption Market." *Social Text* 74 (2003): 83–109. Print.

Casalilla Galán, Juan Alonso, Fernando Antonio Bermejo Cuadrillero and Asunción Romero González. *Manual Para La Valoración De La Idoneidad En Adopción Internacional*. Madrid: Instituto Madrileño del Menor y la Familia, 2008. Print.

Castañeda, Claudia. "Adopting Technologies: Producing Race in Trans-Racial Adoption." *Scholar and Feminist Online* 9.1/9.2 (2011): 1–5.

Cheng, V.J. *Inauthentic: The Anxiety over Culture and Identity*. New Brunswick: Rutgers UP, 2004. Print.

Colomer, Teresa, Bettina Kümmerling-Meibauer and Cecilia Silva-Diaz. *New Directions in Picturebook Research*. Taylor & Francis, 2012. Print.

Colomer, Teresa. *Andar Entre Libros. La Lectura Literaria En La Escuela*. Mexico: Fondo de Cultura Económica, 2005. Print.

Colomer, Teresa and Martina Fittipaldi. *La Literatura Que Acoge: Inmigración Y Lectura De Álbumes*. Eds. Colomer, Teresa and Martina Fittipaldi. Barcelona: Banco del Libro, Gretel, 2012. Print.

Cooperative Children's Book Center. "Publishing Statistics on Children's Books About People of Color and First/Native Nations and by People of Color and First/Native Nations." 2015. Web.

Corkill, David. "Multiple Identities, Immigration and Racism in Spain and Portugal." *Nation and Identity in Contemporary Europe*. Eds. Jenkins, Brian and Sofos Spyros. London: Routledge, 1996. 155–71. Print.

Coy, Patrick and Lynne Woehrle. *Social Conflicts and Collective Identities*. Rowman & Littlefield Publishers, 2000. Print.

Crago, Hugo. *"Can Stories Heal?" Understanding Children's Literature*. London: Routledge (1999). Print.

Crenshaw, Kimberlé Williams. "Mapping the Margins: Intersectionality, Identity, Politics, and Violence against Women of Color." *Critical Race Theory: The Key Writings That Formed the Movement*. Ed. Crenshaw, Kimberlé Williams and Neil Gotanda, Gary Peller and Kendall Thomas. New York: New York P, 1995. Print.

Dahlen, Sarah Park. "Evaluating Children's Books About Transracial Asian Adoption." *Diversity in Youth Literature: Opening Doors through Reading*. Ed. Dahlen, Jamie Campbell Naidoo and Sarah Park. Chicago: ALA Editions, 2013. Print.

Dahlen, Sarah Park and Lies Wesseling. "On Constructing Fictions and Families." *Children's Literature Association Quarterly* 40.4 (2015): 317–21. Print.

Davis, Kathy. "Intersectionality as Buzzword: A Sociology of Science Perspective on What Makes a Feminist Theory Successful." *Feminist Theory* 9.1 (2008): 67–85. Print.

Davis, M.A. *Children for Families or Families for Children: The Demography of Adoption Behavior in the U.S.* Springer, 2011. Print.

De Graeve, Karin. "The Limits of Intimate Citizenship: Reproduction of Difference in Flemish-Ethiopian 'Adoption Cultures'." *Bioethics* 24.7 (2010): 365–72. Print.

de Sousa Santos, Boaventura. *Toward a New Legal Common Sense: Law, Globalization, and Emancipation.* Butterworths, 2002. Print.

Del Olmo, Margarita. "La Articulación De La Diversidad En La Escuela: Un Proyecto De Investigación En Curso Sobre Las 'Aulas De Enlace'." *Revista de dialectología y tradiciones populares* 62.1 (2007): 187–203. Print.

Delgado, Richard and Jean Stefancic. *Critical Race Theory: An Introduction.* New York UP, 2012. Print.

Derksen, Maarten. "Race." *Imagology: The Cultural Construction and Literary Representation of National Characters: A Critical Survey.* Eds. Beller, M. and J.T. Leersen. Amsterdam/New York: Rodopi, 2007. Print.

Donald, James and Ali Rattansi. *Race, Culture and Difference.* SAGE Publications, 1992. Print.

Dorow, Sara K. "Racialized Choices: Chinese Adoption and the 'White Noise' of Blackness." *Critical Sociology* 32.2–3 (2006): 357–79. Print.

———. *Transnational Adoption: A Cultural Economy of Race, Gender, and Kinship.* New York UP, 2006. Print.

Doughty, Steve. "Revealed: How 500,000 Immigrants Have Been Given Social Housing in Last Decade as Number of Families on Waiting List Hits Record High." *Mail Online* (2013). Web. 10.08.2015.

DuBois, Laurent. *Soccer Empire: The World Cup and the Future of France.* U of California P, 2010. Print.

Dyer, Richard. *White.* Taylor & Francis, 1997. Print.

Eagleton, Terry. *Ideology: An Introduction.* Verso, 1991. Print.

Eccleshare, Julia. "Are There Any Good Books for Children About Homelessness?" *The Guardian* 10.08.2015 2015. Print.

Eng, David L. "Transnational Adoption and Queer Diasporas." *Social Text* 21.1 74 (2003): 1–37. Print.

Eurostat. "Migration and Migrant Population Statistics." (2012). Print.

Ewers, Hans Heino. *Fundamental Concepts of Children's Literature Research: Literary and Sociological Approaches.* Routledge, 2011. Print.

Fabian, Johannes. *Time and the Other: How Anthropology Makes Its Object.* Columbia UP, 1983. Print.

Fish, Stanley. "Boutique Multiculturalism, or Why Liberals Are Incapable of Thinking About Hate Speech." *Critical Inquiry* 23.2 (1997): 378–95. Print.

Fisher, Walter R. *Human Communication as Narration: Toward a Philosophy of Reason, Value and Action.* U of South Carolina P, 1989. Print.

Fonseca, Claudia, Diana Marre, Anna Uziel and Adriana Vianna. "El principio del 'interés superior' de la niñez tras dos décadas de prácticas: perspectivas comparativas" *Scripta Nova. Revista Electrónica de Geografía y Ciencias Sociales.* [En línea]. Barcelona: Universidad de Barcelona" XVI. 395 (2012). Web.

Fox, Dana and Kathy Short. *Stories Matter: The Complexity of Cultural Authenticity in Children's Literature.* National Council of Teachers of English, 2003. Print.

Friedman, Michael. "Ernst Cassirer." *The Stanford Encyclopedia of Philosophy*. Spring (2011). Web. 15.05.2014.

Fulcher, James and John Scott. *Sociology*. OUP Oxford, 2011. Print.

García Alonso, Mariemma. "Recursos Bibliográficos Y Documentales Para Tratar La Inmigración En Las Aulas." *Tabanque: Revista pedagógica* 22 (2009): 71–85. Print.

García Castaño, F. Javier, Antolín Granados Martínez and Lorenzo Capellán de Toro. "Presencia E Imagen De La Inmigración Extranjera En Andalucía." *Perspectivas De La Inmigración En España: Una Aproximación Desde El Territorio*. Eds. Gemma, Aubarell and Albert Roca Parés. Barcelona: Icaria Editorial, 2003. Print.

García González, Macarena and Elisabeth Wesseling. "Stories We Adopt By: Tracing 'the Red Thread' in Adoption Narratives, 1990–2010." *The Lion and the Unicorn* 37.3 (2013). Print.

Geertz, Clifford. *Local Knowledge: Further Essays in Interpretive Anthropology*. Basic Books, 1983. Print.

Geiger, Martin. "Exclusion and Inclusion of the Morrocan Immigrants: Empirical Evidences from Almería, Spain." *Migration, Mobility and Human Rights at the Eastern Border of the European Union - Space of Freedom and Security*. Ed. Silasi, G. Timisoara: Ed. University de Vest, 2008. 217. Print.

Giroux, Henry. "Living Dangerously: Identity Politics and the New Cultural Racism: Towards a Critical Pedagogy of Representation." *Cultural Studies*. Ed. Giroux, Henry: Taylor & Francis, 1993. Print.

González Alcantud, J.A. *Racismo Elegante: De La Teoría De Las Razas Culturales a La Invisibilidad Del Racismo Cotidiano*. Barcelona: Bellaterra, Ediciones S.A., 2011. Print.

González-Enríquez, Carmen. "Spain: Irregularity as a Rule." *Irregular Migration in Europe: Myths and Realities*. Ed. Triandafyllidou, A.: Ashgate Publishing, 2010. 247–66. Print.

Greimas, Julien. *On Meaning: Selected Writings in Semiotic Theory*. London: Frances Pinter, 1987. Print.

Hall, Stuart. "Introduction. Who Needs Identity?" *Questions of Cultural Identity*. Eds. du Gay, P. and S. Hall: SAGE Publications, 1996. Print.

———. "New Ethnicities." *Stuart Hall: Critical Dialogues in Cultural Studies*. Eds. Morley, D., D.M. Kuan-Hsing Chen and S. Hall: Taylor & Francis Group, 1996. 442–51. Print.

———. *Representation: Cultural Representations and Signifying Practices*. SAGE Publications, 1997. Print.

Happonen, Sirke. "On Representation, Modality and Movement in Picture Books for Children." *Visual History: Images of Education*. Eds. Mietzner, U., K. Myers and N. Peim: P. Lang, 2005. 55–84. Print.

Herman, David. *Basic Elements of Narrative*. Wiley, 2011. Print.

Hierro, Lola. "La Adolescencia De Las Niñas Mei Ming." *El País* 2014. Print.

Hillel, Margot. "'A Little Child Shall Lead Them' the Child as Redeemer." *Children's Literature and the Fin De Siècle*. Ed. McGillis, R.: Praeger, 2003. Print.

Hirsch, Marianne. *Family Frames: Photography, Narrative, and Postmemory*. Harvard UP, 1997. Print.

Hollindale, Peter. *Ideology and the Children's Book*. Thimble Press, 1988. Print.

Homans, Margaret. "Adoption Narratives, Trauma, and Origins." *Narrative* 14.1 (2006): 4–26. Print.

Home Affairs Division of the European Commission. "Family Reunification." 2013. Web. 04.10 2013.

Horning, Kathleen T., Merri V. Lindgren and Megan Schliesman. "A Few Observations on Publishing in 2012." Cooperative Children's Book Center (2013). Web.

Horskotte, Silke. "Seeing or Speaking: Visual Narratology and Focalization, Literature to Film." *Narratology in the Age of Cross-Disciplinary Narrative Research*. Eds. Heinen, S. and R. Sommer: Walter de Gruyter, 2009. Print.

Howell, Signe. *The Kinning of Foreigners: Transnational Adoption in a Global Perspective*. New York-Oxford: Berghahn Publishers, 2006. Print.

Howell, Signe and Diana Marre. "To Kin a Transnationally Adopted Child in Norway and Spain: The Achievement of Resemblances and Belonging." *Ethnos* 71.3 (2006): 293–316. Print.

Howell, Signe and Melhuus. "Mixed Race Families - Do They Exist? Some Criteria for Identity and Belonging in Contemporary Norway." *Race, Ethnicity and Nation: Perspectives from Kinship and Genetics*. Ed. Wade, P.: Berghahn Books, 2007. 73–94. Print.

Hübinette, Tobias. "Disembedded and Free-Floating Bodies out-of-Place and out-of-Control: Examining the Borderline Existence of Adopted Koreans." *Adoption & Culture: The Interdisciplinary Journal of the Alliance for the Study of Adoption and Culture* 1.1 (2007): 129–62. Print.

———. "International Adoption Is Harmful and Exploitive." *Issues in Adoption. Current Controversies*. Ed. Dudley, William. Farmington Hills: Greenhaven Press, 2006. 66–71. Print.

Hughes, Diane, James Rodriguez, Emilie P. Smith, Deborah J. Johnson, Howard C. Stevenson, Paul Spicer. "Parents' Ethnic-Racial Socialization Practices: A Review of Research and Directions for Future Study." *Developmental Psychology* 42.5 (2006): 747. Print.

Ibrahim, Maggie. "The Securitization of Migration: A Racial Discourse." *International Migration* 43.5 (2005): 163–87. Print.

International, Amnesty. *Stop Racism, Not People. Racial Profiling and Immigration Control in Spain*. London 2011. Print.

Jacey, Fortin. "Adopting from Africa: The Complicated Truth Behind a Celebrity Fad." *International Business Times* (2012). Web. 21.08.2015.

Jacobson, Heather. *Culture Keeping: White Mothers, International Adoption, and the Negotiation of Family Difference*. Vanderbilt UP, 2008. Print.

Jerng, Mark C. *Claiming Others: Transracial Adoption and National Belonging*. U of Minnesota P, 2010. Print.

Jiménez, Yasmina. "Sale a La Venta 'Wamba Y El Viaje De La Miel', Un Cuento Para Acercar a Los Niños El Drama De La Inmigración." *El Mundo* 2005. Print.

Joppke, Christian. "The Retreat of Multiculturalism in the Liberal State: Theory and Policy." *The British Journal of Sociology* 55.2 (2004): 237–57. Print.

Jung, S.J. *Piel Color Miel*. Girona: Rosell, 2008. Print.

Keeley, Brian. *International Migration: The Human Face of Globalization*. OECD Insights, 2009. Print.

Kim, Wun Jung. "International Adoption: A Case Review of Korean Children." *Child Psychiatry and Human Development* 25.3 (1995): 141–54. Print.

Kimball, Melanie A. "From Folktales to Fiction: Orphan Characters in Children's Literature." *Library Trends* 47.3 (1999): 558–78. Print.

Kleiner-Liebau, Desiree. *Migration and the Construction of National Identity in Spain*. Iberoamericana, 2009. Print.

Koss, Melanie D. "Diversity in Contemporary Picturebooks: A Content Analysis." *Journal of Children's Literature* 41.1 (2015): 32. Print.

Kress, Gunther and Theo Van Leeuwen. *Reading Images: The Grammar of Visual Design*. Taylor & Francis, 2006. Print.

Kuzmany, Stefan. "Preußler Und Die Kinderbuchdebatte: Sprachkampf Um Die "Hexe." Der Spiegel 2013: http://www.spiegel.de/kultur/literatur/otfried-preussler-und-die-debatte-ueber-veraltete-sprache-im-kinderbuch-a-884511.html. Print.

Lakoff, George. *Moral Politics: How Liberals and Conservatives Think*, Second Edition. U of Chicago P, 2002. Print.

Lakoff, George and Mark Johnson. *Metaphors We Live By*. Chicago: U of Chicago P, 2003. Print.

Langellier, Karin and Eric Peterson. *Storytelling in Daily Life: Performing Narrative*. Temple UP, 2004. Print.

Lanzieri, Giampaolo and Veronica Corsini. *Statistics in Focus: Eurostat*, 2006. Print.

Lee & Low Books. "Why Hasn't the Number of Multicultural Books Increased in Eighteen Years?" A blog on race, diversity, education, and children's books. The Open Book 2013. Web.

Leerssen, Joseph. "Imagology: History and Method." *Imagology: The Cultural Construction and Literary Representation of National Characters: A Critical Survey*. Eds. Beller, M. and J.T. Leersen. Amsterdam/New York: Rodopi, 2007. 17–32. Print.

Leersen, Joseph T. and Menno Spiering. *National Identity: Symbol and Representation*. Rodopi, 1991. Print.

Lejeune, Phillipe. *Le Pacte Autobiographique*. Seuil, 1975. Print.

Lentin, A., and G. Titley. *The Crises of Multiculturalism: Racism in a Neoliberal Age*. Zed Books, 2011. Print.

Lesnik-Oberstein, Karin. *Children's Literature: Criticism and the Fictional Child*. Clarendon Press, 1994. Print.

———. "Defining Children's Literature and Childhood." *International Companion Encyclopedia of Children's Literature*. Ed. Hunt, P.: Taylor & Francis, 2013. 15–29. Print.

Lewis, David. *Reading Contemporary Picturebooks: Picturing Text*. Taylor & Francis, 2001. Print.

Lewis, Reina. *Gendering Orientalism: Race, Femininity and Representation*. Taylor & Francis, 1995. Print.

Lo, Malinda. "2014 LGBT YA by the Numbers." http://www.malindalo.com 2014. Web.

———. "Perceptions of Diversity in Book Reviews." http://www.malindalo.com 2015. Web.

Lowery, Ruth McKoy. *Immigrants in Children's Literature*. P. Lang Publisher, 2001. Print.

MacCann, Donnarae. "Editor's Introduction: Racism and Antiracism: Forty Years of Theories and Debates." *The Lion and the Unicorn* 25.3 (2001): 337–52. Print.

Maclay, G.R. *The Social Organism: A Short History of the Idea That a Human Society May Be Regarded as a Gigantic Living Creature.* North River Press, 1990. Print.

MacLeod, Anne Scott. *American Childhood. Essays on Children's Literature of the Nineteenth and Twentieth Centuries.* University of Georgia Press, 1995. Print.

Mac Naughton, Glenda and Karina Davis. "Discourses of 'Race' in Early Childhood: From Cognition to Power." *"Race" and Early Childhood Education.* Eds. Mac Naughton, Glenda and Karina Davis: Palgrave Macmillan, 2009. Print.

———. "Introduction: Thinking Differently: The Call and the Desire." *"Race" and Early Childhood Education.* Eds. Naughton, G.M. and K. Davis. New York: Palgrave Macmillan, 2009. Print.

———. *"Race" and Early Childhood Education: An International Approach to Identity, Politics, and Pedagogy.* Palgrave Macmillan, 2009. Print.

Mac Naughton, Glenda and Karina Davis and Kylie Smith. "Exploring 'Race-Identities' with Young Children." *"Race" and Early Childhood Education.* Eds. Naughton, G.M. and K. Davis: Palgrave Macmillan, 2009. 31–48. Print.

Maddy, Yulisa Amadu and Donnarae MacCann. *Neo-Imperialism in Children's Literature About Africa: A Study of Contemporary Fiction.* Taylor & Francis, 2008. Print.

Mail, Daily. "Nicolas Sarkozy Joins David Cameron and Angela Merkel View That Multiculturalism Has Failed." *Daily Telegraph* 2011. Print.

Marre, Diana. "'I Want Her to Learn Her Language and Maintain Her Culture': Transnational Adoptive Families' Views of 'Cultural Origins'." *Race, Ethnicity and Nation: Perspectives from Kinship and Genetics.* Ed. Wade, P.: Berghahn Books, 2007. 73–94. Print.

Marre, Diana and Beatriz San Román. El "interés superior de la niñez" en la adopción en España: entre la protección, los derechos y las interpretaciones. *Scripta Nova. Revista Electrónica de Geografía y Ciencias Sociales.* [En línea]. Barcelona: Universidad de Barcelona. XVI. 395 (2012). Web.

Martin, Michelle. *Brown Gold: Milestones of African American Children's Picture Books, 1845–2002.* Taylor & Francis, 2004. Print.

Mattix, April A., and Patricia A. Crawford. "Connecting the Dots: Exploring Themes in Adoption Picturebooks." *Early Childhood Education Journal* 39.5 (2011): 313–21. Print.

McAdams, D.P., R. Josselson, and A. Lieblich. *Identity and Story: Creating Self in Narrative.* American Psychological Association, 2006. Print.

McCallum, Robyn and Stephens John. "Ideology and Children's Books." *Handbook of Research on Children's and Young Adult Literature.* New York: Routledge, 2010. Print.

McGillis, Roderick. *Voices of the Other: Children's Literature and the Postcolonial Context.* Taylor & Francis, 2013. Print.

Medina, José. *Language: Key Concepts in Philosophy.* Bloomsbury Publishing, 2010. Print.

Merino Sanz, María Jesús. *Inmigración Y Consumo. Estilos De Vida De Los Inmigrantes En España.* ESIC Editorial, 2009. Print.

Mernissi, Fatima. *Scheherazade Goes West.* Washington: Washington Square Press, 2001. Print.

Mignolo, Walter. "The Geopolitics of Knowledge and the Colonial Difference." *SAQ* 101.1 (2002): 56–96. Print.

Minguez López, Xavier. "La Interculturalitat En La Lij Catalana." *Caplletra* 63 (2017). Print.

Minkenberg, Michael. "Religious Legacies and the Politics of Multiculturalism." *Immigration, Integration, and Security: America and Europe in Comparative Perspective.* Eds. d'Appollonia, A.C. and S. Reich: U of Pittsburgh P, 2008. 44–66. Print.

Mitchell, W.J.T. *What Do Pictures Want?: The Lives and Loves of Images.* U of Chicago P, 2005. Print.

Moebius, William. "Picturebooks." *Keywords for Children's Literature.* Eds. Nel, P. and L. Paul: New York UP, 2011. 169–74. Print.

Moore, Opal and Donnarae MacCann. "Paternalism and Assimilation in Books About Hispanics: Part One of a Two-Part Essay." *Children's Literature Association Quarterly* 12.2 (1987). Print.

Myers, Christopher. "The Apartheid of Children's Literature." *New York Times* (2014). Print.

Naidoo, Jamie Campbell. *Celebrating Cuentos: Promoting Latino Children's Literature and Literacy in Classrooms and Libraries.* ABC-CLIO, 2011. Print.

Nelson, Claudia. *Little Strangers: Portrayals of Adoption and Foster Care in America, 1850–1929.* Indiana UP, 2003. Print.

Nieto, Sonia. "Foreword." *Critical Multicultural Analysis of Children's Literature: Mirrors, Windows, and Doors.* Eds. Botelho, M.J. and M.K. Rudman: Taylor & Francis, 2009. Print.

———. "We Have Stories to Tell: A Case Study of Puerto Ricans in Children's Books." *Teaching Multicultural Literature in Grades K-8* (1992): 171–201. Print.

Nikolajeva, Maria. "Exit Children's Literature?" *The Lion and the Unicorn* 22.2 (1998): 221–36. Print.

———. *Power, Voice and Subjectivity in Literature for Young Readers.* Taylor & Francis, 2009. Print.

———. "Theory, Post-Theory, and Aetonormative Theory." *Neohelicon* 36.1 (2009): 13–24. Print.

Nikolajeva, Maria and Carole Scott. "How Picturebooks Work." New York: Garland, 2001. Print.

Nodelman, Perry and Mavis Reimer. *The Pleasures of Children's Literature.* Boston: Allyn and Bacon, 2003. Print.

Nodelman, Perry. "Decoding the Images: Illustration and Picturebooks." *Understanding Children's Literature: Key Essays from the International Companion Encyclopedia of Children's Literature.* Ed. Hunt, Peter. London; New York: Routledge, 1999. x, 188 p. Print.

———. "The Eye and the I: Identification and First-Person Narratives in Picture Books." *Children's Literature* 19 (1991): 1–30. Print.

———. "The Other: Orientalism, Colonialism, and Children's Literature." *Children's Literature Association Quarterly* 317.1 (1992): 29–35. Print.

———. *Words About Pictures: The Narrative Art of Children's Picture Books.* U of Georgia P, 1990. Print.

Novy, Marianne. *Imagining Adoption: Essays on Literature and Culture.* U of Michigan P, 2004. Print.

———. *Reading Adoption: Family and Difference in Fiction and Drama.* Ann Arbor, MI: U of Michigan P, 2005. Print.

Nussbaum, Martha. *Cultivating Humanity*. Harvard UP, 1998. Print.

O'Sullivan, Emer. "Imagology Meets Children's Literature." *International Research in Children's Literature* 4.1 (2011): 1–14. Print.

Oh, Arissa. *To Save the Children of Korea: The Cold War Origins of International Adoption*. Stanford UP, 2015. Print.

Ortiz, Ana Teresa and Laura Briggs. "The Culture of Poverty, Crack Babies, and Welfare Cheats: The Making of the 'Healthy White Baby Crisis.'" *Social Text* 76.21 (2003): 39–57. Print.

Park, Sarah. *Representations of Transracial Korean Adoption in Children's Literature*. U of Illinois at Urbana-Champaign, 2009. Print.

Pearce, Sharyn. "Messages from the Inside?: Multiculturalism in Contemporary Australian Children's Literature." *The Lion and the Unicorn* 27.2 (2003): 235–50. Print.

Pesonen, Jaana. "Anti-Racist Strategies in Finnish Children's Literature: Physical Appearance and Language as Signifiers of National Belonging." *Children's Literature in Education* 44.3 (2013): 238–50. Print.

Peters, Laura. *Orphan Texts: Victorian Orphans, Culture and Empire*. Manchester UP, 2001. Print.

Philipps, Carolin. *El Precio De La Verdad*. Bruño, 2006. Print.

Pinsent, Pat. *Children's Literature and the Politics of Equality*. David Fulton, 1997. Print.

Porter Abbott, Herman. "The Cambridge Introduction to Narrative." Cambridge: Cambridge University Press, 2008. Print.

Pratt, Mary Louise. *Imperial Eyes: Travel Writing and Transculturation*. Routledge, 2007. Print.

Prins, Baukje. "Narrative Accounts of Origins: A Blind Spot in the Intersectional Approach?" *European Journal of Women's Studies* 13.3 (2006): 277–90. Print.

Räthzel, Nora. "Developments in Theories of Racism." *Europe's New Racism: Causes, Manifestations, and Solutions*. Ed. Foundation, Evens. New York: Berghahn Books, 2002. Print.

Rattansi, Ali. "Racism, "Postmodernism" and Reflexive Multiculturalism." *Critical Multiculturalism: Rethinking Multicultural and Antiracist Education*. Ed. May, S.: Falmer Press, 1999. Print.

———. *Racism: A Very Short Introduction*. Oxford UP, USA, 2007. Print.

Reinoso, Marta, et al. "Internationally Adopted Children's General and Adoption-Specific Stressors, Coping Strategies and Psychological Adjustment." *Child & Family Social Work* 21.1 (2013): 1–13. Print.

Richter, M.V. *Creating the National Mosaic: Multiculturalism in Canadian Children's Literature from 1950 to 1994*. Rodopi, 2011. Print.

Rose, Jacqueline. *The Case of Peter Pan, or, the Impossibility of Children's Fiction*. U of Pennsylvania P, 1984. Print.

Rosello, Martha. "Conviviality and Pilgrimage: Hospitality as Lnterruptive Practice." *The Conditions of Hospitality: Ethics, Politics, and Aesthetics on the Threshold of the Possible*. Ed. Claviez, T.: Fordham University Press, 2013. 127–44. Print.

Rudd, David. "Theorising and Theories. How Does Children's Literature Exist." *Understanding Children's Literature*. Ed. Hunt, P.: Taylor & Francis, 2006. Print.

Salih, Sarah. *Judith Butler.* Routledge, 2002. Print.

San Román, Beatriz and Diana Marre. "De 'Chocolatinas' Y 'Princesas De Ojos Rasgados': Sobre La Diferencia 'Fisonómica' En La Adopción Transracial En España." *Nuevas Maternidades.* Barcelona: Editorial Bellaterra, 2013. 123–42. Print.

San Román, Beatriz. "'I Am White, Even If I Am Racially Black', 'I Am Afro-Spanish': Confronting Belonging Paradoxes in Transracial Adoptions." *Journal of Intercultural Studies* 34.3 (2013): 229–45. Print.

Santamaría, Enrique. "Inmigración Y Barbarie. La Construcción Social Y Política Del Inmigrante Como Amenaza." *Papers* 66 (2002): 59–75. Print.

Schiller, Nina Glick, Linda Basch, and Blanc Cristina Szanton. "From Immigrant to Transmigrant: Theorizing Transnational Migration." *Anthropological Quarterly* 68.1 (1995): 48–63. Print.

Schneider, Jens and Maurice Crul. "New Insights into Assimilation and Integration Theory: Introduction to the Special Issue." *Ethnic and Racial Studies* 33.7 (2010): 1143–48. Print.

Selman, Peter. "From Bucharest to Beijing: Changes in Countries Sending Children for International Adoption 1990 to 2006." *International Advances in Adoption Research for Practice.* Eds. Wrobel, G. and E. Neil. London: John Wiley, 2009. 41–69. Print.

———. "Global Trends in Intercountry Adoption: 2001–2010." *Adoption Advocate* 44 (2012): 1–19. Print.

———. "Intercountry Adoption in the New Millennium; the 'Quiet Migration' Revisited." *Population Research and Policy Review* 21 (2002): 205–25. Print.

———. "The Movement of Children in International Adoption. Development and Trends in Receiving States and States of Origin 1998–2004." *International Adoption Global Inequalities and the Circulation of Children.* Eds. Marré, D. and L. Briggs. New York and London: New York UP, 2009. Print.

Short, Kathy G. "Critically Reading the Word and the World: Building Intercultural Understanding through Literature." *Bookbird: A Journal of International Children's Literature* 47.2 (2009): 1–10. Print.

Singer, A.J. *Teaching Global History: A Social Studies Approach.* Taylor & Francis, 2012. Print.

Sipe, Lawrence R. "Revisiting the Relationships between Text and Pictures." *Children's Literature in Education* 43.1 (2012): 4–21. Print.

Smedley, Audrey and Brian D. Smedley. *Race in North America: The Origin and Evolution of a Worldview.* Westview Press, 2012. Print.

Smith, Michael Peter and Luis Eduardo Guarnizo. *Transnationalism from Below.* Transaction Publishers, 1998. Print.

Solomos, John and Les Back. "Introduction: Theorising Race and Racism." *Theories of Race and Racism. A Reader.* Eds. Back, Les and John Solomos. London and New York: Routledge, 2000. Print.

Somers, Margaret R. "The Narrative Constitution of Identity: A Relational and Network Approach." *Theory and Society* 23.5 (1994): 605–49. Print.

Spivak, Gayatri. "Can the Subaltern Speak, Revised Edition." *Can the Subaltern Speak?: Reflections on the History of an Idea.* Ed. Morris, R.C.: Columbia UP, 2010. 21–80. Print.

Stainton, R.J. *Perspectives in the Philosophy of Language: A Concise Anthology.* Broadview Press, 2000. Print.

Stephens, John. "Advocating Multiculturalism: Migrants in Australian Children's Literature after 1972." *Children's Literature Association Quarterly* 15.4 (1990): 180–85. Print.

———. *Language and Ideology in Children's Fiction.* Longman, 1992. Print.

———. "Multiculturalism in Recent Australian Children's Fiction:(Re) Connecting Selves through Personal and National Histories." *Other Worlds, Other Lives: Children's Literature Experiences.* Ed. Myrna Machet, Sandra Olën, Thomas Van der Walt: U of South Africa, 1996. 1–19. Print.

———. "Schemas and Scripts: Cognitive Instruments and the Representation of Cultural Diversity in Children's Literature." *Contemporary Children's Literature and Film: Engaging with Theory.* Eds. Mallan, K. and C. Bradford: Palgrave MacMillan, 2011. Print.

Storey, John. *Cultural Theory and Popular Culture: A Reader.* Vol. 1: Pearson Education, 2006. Print.

Teuscher, Simon. "Flesh and Blood in the Treatises on the Arbor Consanguinitatis (Thirteenth to Sixteenth Centuries)." *Blood And Kinship: Matter for Metaphor from Ancient Rome to the Present* (2013): 83–104. Print.

Thiele, Jens. *Das Bilderbuch: Aesthetik, Theorie, Analyse, Didaktik, Rezeption.* Isensee Florian GmbH, 2000. Print.

Thompson, N.S. "Hague Is Enough? A Call for More Protective, Uniform Law Guiding International Adoptions." *Wisconsin International Law Journal* 22.2 (2004): 441. Print.

Thomson, Stephen. "The Child, the Family, the Relationship." *Children's Literature: New Approaches.* Ed. Lesnik-Oberstein, K.: Palgrave Macmillan, 2004. 144–67. Print.

Tobella Mayans, Alba. "¿Cómo Vas a Ser Del Atleti Si Eres Negro?" *El País* 06.01.2014. Print.

Tomlinson, Alan and Christopher Young. *National Identity and Global Sports Events: Culture, Politics, and Spectacle in the Olympics and the Football World Cup.* State U of New York P, 2006. Print.

Trenka, Jane Jeong. *Language of Blood: A Memoir.* Sant Paul, MN: Minnesota Historical Society Press, 2003. Print.

Triandafyllidou, Anne. *Immigrants and National Identity in Europe.* Taylor & Francis, 2004. Print.

van Dijk, Teun. *Ideology: A Multidisciplinary Approach.* SAGE Publications, 1998. Print.

———. "New(S) Racism: A Discourse Analytical Approach." *Ethnic Minorities and the Media.* Ed. S. Cottle: Open University Press, 2000. 33–49. Print.

———. *Racism and Discourse in Spain and Latin America.* John Benjamins Publishing, 2005. Print.

van Dijk, Teun and Encarnación Atienza. "Knowledge and Discourse in Secondary School Social Science Textbooks." *Discourse Studies* 13.1 (2011): 93–118. Print.

Verkuyten, Maykel. "Immigration Discourses and Their Impact on Multiculturalism: A Discursive and Experimental Study." *British Journal of Social Psychology* 44 (2005): 223–40. Print.

Vertovec, Steven and Susanne Wessendorf. *Multiculturalism Backlash: European Discourses, Policies and Practices.* Taylor & Francis, 2010. Print.

Vicente, T.L. "Latin American Immigration to Spain Evolution and Legal Status of Latin American Immigrants in Spain (1999–2009)." *Migration Citizenship Education* (2010). Web.

Vich-Bertran, Júlia. "La historia del hilo rojo: un estudio etnográfico multisituado sobre el campo adoptivo transnacional China-España". *Parentescos: Modelos Culturales de Reproducción.* Eds. J. Grau, D. Rodríguez & H. Valenzuela. Editorial PPU, Barcelona, 2001. 311–43. Print.

Volkman, Toby Alice. *Cultures of Transnational Adoption.* Duke University Press Books, 2005. Print.

Volkman, Toby Alice. "Introduction: Transnational Adoption." *Social Text* 21.1 (2003): 1–5. Print.

Wall, Barbara. *The Narrator's Voice: The Dilemma of Children's Fiction.* Macmillan, 1991. Print.

Weil, Richard H. "International Adoptions: The Quiet Migration." *International Migration Review* 18.2 (1984): 276–93. Print.

Weinreich, Torben. *Children's Literature: Art or Pedagogie?* Roskilde UP, 2000. Print.

Welsch, Wolfgang. "Transculturality: The Puzzling Form of Cultures Today." *Spaces of Culture: City, Nation, World* (1999): 194–213. Print.

Woodward, Kathryn. *Understanding Identity.* Bloomsbury USA, 2003. Print.

Yngvesson, Barbara. "Going 'Home': Adoption, Loss of Bearings, and the Mythology of Roots." *Social Text* 21.1 (2003): 7–27. Print.

———. "Placing the 'Gift Child' in Transnational Adoption." *Law & Society Review* 36.2 (2002): 227–56. Print.

Yokota, Junko. "Issues in Selecting Multicultural Children's Literature." *Language Arts* (1993): 156–67. Print.

———. "Realism in Picture Books for Children: Representations of Our Diverse World." *Filoteknos* 4 (2014): 64–72. Print.

Yuval-Davis, Nira. *Gender & Nation.* Sage Publications, 1997. Print.

———. "Intersectionality and Feminist Politics." *European Journal of Women's Studies* 13.3 (2006): 193–209. Print.

———. *The Politics of Belonging: Intersectional Contestations.* SAGE Publications, 2011. Print.

Zamudio, Margaret, Christopher Russel, Francisco Rios and Jacquelyn L. Bridgeman. *Critical Race Theory Matters: Education and Ideology.* Taylor & Francis Group, 2011. Print.

Zapata-Barrero, Ricard. "Managing Diversity in Spanish Society: A Practical Approach." *Journal of Intercultural Studies* 31.4 (2010): 383–402. Print.

———. "Policies and Public Opinion Towards Immigrants: The Spanish Case." *Ethnic and Racial Studies* 32.7 (2009): 1101–20. Print.

Zipes, Jack. "Why Fantasy Matters Too Much." *Journal of Aesthetic Education* 43.2 (2009): 77–91. Print.

Index

LF093571338

39229670R00112